A COUPLE'S GUIDE TO

happy
retirement

Endorsements and Reviews

"This book discusses the psychology of retirement with case examples. This topic will become increasingly discussed as the 77 million Boomers enter the retirement age. The dynamics between couples going through retirement are not well known. The psychological changes each spouse feels individually as their life matures and as they relate to each other are individually surprising, unrecognized, and can be devastating as the author points out. This is a terrific book for couples entering this phase of life. Where can you get this information anywhere else? Very little is said about it in public. Retirement will become known as a disease in the coming years. …The book is very helpful in providing a perspective on this phase of life."

James I. Ausman, MD, PhD
Executive Producer,
The Leading Gen: What will you do with the rest of your life?
Public Television Series, Fall 2009

A COUPLE'S GUIDE TO

happy retirement

For Better or for Worse…
but Not for Lunch

Second Edition

SARA YOGEV, Ph.D

Published by Familius LLC, www.familius.com
First Published in 2001 by Contemporary Books,
a Division of The McGraw-Hill Companies.

Familius books are available at special discounts for bulk purchases for sales promotions, family or corporate use. Special editions, including personalized covers, excerpts of existing books, or books with corporate logos, can be created in large quantities for special needs. For more information, contact Premium Sales at 801-552-7298 or email specialmarkets@familius.com

Library of Congress Control Number: 2012947939

pISBN 978-1-938301-12-4
eISBN 978-1-938301-11-7

Printed in the United States of America

Book design by Kurt Wahlner
Cover design by David Miles
Edited by Edith Songer and Christopher Robbins

10 9 8 7 6 5 4 3 2 1
digital version

Second Edition

Table of Contents

Foreword   6

Introduction to the Second Edition   9

Chapter One
Making Yourself and Your Marriage
    Ready for Retirement   17

Chapter Two
Learning to Let Go of Work and Making
    the Psychological Shift to Retirement   33

Chapter Three
Finding Your Purpose in Retirement   50

Chapter Four
Readjusting the Togetherness-Separation Balance   72

Chapter Five
The Psychological Meaning of Money   97

Chapter Six
The Household Arena   120

Chapter Seven
Friendship   135

Chapter Eight
Family Matters   156

Chapter Nine
Gendered Retirement: The Different
    Responses of Men and Women   176

Chapter Ten
The Transition: Making It Easier
    for Yourself and Your Marriage   193

Chapter Eleven
Relocation   212

Chapter Twelve
The Best Retirement   231

Acknowledgements   246

Selected Bibliography   248

Index   251

About the Publisher   255

Foreword

Creatively combining individual case studies with the latest research, *A Couple's Guide to Happy Retirement* challenges all of us who have retired, or ever will retire. It describes a myriad of ways—many of which probably have never occurred to most of us—stopping work affects us and our relationships with the people around us, especially our spouses. Through the stories of people we recognize, we see that retirement prompts some subtle, and some not so subtle, changes in how we experience our sense of purpose in life, our feelings about togetherness, travel, money, housework, old and new friendships, parenting and grandparenting, volunteering, and more. The research presented offers a sensible, intellectual framework and concepts that we can cling to as we go through the innovative exercises at the end of most chapters. It is through these exercises that we come to the realization that retirement is just the beginning of a process that will require readjustments in much of our thinking and behavior, and a *lot* of renegotiation with others.

Since writing the Foreword eleven years ago for the first edition of this book, I have retired. I started gradually, by reducing my teaching time. I was fortunate to be able to take advantage of a long-established right at the University of Washington for retiring faculty to teach 40 percent time for up to five years. I taught part time for three years, and during that time continued with most of my other outside activities such as serving on boards, exercising, writing, meeting friends for lunch, going on trips with my (unretired) husband whenever he had time, and enjoying my hobbies and seeing our children establish themselves securely in their own careers. In short, I continued to be busy and over-committed, as I usually had been during my full-time career employment.

Then there was an event that seemed to change everything, at least in my attitudes toward work. Our then 41-year-old daughter, a full-time lawyer married to a man in the midst of dramatically changing his career, gave birth to her first child, and I wanted to be available to help as needed. I offered to babysit on a regular basis, and other times as well. I enjoyed my time with the new baby immensely, as well as the extra moments it gave me with our daughter and her family at this time that was so important to them, too. When the baby was just a couple of months old, I had to decide whether I was going to teach part time again the fourth year. I declined, and a year later I declined for the fifth year.

It was about then that I realized I needed to reread Dr. Yogev's book, and to fully engage the exercises at the end of chapters. I realized that I had put off planning exactly *how* I wanted to be fully retired. I knew that I would spend some time grandparenting, and that my relationship with my adult married children would be different but I wasn't sure how. I also hadn't seriously considered how my relationship to my husband would change. And despite having read Dr. Yogev's book years earlier, I found I wasn't prepared for the psychological consequences of fully retiring hurriedly *without* much of a plan. I felt both threatened and comforted by this book. It pushed me to confront a number of issues, many of which were uncomfortable for me and that I had managed to avoid.

Very recently, my husband retired too, and is spending more time at home, much of it devoted to going through materials he has collected over forty years of teaching and research. He is wisely continuing to work on research projects and to volunteer on boards of organizations he believes are serving the community. I now realize that although we have already negotiated a lot during our 42-year marriage, we need to negotiate more. I am certain it will be useful for us to do together the exercises Dr. Yogev has provided. *A Couple's Guide to Happy Retirement* can guide us as we consider such things as non-work related trips we might take, and whether and how to downsize. In short, this is one of those books I will keep and reread as the dynamics in my life change and when I am experiencing feelings I don't understand.

A Couple's Guide to Happy Retirement also has much broader implications for our society because there are so many "boomers" who are nearing retirement age and because so many are living longer. The ideas put forth in the book, therefore, suggest both the need for some changes in public policy and some creative opportunities for not-for-profit or non-governmental organizations. For example, Dr. Yogev illustrates with individual cases how retirement-related depression affects relationships and well-being. It stands to reason that in many cases such depression could also have physical repercussions, and that there could easily be additional costs incurred for both psychiatric and physical treatment. It seems that it would be reasonable, and perhaps cost effective, for those in the public policy arena to encourage the development of psychological preparation and planning for retirement, and thus complement the already widespread pre-retirement financial planning work-shops and other activities devoted to the care and nurture of money.

Further, it seems to me, there are enormous implications for the plethora of non-profit organizations that need and depend on volunteers for the growth and sustenance of their operations. *A Couple's Guide to Happy Retirement* is replete with examples of retirees whose needs for a new or revised purpose in life have been satisfied by volunteer work. Non-profit organizations can help themselves by helping retirees identify the organizations that will satisfy their personal needs for new purposes in life.

Margaret T. Gordon
Dean and Professor Emeritus
Evans School of Public Affairs
University of Washington

Introduction
to the Second Edition

Traditional retirement is obsolete. The definition of retirement as workers' final exit from the labor force is increasingly outdated as people move in and out of the labor force. Thus the boundary separating employment and retirement is blurred and less clear cut. For most people today, retirement is a process occurring over time with different stages rather than a one-time event. New careers, self-employment, part-time work, or consulting are common occurrences for people who "retire" from a long-time, primary job or career.

Past research suggested that the transition to retirement enhances marital satisfaction as a result of reduced workload. However, more recent research has found retirement often produces a temporary decline in marital satisfaction for both husbands and wives. Newly retired individuals report the lowest marital satisfaction and highest marital conflict compared with those who are retired for a long time or are not yet retired and still employed. After two years in retirement, once couples are settled into this new life stage, marital satisfaction is higher.

The Gray Divorce Phenomenon (divorce among those 50 years old and older) provides a cautionary lesson for every couple entering retirement. While overall national divorce rates have declined since spiking in the 1980s, gray divorce has risen to its highest level on record. In 1990 only 1 in 10 people who got divorced was 50 or older, by 2009 the number was roughly 1 in 4. More than 600,000 people ages 50 and older got divorced in 2009.

According to *The Wall Street Journal's* March 3, 2012 article about gray divorce, based on current trends, this number is predicted to top 800,000 by 2030. With Americans staying healthier longer and living longer, the retirement years are stretched out, giving couples more time together. Among many couples, retirement often creates friction, weakening even the strongest ties. The increased togetherness exacerbates existing problems, bringing tension bubbling to the surface. Without child-raising duties and demanding job responsibilities to provide distraction, structure, and escape, people are more vulnerable to conflict. There is no longer a way to ignore or avoid addressing long-term unresolved issues as well as newly created issues. Many retirees refuse to settle for retirement filled with marital discord.

According to Deirdre Bair, author of *Calling It Quits; Late-Life Divorce and Starting Over*, a chronicle of nearly 400 interviews with people getting divorced in midlife, boomers in unhappy marriages often look at each other and think: "I may have another 25 to 35 years to live. Do I want to spend it with this person?" They have an urgent feeling to get divorced now or they'll never have the chance again. Indeed, the divorce rate among Americans older than 65 grew from 6.7 percent in March 2000 to 9.7 percent in 2009, according to US Census figures.

This marital problem seems to be international as we hear about "Retired Husband Syndrome" in Japan—Japanese women experiencing depression as their husbands retire (*Chicago Tribune* October 19, 2005)—as well as in Spain where in February 2006 *Sur* newspaper reported about the difficulties wives face as their retired husbands infringe on their turf and autonomy.

Most retirement planning programs and publications are geared exclusively or predominantly to financial matters. While having enough money in retirement is important, adjusting to this new stage of life requires a more holistic approach. Other retirement books, articles and advice-giving mediums, particularly those written before the last economic crisis, focus on leisure advice, and it's entirely possible that this isn't what you or your spouse wants.

Erik Erikson, the great psychologist on adulthood, said that the hallmark of well-being in older people could be encapsulated in the phrase, "I am what survives of me." It is important and ever more challenging to find a way to balance the books while remaining true to one's "generativity," the psychological task of the advanced age (see more on that in Chapter 1).

Given the changing definition of retirement, particularly during an economic upturn and a booming economy, financial concerns are not the singular or dominant concerns that guide people's behaviors. Other needs like growth, identity, generativity, and relatedness have as much influence.

Indeed, Mark Freedman, author of the 2008 book *Encore: Finding Work That Matters in the Second Half of Life* wrote before the current economic crisis "The reality is that the end of middle age is no longer, for most people, attached to the beginning of either retirement or old age. We need a call to action for creating an "encore" stage of life characterized by purpose, contribution and commitment, particularly to the well-being of future generations."

However, it is worth noting that the altruistic and idealistic redefinitions of retirement proposed earlier, need to be reassessed in light of the economic downturn. The predictions that baby boomers would revolutionize retirement and would devote their golden years to social activism and life-long learning are not happening due to economic pressure.

In the eleven years since this book was first published, a lot has changed. The current economic crisis has impacted retirement in many ways. Many retirement plans have dwindled, and not because individuals have spent indiscriminately. Whether invested in mutual funds, blue-chip stocks, certificates of deposit or dividend-paying stocks, almost everyone has found their assets diminished. Many people in retirement age now worry that they will outlive their savings and won't have enough money for a comfortable retirement. McKinsey & Company, a large consulting firm, predicts that the typical American family faces a 37 percent shortfall in their income for retirement. Other retired age individuals feel pressured to work beyond traditional retirement age because they believe they cannot rely on Social Security. In addition, with unemployment and homelessness rates at high levels, the younger generations are frequently looking to retirees for help.

Thus, the phenomenon of older men and women choosing to remain in the workforce or returning to work is on the rise. It's not surprising to find a gray-haired man or women serving you lattes at Starbucks or working the register at Whole Foods. In some places e.g. Fort Lauderdale, Florida, people in their 60s and 70s compete against their grandchildren for entry-level jobs like supermarket cashiers or receptionists in medical offices.

The *New York Times* on May 18, 2012 reported that according to Labor Department figures the percentage of workers over the traditional retirement age of 65 is at a record high. More than one-third of men ages 65-69 are working as are more than one-fourth of women. For the first time since government began keeping track of numbers and probably the first time ever, one in nine American men over the age of 75 and one in 20 women over that age were working in April 2012. This could mean that the retirement dream is further away for a lot of baby boomers as they can't afford to retire or for those who choose to continue to work, but not out of financial necessity.

Therefore, publications like *Monitor on Psychology*, November 2004, and *US News and World Report* in June 12, 2006, June 3 2002, and June 4 2001 that focused on non-financial aspects of life in retirement are not that relevant any longer. While many innovative volunteer/social activist programs for retirees still exist, many people are more focused on feeding themselves rather than others. It has become clearer than ever before that the challenge for many retirees involves both money and fulfillment. Therefore in this second edition "bridge employment" is discussed (see chapter 3), a new concept that didn't appear in the literature before.

What all this means is that people need to spend more energy on psychological planning for retirement. We plan our career but don't plan our retirement, which can last 20-30 years. We need to see retirement as a passage to new opportunity that requires thought and discussion about everything from purpose to pleasure, from contributing to society to contributing to family—not just a financial plan. Reflecting upon and talking about the impact of these issues on your identity and relationships is crucial. Retirement is not just walking away from work; it is also walking toward something new.

Professor Lorraine Dorfman from the University of Iowa reported that planning for retirement was the second most important factor (after health) for people who expressed satisfaction with retirement. *American Psychologist* April 2011 special section on Retirement stresses the need for more careful attention to this life stage which involves a sequence of decisions over several years. This confirms my experience that clients who have created psychologically astute plans for their retirement years tend to adjust better, both as individuals and as couples. Specifically, a good retirement plan should encompass constructive use of time, purposefulness, and interpersonal issues, all of which can increase satisfaction and relationship building.

My hope is that this book will assist you in creating a good plan, and in your pursuit of whatever you deem important in your life. Marital bliss in retirement is the goal of this book, and to achieve it, you and your partner need to look at all your options rather than focus on the traditional measures of retirement happiness.

Therefore, I want to emphasize in this second edition the importance of balance for individuals and couples in retirement. My goal is to help retirees find a way to live together happily ever after, recognizing that how people interpret that phrase may have changed a bit. Most people are searching for the right mix of money with meaning, of profits with purpose, of using their many experiences in ways that aren't just contained in photo albums but are significant and memorable. In other words, they seek an intersection of continued income, with purpose and impact, something they will be remembered for.

When I work with my clients on retirement planning, I stress that retirement is affecting both spouses, not just the retired one. I also emphasize that retirement is experienced differently by each person. We've learned a lot in recent years about the links between retirement, marital satisfaction, and gender. Knowing the gestalt of the entire relationship—not just what's happening with an individual in the relationship—improves our understanding of changes in marital satisfaction around the retirement transition. Therefore, good communication and conflict resolution skills are essential. The questions at the end of each chapter in this book are intended to help couples engage in constructive discussion of common conflict-producing issues.

This book is based upon my accumulated psychological knowledge that came from two different sources. It contains the collected wisdom of countless dedicated researchers in the areas of work, family, retirement, aging, and marital dynamics, whose works have influenced my thinking. It also reflects the collected personal experiences of many individuals and couples. In interviews for my research or in my clinical and coaching practice, people have shared with me their joys and pains and, by allowing me to be their guide, touched, enriched, and contributed to my growth as well. May their stories, struggles, and victories be an inspiration to others. The identities of the people described in this book were protected by altering names and other recognizable characteristics, but the basic psychological dynamics have been preserved. At times the therapeutic scenarios and complexities have been simplified in order to make a point clearer. Any similarity to actual people is completely coincidental.

Some of the terms used throughout this book need clarification. The terms work and employment are used as synonyms and when not working is mentioned it means not employed. In no way does it mean to discount homemaker's contribution or the value of any other non-paid work. The terms wife, husband, spouse, partner, relationship, and marriage are used interchangeably with the intention of including all couples, married or not. In no instance are the terms meant to exclude anyone. My professional experience has been primarily with male/female couples, and most of the examples in the book are based on such interactions. Yet, it is my hope that this book will prove helpful to any individual who is engaged in an ongoing love relationship of any type and who is preparing for, facing, or going through retirement.

This book focuses on how to shorten and reduce the difficult post-retirement transition so that the negative individual and marital impact will be minimal. In this updated edition, I have added new sections that address events and trends that have arisen in recent years, including bridge employment (Chapter 3), sexuality among older couples (Chapter 4), forced/involuntary retirement (Chapter 10) and relocation (Chapter 11). You will also find relevant, new and recent research in many of the chapters.

Many readers have written or told me about how helpful the first edition of this book was for their own wellbeing as well as for their marriage after one or both spouses retired. I hope this second edition is at least equally helpful by providing the latest information on the issues that impact the happiness and satisfaction of couples at this stage of their lives. I trust this book provides you with the information and tools you will need for yourself and your relationship to thrive in retirement. In other words, that both you and your partner will experience a genuine happy " For Better Or For Worse, But Not For Lunch" life stage.

A COUPLE'S GUIDE TO

happy
retirement

CHAPTER ONE

Making Yourself and Your Marriage Ready for Retirement

After 37 years of marriage that included three children and two successful careers, Gary and Anna were looking forward to Gary's retirement. Anna had retired from her job as a teacher five years before, and Gary, a patent attorney with a major law firm, was now calling it quits at age 63. It wasn't that he had to retire or was sick of his job—far from it. It was simply that he and his wife had spent years talking about the places they wanted to visit and how, when he retired, they could fulfill this dream.

In addition, Gary's demanding job had always prevented him from spending as much time with Anna and the kids as he would have liked. He intended to make up for all the experiences on which he had missed out by visiting his adult children—two of whom lived in other cities—and playing with his grandchildren. Because he had reaped the benefits of being a partner in the firm and invested wisely, they could do what they wanted without agonizing about finances.

During the first six months of retirement, the experience proved to be even better than they had expected. They took wonderful vacations to South America, Alaska, and Tuscany; they visited with their children and grandchildren; and they delighted in being together without the pressure of work impeding them. Then an ill wind began to blow.

Not overnight, but over time, the joys and possibilities of being home together diminished. Little tensions crept into their daily conversations. Gary resented the fact that Anna had a group of friends with whom she did things;

she was a member of an all-women's book club and regularly had lunch with two close friends. Gary felt that he was being excluded and told Anna so. To placate him, she invited him to join her and her friends the next time they had lunch, but it was a disaster; Anna told him that his presence somehow upset the chemistry of their little group, and an all-out argument ensued.

Gary was becoming increasingly bored and frustrated. It wasn't that he didn't have friends, but the vast majority of them were former business colleagues. Not only was it difficult to get together with them regularly, but also when they did get together, their conversations were often strained and stilted— he was out of the work loop.

Anna felt that Gary's problem was more than just not working; he wasn't willing to adjust his life to retirement, to develop new interests and goals. As Gary became more irritable and argumentative, Anna was more inclined to do things without him, which heightened the relationship's tension. Once, when their daughter in another city needed help with her children for a week, Anna insisted on going by herself, telling Gary he would just get in the way. In reality, she was set on spending time away from his sour moods.

Within a year, the relationship was strained to the breaking point. Gary and Anna had tried to take another vacation together, hopeful that a trip to the south of France would re-instill the magic of their earlier travels, but they discovered that their problems traveled with them. They ended up not staying as long as anticipated, both of them now eager to get away from the other. It wasn't long after this trip that Anna contacted a divorce lawyer, who referred her to me.

In the course of 12 months, Anna and Gary watched a relationship that had thrived for 37 years fall apart before their eyes. Both were completely unprepared for the psychological impact that retirement would have on their partnership.

A Troubling Trend

Over the years, I have seen many couples like Anna and Gary who enjoyed a long, happy marriage only to be thwarted by serious marital problems when one or both people retired. As a psychologist who specializes in work–family issues, I'm acutely aware of this phenomenon. Many couples are frustrated and disappointed to discover that retirement's golden years can tarnish a marriage. Instead of being able to capitalize on the fruits of their labor, their good health, and their savings, couples are angry and rueful about what's happened to their marriage. Some people find themselves having more fights than ever before, while others sulk around feeling alienated from their spouses.

I've also observed this phenomenon from the perspectives of adult children who are in therapy with me. They are concerned that their parents' marriages have deteriorated after retirement and are trying to prevent them from fighting all the time or even divorcing. In the last few years, I've heard a growing number of young adults decrying how retirement has "wrecked" their parents' marriages, an issue we'll return to later.

From my work as therapist and the numerous studies I've read, I'm convinced that a troubling trend has emerged that will bedevil retiring couples for years to come. While the marketplace overflows with advice on how people can plan financially for retirement, there's an information gap in planning for the psychological aspects of retirement and its impact on marriage. Because of this emphasis on financial planning, people seldom mull over the psychological adjustment and related changes they will need to make in their relationships.

Awareness of the ramifications and dialogue about the problems can go a long way toward keeping relationships strong in the absence of work. Throughout the following chapters, I provide case histories from my files like that of Gary and Anna, illustrating common conflicts as well as conflict-resolving techniques.

Retirement can alter the marital dynamic in countless ways, from increasing the amount of time couples spend together to forcing decisions about relationships with adult children and about friends, money, and the division of housework. Each chapter explores a critical aspect of the retirement/relationship issue and offers ideas for preventing or resolving the problems that result.

Retirement as a Psychological Process

As a relatively recent development in our culture, retirement has not yet acquired the importance or symbolism of other milestones such as marriage or childbirth or of "coming-of-age" events such as bar mitzvahs, confirmations, or obtaining a driver's license. As a result, people sometimes underestimate its impact and view it as a one-day transition without ongoing lifelong consequences.

Retirement is not just an action by which you *summarily* withdraw yourself from paid employment. It is more than one day in your life when you stop working. If it were only a transient event in a life filled with events, people wouldn't have a problem with it. But because it's an ongoing process that has tremendous psychological implications, its impact is significant and long lasting.

As Robert Atchley states in his classic 1982 work "The Process of Retirement," the retirement process has six stages:

- **Pre-retirement:** plans are made for and attitudes are formed about retirement.
- **Retirement event:** this often is marked by a celebration of some sort.
- **Honeymoon:** the period immediately following retirement, which can last a few months or up to a year, in which people often feel free, relaxed, and happy, with no more work demands, daily time structure and less stress.
- **Disenchantment:** the letdown following the honeymoon, in which people feel lack of purpose, lost, confused, and a sense of void. They realize they need to reorient themselves, set realistic lifestyle goals, and develop a new, satisfying routine.
- **Reorientation:** people start adjusting to a retirement lifestyle and change their attitudes and behaviors to cope more effectively.
- **Routine:** individuals develop a new routine that meets their personal and marital needs.

Much of this book delves into the disenchantment stage, since this is where individuals often linger too long or even become trapped and depressed. More to the point, this is the stage in which couples notice their marital satisfaction decreasing as one or both partners have difficulty making the transition to a satisfying retirement lifestyle. As you'll discover, it's possible to shorten and even bypass this stage by preparing psychologically for retirement. This psychological preparation also facilitates your reorientation and helps you establish a viable routine.

Retirement can be both heaven and hell. On the negative side, it can be one of the most stressful events in life, since it means coping with loss—loss of constructive activity, routine, work companions, income, and even status. On the positive side, retirement can be an opportunity to enjoy life in a new way, the right to stop work and do the 1,001 things you've always wanted to do but never had time for, and a chance to give yourself over to new challenges and adventures. Whether retirement is heaven or hell for you as an individual and as a couple depends to a certain extent on how aware you are of the psychological realities of retirement as opposed to the myths.

A Major Life Transition

The idea of retirement is relatively new; it really started only about a hundred years ago. The Social Security program, which is approaching its eighth decade, made retirement financially feasible for many American workers.

In the same way that prior generations assumed that they didn't need books about parenting because they "intuitively" knew how to raise their kids, many people mistakenly assume that they know what to do as retirees without much application of thought or groundwork. What they fail to realize is that for their parents or grandparents, retirement was a relatively short phase— often people worked as long as they could and retired because of poor health. For them, retirement was the beginning of the end.

In the year 1900, the average life expectancy was 46.3 years. Workers continued to work until they drew their last breath and literally died with their boots on. The few that made it to age 65 could expect to live only 1.2 more years as retirees.

In the year 2000, the average life expectancy was 73.5 years for men and 80.4 years for women. Longevity numbers continue to improve as can be seen from the 2012 U.S. Census, which projects life expectancy of 75.7 years for men and 80.8 years for women. With increased longevity and life expectancy, thanks to improved nutrition and medical care, many people can expect to enjoy good health well into their 80s and to spend 10, 20, or even more years as retirees. Thus, retiring at around age 62 when one is eligible to draw Social Security benefits means *spending a significant percentage, one-fourth to one-third, of one's life in retirement.*

Given the swelling ranks of retirees as well as the amount of time spent in retirement, it's logical to suppose that people would make it their business to educate themselves about retirement realities.

Unfortunately, many people are caught up in the myth of retirement as a perpetual honeymoon. While this is definitely a phase of retirement, it is a passing one. After the initial excitement lapses, people struggle because they're not emotionally prepared to deal with who they are without work and don't know how to feel productive, worthwhile, and valuable without a job. As a result, they often take a psychological pounding that can set their marriage on edge.

In fact, researchers consistently report that at least one-third of retirees experience difficulties with the transition to retirement. When baby boomers start to retire in droves—a process that's already beginning—it's a reasonable assumption that roughly the same percentage of these 66 million boomers will experience relationship problems. So, we are talking about 22 million people who will wrestle with the transition.

Erik Erikson, a leading psychologist in the area of human development, describes seven stages over the life span. The seven stages are helpful in understanding retirement and why the absence of the occupational role can be a severe threat to a retiree's sense of identity. In Erikson's writings, *identity* refers to how we see ourselves and is subject to existential issues throughout life while *self* is primarily determined by how others see us.

Stage 1: Trust vs. mistrust: feeling of uncertainty about the future—doubt as to how retirement will turn out. Anxiety about trusting oneself to make the right decision can lead to procrastination of retirement and conversely to an opposite impulsive decision to retire.

Stage 2: Autonomy vs. shame and doubt: fear of inability to take care of oneself with increasing age. Deterioration of vision, hearing and memory can threaten personal autonomy.

Stage 3: Initiative vs. guilt: finding the right answers to the question of what do I do with my retirement apart from leisure, hobbies, travel, etc. Busy schedule of recreational activities does not provide long term meaning. Not all retirees face these questions. For those who do, meaning and life satisfaction rather than economic success and ambition are more important to finding the right activities.

Stage 4: Industry vs. Inferiority: in retirement being industrious is optional. Yet it is a source of meaning. Busyness should not be mistaken for engagement. Busyness can be a defense against the challenge of finding meaning. Feeling industrious is almost a prerequisite for success in retirement. Activities that are meaningful for both retirees and the recipients of their labor are desirable forms of engagement—mentoring, coaching and other volunteer activities. The fourth stage of industry often overlaps with the seventh stage of generativity.

Stage 5: Identity vs. Role Confusion: the challenge of finding balance between the pressure to conform to values of one's community and one's authenticity. Finding self directed roles with membership in community. Some of these roles can be a continuation of involvement in activities that occurred outside the work place prior to retirement e.g. elder in the church or being on a board of non-profit organization.

Stage 6: Intimacy vs. Isolation: Finding balance between independence and dependence in the marriage. Some men are not used to being home alone and put pressure on their wives to have fewer activities without them. Some retirees of both genders prefer fewer but closer friends. The social network they were part of is left behind and can cause additional loss. It is important to develop "my world," "your world," and "our world," as three distinct entities in order to solve the dangers of co-dependency and isolation in retirement.

Stage 7: Generativity vs. Stagnation: Commitment to help and contribute to the well-being of the community and other vs. narrow self interest. This involves an investment in making a better world by volunteering, coaching, mentoring, etc. Pouring one's heart and soul into humanity is definitely better than chasing pleasurable pursuits such as tennis, travel, and other enjoyable activities exclusively. Fulfillment doesn't occur on the golf course.

In other words, retirees need to find new sources of identity—develop a diversified portfolio of "selves" that replace work identities lost by retirement. Retirement often catalyzes a look backwards, promotes life review and spotlights concerns such as whether retirees fulfilled goals related to their career, family and social relationships. Being closer to the end of life can also trigger death anxiety and questions like "Who am I apart from the roles I have been playing as spouse, parent, and employee and what will I do with my life from now on?"

Why Individuals Have Difficulty With This Major Life Transition

Though you don't need to have a psychologist's or sociologist's understanding of all the factors that make retirement so challenging for people, it's worth taking a moment to consider the following factors that are involved with and impact this process.

Ageism and negative connotations to growing old:

Not so long ago, the elderly members of society were objects of great respect, and their many years on the planet were thought to grant them certain wisdom. Today our society places great value on youth and vitality and often labels old people as useless, decrepit, and possessing diminished responsibilities and status. This largely negative view of elderly people causes some retirees to see themselves as somehow "diminished" when they stop working; they believe they shift from being a productive member of society to an unproductive one.

In addition, a growing number of elderly people are neglected, abandoned, or disrespected by their families. These negative reactions are often due to the societal stigma of old age; we associate elderly people with death and withdraw from them because they make us uncomfortable. Or rather, we're uncomfortable with the notion of growing old and don't want to be reminded of our own mortality.

Increasingly meaningful work:

For many years, work goals revolved around salary, perks, and job security, while non-work activities such as hobbies and family relationships offered much more fulfillment. With the relatively recent emphasis on finding value in work, the landscape has changed. Society now has placed enormous emphasis on employment as a source of self-esteem and satisfaction. Today people often define themselves by what they do; they feel productive and important because of their jobs. When they retire, they lose their sense of identity and life purpose.

Therefore, we see today many people who retire from one job and begin a new job…or a new career…or start their own business. As more and more organizations turn to outsourcing, they are also turning to experienced ex-employees to provide this service, and many of them are retirees. Another major change: The retired population has become more diverse and now includes individuals who enjoy greater health, education, wealth and lifespan.

Many individuals now expect their retirement to be a period of growth and development. The beginning of retirement and the end of an occupation is often fluid and ill-defined. Some people retire in stages, going from full-time to part-time status. Others are downsized into retirement, obtain a new job, are downsized again and finally retire completely. Still others may see themselves transitioning from working to consulting or freelance work.

Money, too, takes on a different meaning in retirement. While finances remain important, financial criteria often are not the singular or dominant need as they were in the earlier life stage when they were an important motivator for continued work. Instead, individuals have a number of personal needs that are associated with well-being in work and retirement like growth, identity relatedness and generativity.

The amorphous nature of this transition, then, can create anxiety because we occupy a no-man's land between working and not working, in particular when there is lack of goals continuity from one's primary work to the next stage.

Indeed, a 2009 research study about continuity theory in retirement provides support to Atchley's belief in the importance of goals continuity in retirement. The authors state that it's a mistake to assume that people who are of retirement age lack the same goals as they had earlier. In fact, individuals who retire at late ages have a greater desire for personal growth, development in their work, and satisfaction with growth opportunities their work provides than individuals who retire early. They also see their work as meaningful, a place where they experience generativity, making contributions and positively affecting the development of others. They also report satisfaction with the degree of autonomy in making work decisions. Their work also fulfills the goal of finances, engendering identity and providing opportunity for relatedness.

The continuing need for meaning, growth, and autonomy experienced in rewarding careers provide an incentive for people to continue to work beyond normal retirement age.

On the other hand, individuals who intend to retire early report that they are less likely to attain generativity or other personal meaningful goals from their work. They expect that retirement, rather than their job, will better fulfill the goals of identity, growth, and relatedness as, for example, their identity needs may shift from work to grandchildren and community.

Therefore, a central objective of retirement and career planning should be to clarify the individual's values: Are they likely to experience purpose and growth through continued employment beyond normal retirement age or are non-work activities more likely to provide meaning. Employers who are interested in retaining workers beyond normative retirement age should create work environments that engender identity, allow autonomy, encourage growth, development and relatedness, and provide opportunities for meaningful and generative acts.

A 2007 study about life satisfaction in retirement found that there is no uniform transition. The study authors described three groups:

- Group One experienced a decline in life satisfaction at retirement but continued on a stable pattern afterwards.
- Group Two experienced the honeymoon stage followed by decline in subjective well-being—in accordance with Atchley stages.
- Group Three showed little change and a more stable pattern of life satisfaction. They had many resources to compensate for the loss of the work role, e.g., high self-esteem, being married and in good

health. They were also more likely to maintain non-work activities as sources of their high and relatively stable life satisfaction.

Thus, it is important to remember that people react differently to retirement. Having continuity in social roles in retirement and being able to adapt to changes, causes less decline in life satisfaction in retirement. Therefore it is important for individuals to prepare for a time in their lives when they don't go to work in order to experience less difficulty adjusting to this life change.

Rising retirement expectations:

In the past, people had more modest expectations; they had manageable, easy-to-achieve goals such as spending more time with and helping other family members, or working at a hobby. Simply arriving at retirement in relatively good health was considered an achievement.

Today expectations are much higher, in part because people have much more money to fuel expectations about grand vacations, moving to idyllic communities, and living life free of pressure. They're also higher because baby boomers want and expect more of retirement, just as they wanted and expected more out of earlier life stages than previous generations did.

Because people are in better physical and financial condition, they have great dreams about what retirement will be like. Unfortunately, these are pipe dreams because people have not realistically assessed what retirement will be like from a psychological standpoint.

Lack of role-models:

Since retirement at the point of two-thirds of our lifespan is a relatively new phenomenon, most people do not have a parent or someone from a previous generation whose retirement can serve as a model for them. The 70-year-old who just finished college or the 82-year-old who still participates in triathlons may receive publicity for his or her accomplishments, but these aren't types of role models with which most people can identify.

As a society, we have not yet developed appropriate norms for retirees. Many people don't realize that retirement is an opportunity for further self-development, new learning, and meeting challenges. Individuals need role models who demonstrate how to find purpose and meaning in the absence of work.

The women's movement:

Women are leading more independent lives than ever before and have become more assertive and outspoken. As women found their voices, they became much more willing to express their opinions about retirement goals—opinions that sometimes created conflict with their husbands' goals. For instance, a woman may want to spend more time visiting her adult children and grandchildren in various cities, while her spouse wants to spend more time golfing; she is interested in relocating to a warmer climate, while he wants them to stay where they are. While women's willingness to express their retirement goals is a positive trend, it can also lead to more marital discord as it sometimes creates a lack of consensus about retirement.

Moreover, many women today lead more independent lives than in the past. Their activities don't revolve around their husbands' interests and sometimes don't include their spouses. The result of this independence is that when men retire, they're surprised to find that their wives don't have much time for them. Men who feel neglected often respond with bitterness and anger.

Dual-career couples:

Until relatively recently, most women derived satisfaction primarily from family, and everything else was a lower priority. Back then, work was a way for them to earn additional money rather than a career. They also perceived a man's career to be more important than a woman's job. In the past, when the roles were set in place, either women retired before their mates or they never worked. When the man retired, his wife was already at home willing to structure her schedule around his.

As the women's movement grew, new notions about work and life took shape. Many women are now working at professional, prestigious jobs that build their self-esteem. Many also continue working after their husbands retire, creating tension because of role reversal—wives expect their retired husbands to take on cleaning, cooking, and other tasks. The new order also means that women who had meaningful careers retire and experience the same emptiness as men who had fulfilling jobs; they too lose their identity and become anxious, irritable, and depressed.

Some of these trends and attitudes cause individual problems with retirement that in turn produce conflict with the spouse. Others result in more direct marital conflicts. Together, they've created relationship tensions that are far more common today than in years past.

There is a complex link between various transition patterns to retirement, marital satisfaction and gender. Knowing couples' interrelated circumstances – not just those of individuals – improves our understanding of changes in marital satisfaction around the retirement transition.

Why Couples Are
Having Problems in Retirement

While there probably have always been couples whose relationships were negatively impacted by retirement, more marriages are being adversely affected today due to a variety of trends and attitudes.

Past research concluded that the transition to retirement enhanced marital satisfaction as a result of reduced workload. However, Phyllis Moen, a leading researcher on retirement, found retirement transition (from one's primary career) is related to temporary decline in marital satisfaction for both husbands and wives. Newly retired individuals report lowest marital satisfaction and highest marital conflict compared with those who are retired for a long time or not yet retired and still employed. After two years in retirement once couples are settled into retirement, marital satisfaction is higher.

Becoming retired is related to heightened marital conflict when one's spouse remains employed regardless of gender. Both spouses experience less conflict if their spouse is also retired. Not-yet-retired women experience highest marital conflict and lowest marital satisfaction if their husband is retired. Thus experiencing retirement together is related to higher marital satisfaction.

In my practice, I've already ministered to my share of men and women suffering from retirement-related depression and marriages in tatters when work is no longer a factor. I fear that we're on the cusp of a crisis. Since depression is the most serious problem among older adults, affecting their marriages and mortality on top of their mental health, people must prepare themselves psychologically for what could be a period of twenty or more years – a quarter to third of their lives.

Depression and marital distress are closely connected at all life stages. After retirement, this coil tightens because spouses spend more time together and less time with other people. The depressed mood of one person weighs heavily on a partner because of their increased time together. In turn, the non-depressed partner tries to "cure" the depressed one and pressures the other to get over the depression. When the "cure" fails and the depression lingers, resentment builds.

Depressed people tend to be critical and negative, and the spouse is often an easy target. After a number of futile attempts to help depressed spouses, their partners can also become depressed or angry. Marital satisfaction suffers, and at its worst, couples divorce after years of marital happiness.

Gender also is a significant factor during this major life transition. Women both in and out of the workforce were socialized to be the caretakers of people and relationships, and they can become upset when they can't help their husbands reorient themselves and find meaning and satisfaction after retirement. Women may start to blame themselves for not being "good enough" and, over time, join their husbands in feeling depressed. Similarly, some women who worked and had careers are shaken by their retirement and take even longer than their husbands in adjusting. As you can imagine, when both spouses are struggling with retirement, all sorts of relationship tensions can develop.

Not only do many couples fail to anticipate the depression that can cause marital strife, but also they don't recognize that retirement is a new stage in their relationship. Through therapy, consultation, and coaching, I have helped many couples who were battered in their passage from one marital stage to the next. The birth of the first child, for instance, often causes stress and marital tension as the focus shifts from the couple to the child. Empty nesters go through another relationship stage as children leave home and a couple is alone for the first time in years. Retirement is the next stage—no more kids and no more work.

As a result, the focus on the marriage intensifies, and many of the rules the couple had over the years regarding intimacy, togetherness, division of housework, finances, and so on, no longer apply, and new rules need to be negotiated. In addition, the narrowing of focus on the marital bond combined with the greater amount of time spent together often raises unresolved issues that had lain dormant while work or children were the thrust of the relationship.

For example, dissatisfaction with emotional intimacy can no longer be explained and excused; the days are over when the woman could dismiss her husband's emotional reserve by saying to herself, "He's just too consumed by work to give more than he's giving now." Similarly, a husband can no longer rationalize his wife's unwillingness to do things with him by saying, "She's such a good parent that she doesn't want to take any time away from the kids."

And of course, couples in retirement sometimes find that what used to be tolerable traits when they worked and spent less time together turn into irritating flaws; a husband's affinity for watching sporting events goes from an acceptable habit to a symbol of his tendency to waste time and ignore his wife.

Preventing and Resolving Relationship Issues

The following pages will guide you through a variety of issues, from maintaining the together–separate balance to negotiating around gender-based roadblocks to diffusing conflicts that revolve around family. You'll find information to help you enjoy an easy and satisfying transition to retirement as an individual and as a couple.

What you won't find is information about the following two subjects: financial planning and dealing with declining health. The absence of financial planning information is due to the surplus of books, articles, and the like on this subject. The health aspects often are largely out of people's control, and so there isn't much advice I can offer on this front. Obviously, health can have a major impact on relationships in retirement, but my focus is on areas where we have more personal control and ability to prevent or solve problems.

I should also point out that this new edition has a section (that was not addressed in the first edition) on involuntary retirement; a problem that is not preventable but can be addressed effectively. This subject has become particularly relevant during and after the recent financial downturn. You'll find information on it in Chapter 10.

As you'll learn, I'm most concerned with those to whom gerontologists refer as the "young-old": healthy, vigorous people who chose to retire and are able to afford it. They are generally active and well integrated in the lives of their families and communities. They may be older in years, but they retain the desire to live a happy, fulfilling life. I assume that you're one of these young-old individuals, and that if your relationship is suffering in retirement, you recognize that things can get better.

As you read, I hope you'll also keep in mind that I'm writing not just to help you better manage your own personal retirement but also to help you develop an awareness and sensitivity to whatever turmoil your spouse is facing. This book will emphasize how crucial it is to think about the transition to retirement from a couple's perspective. The fact that you have an easy adjustment does not mean that you'll be able to enjoy your retirement if your partner is blocked and unable to find joy in this new life stage. The stuck partner can't be ignored. Even when only one spouse has difficulties adjusting to retirement, the quality of life for both partners as well as the marriage will be negatively impacted.

Therefore, throughout the book you'll find suggestions that will help you develop a better ability to move through this transition as an individual and as part of a couple. For example, many people are so wrapped up in their own anxiety about retirement that they are oblivious to their partner's process and do not allow their spouses the time and space they need for a successful transition. Too often, they're unaware of the gap between their retirement needs and their spouse's expectations. Therefore, they're knocked for a loop by the way the partner is responding to retirement and sometimes have difficulty recovering. Ideally, couples will prevent this from happening by addressing issues proactively, before they retire. Realistically, many people will wait until after retirement and come to this book eager to rescue the relationship.

While reading, instead of assuming that my suggestions are "one size fits all," please consider that different individuals and couples will receive varying benefits from this book. What is extremely helpful and meaningful for one might not be so important to another. Trust your own experiences and what feels right to you. Most important, read this book not only from your head, but also from your heart. Over the years, I've developed a set of techniques and tools that I share with readers. The coverage of topics in each chapter is based on my clinical experience and knowledge of the research relevant to retirement transitions and related marital dynamics. At the end of most chapters you'll find exercises and questions that will help you apply the material to your own situation and that can be the basis of productive discussions with your spouse.

Each chapter also includes examples. The case histories you'll read about are drawn from my professional experiences as well as accounts from colleagues and friends. I, of course, disguise the identities of the people whose stories I cite and use composites in some instances. At times, I simplify complex therapeutic situations in order to make examples clear and accessible.

Finally, I want to emphasize that the underlying message of this book is optimistic. The retired couples with whom I've worked respond well to counseling or coaching, which is frequently short-term, and are often able to resolve the problems caused by retirement. If people have enjoyed a strong, solid marriage for many years, there's no reason they can't enjoy a wonderful retirement together.

The key is to bring the deeper sources of relationship problems out into the open and negotiate an equitable solution. Couples who regularly experienced miscommunication during the work years or who are bedeviled by unresolved issues that retirement exposed sometimes need more time to work through and around the obstacles. Even these couples frequently reach new levels of closeness and marital satisfaction as the unresolved issues are finally put to rest in a satisfying manner.

Preparation is the byword. Retirement-preparation programs generally help couples enjoy happier relationships, and I hope this book has the same effect. By preparing for life after work, you'll be able to constructively plan and enjoy this "third age"—after childhood/adolescence and work/child-raising. Your participation in psychologically valid preparation activities such as reading this book reflects the desire to achieve emotional integrity and self-fulfillment in retirement.

Demonstrating that you recognize the psychological challenge of retirement and that you're willing to work to meet this challenge is a good sign. When you're done reading, I believe you'll be able to say, "For better or for worse *and also* for lunch."

CHAPTER TWO

Learning to Let Go of Work and Making the Psychological Shift to Retirement

Work is a funny thing. As much as you may complain about it—the hours, the politics, the lack of recognition, the travel, the competition, the boss, the employees, the customers—you also derive fulfillment and meaning from it. What you do for a living and when, how, why, and where you do it shape this meaning. If you are unaware of the particular relationship you have to your work, you may not be prepared psychologically to retire and are more likely to harm your marriage.

Making the psychological transition to retirement is a challenge, and it's a challenge that cannot be met without first understanding the meaning of work. Gaining this understanding is a more complex endeavor than you may think.

Jim, for instance, was convinced that he knew what work gave him and that he was ready to give it up. A top marketing executive with a Fortune 500 company, Jim initially thrived on the pressure and competitiveness that came with the job, and he did well professionally. Working for three different organizations over the course of his career, he gained power in these companies and prestige within the industry.

At the last company, though, he found himself floundering. He was not as quick as others to pick up on the internet marketing trend, and he knew that young members of the marketing department viewed him as an old fogy.

At 63, he decided to take early retirement. While he intended to do some consulting and "keep his hand in," he primarily wanted to spend more time at his country home fishing, hiking, and sitting on the deck reading a stack of books he'd been meaning to get to for years.

At first, retirement was a relief, and Jim did all the things he'd promised himself he'd do when he left the office whirl. After four months, however, he began to miss the action, the power he had wielded, and the camaraderie of his team. He was faced with too much "unstructured" time to mark.

At work, most of his days had been structured by various meetings, projects, and objectives. He used to daydream about just sitting on the dock behind his country home and waiting for the fish to bite. Now he recognized that this activity as well as others to which he'd been looking forward weren't as all-consuming as in his daydream. Ironically, Jim would sit there fishing and daydream about coordinating an advertising campaign. He was also dissatisfied with the people in his circle. As much as he liked the couples with whom he and his wife shared their time, they seemed to lack the energy and creativity of his former colleagues.

As a result of all this, Jim became irritable, especially around his wife. She was a magnet for his frustrations, sparking them with an offhand comment or even a "look." Their bickering increased, and then Jim became depressed and withdrawn. Part of the problem was that they were spending more time together than they ever had before. Part of it was that his wife had her own life, and he felt like an intruder. But the real source of the problem was that Jim had not prepared psychologically for retirement. He had never really come to terms with what work meant to him, and when his honeymoon stage ended, he was unable to reorient himself. Thus, he was unable to fill up his life in other, equally meaningful ways.

To avoid landing in Jim's predicament and becoming stuck in the disenchantment stage of retirement, you first have to arm yourself with a basic understanding of what work really means to you.

The Four Elemental Meanings

Jim, like many other people, didn't think deeply or perceptively about his work. It's not just "a job" or "fun." It's more than just an opportunity to do what you do well. Work is a complex process that provides different satisfactions for different people. To develop an appreciation of these satisfactions, let's look at the four psychologically relevant aspects of work:

1. Structured time
2. Social interaction
3. Personal identity, accomplishment, and status
4. Life purpose

Structured Time

Dealing with vast stretches of "empty" time is often the first challenge for recent retirees. The person who works the traditional nine-to-five day has a different lifestyle from that of the person who works evenings or nights. Pilots or consultants may work continuously for days or even weeks without a break, while others who have their own businesses may lack specific working hours. With the advent of flextime and telecommuting in the workplace, some people have the freedom to arrange their time according to their needs and preferences. Some individuals stick to 40-hour weeks, while others frequently put in twice that much time working evenings and weekends.

Our work schedules have a significant impact on how we react to retirement. For instance, people who are accustomed to being at work from nine to five, Monday through Friday, may be disconcerted to be home during these hours. For decades, they were at home during the week only when they were sick or on vacation. In fact, at first, nine-to-fivers tend to view their retirement as a vacation, and it's only when the vacation extends far beyond the norm that they become antsy.

Workaholics often are uncomfortable in a non-work environment. For them, work time was "real" time; it imposed a structure on their lives. Retirement is a fantasy, though not in the positive sense of the word. To many workaholics, retirement seems an aimless existence. From their work-focused perspective, there is nothing to do.

People who did some or all of their work at home or who had more flexible schedules often make a smoother transition to retirement. Their lives were not as tightly circumscribed by their work schedules; they didn't automatically associate certain times with work and certain times with non-work activities. Consequently, they aren't thrown off kilter so much by the free time of retirement.

Work imbues our time with a concrete meaning: we bill by the hour; we are accountable to a boss for how we spend our time; we have time frames and time lines that organize our days and weeks; we tote calendars filled with meetings, conferences, and deadlines. Whether or not this is truly meaningful activity is beside the point. It fosters the sense that our time is valuable, and this makes the chaos that lurks on the edge of our vision bearable. When we're no longer working, the eternity of death can be glimpsed much more easily. We begin to question why we were placed on this earth.

In retirement, the symptoms of this malaise aren't necessarily metaphysical discussions. They usually manifest themselves in some mundane event. Many recent retirees recount specific time-related incidents that make them angry or sad.

Denise, for instance, worked as a court reporter for 17 years before she retired, and she couldn't remember ever having taken an entire week off while staying at home. During her work life, she always did the family grocery shopping on Saturday. Shortly after she retired, she went to her neighborhood supermarket on a weekday and was amazed at how empty it was and how much faster she was able to get through her list. She bitterly recalled what an imposition on her time shopping had been in the past, but she was equally bitter when she observed, "Now that I have all the time in the world, I can do the shopping in half the time it took to do it before."

Martin, another recent retiree, had a similar reaction when he went to his bank on a weekday. While he was gratified to be able to complete his transaction more quickly, he felt "as if something was wrong" when he didn't have to stand in line as he had in the past. Perhaps the banking environment reminded him that he was no longer earning a regular paycheck. Whatever the reason, as he breezed in and out of the bank, Martin viewed himself as disengaged from the world and unproductive. At that moment he had the image of himself as "a useless old man."

You need to become aware of your time sensitivities, and these sensitivities vary by individuals. One person may feel blue sitting in a restaurant and watching through the window as commuters stream by for an outbound rush-hour train. Another person's angst may be triggered by seeing children walking to or from school and by realizing he hasn't seen that sight in 30 years. Becoming aware of feelings produced by these situations will help you stop them from spilling over, spoiling your mood, and possibly harming your marriage.

Social Interaction

Work is also a place to meet and develop friendships and a sense of belonging to a group. If you're like most people, you feel that you share interests with colleagues as well as specific experiences that have shaped your work lives. The collegiality of working on the same team, the mutual dislike of the same boss, the achievement of the same career objectives—all these qualities bind people together and provide the social interaction that most of us enjoy.

You've probably gone to a party or other type of social gathering with your spouse and noticed that the people who work together gather together. If you're not part of their work group, you feel like an outsider. Similarly, different professions have specific restaurants or bars where members gather together after work. There are cop bars, journalist hangouts, and places where professional athletes congregate.

If most of your friends and social acquaintances are tied to your work environment, retirement will have more of an impact on you than it would if your friends were mostly from other sources. When people retire, the common thread that work provided and that bound many of their friendships together begins to fray.

Though some people insist that they can sustain their work relationships in retirement, the prospect is dubious. Just think about what percentage of time you spend talking with work friends about non-work activities: it's highly likely that the majority of your conversation focuses on bonuses, work projects, the new boss, a seminar you attended, or an unfair policy. Taking all this away may not end the relationship—you doubtless share other areas of interest—but it probably will diminish it. The friendship won't be as rich or as timely without the events of the workday as fodder for speculation, argument, and consensus.

If you lose this social interaction but find that your spouse still retains his or her own social network of friends, tension is likely. In the past, your mutually exclusive circles of friends balanced each other out. For men especially, the balance can easily tip in the spouse's favor because women tend to have more personal friendships, and husbands can resent this. If you're in this position, you may feel as if your wife is spending all of her time with them and not enough with you, and you may even verbalize this feeling to her. It's no wonder that many retired people cling annoyingly to their spouses in a desperate attempt to replace the social interaction they no longer have.

Personal Identity, Accomplishment, and Status

In our culture, what we do for a living defines to a great extent who we are. When we meet new people, we reflexively ask them what they do for a living. Typically, a university professor is regarded differently from a factory worker; a housewife is regarded differently from a doctor. In every culture, certain occupations are more prestigious than others, and the people who occupy the more prestigious ones are regarded with more respect. Thus, doctors and lawyers receive more respect than nurses and accountants; nurses and accountants receive more respect than receptionists and factory workers.

This occupational caste system carries many subtle but meaningful distinctions. Certainly factory workers or receptionists can find their work meaningful; most people invest great meaning in their chosen professions no matter what they do. Nevertheless, our cultural norms make us acutely conscious of what we do for a living.

In western society, usually the financial rewards are tied to the status level: the greater the prestige of the profession, the more money one earns. The reverse is also true, particularly in American culture: a person who earns a lot of money is regarded with respect, even though the profession itself may not be a prestigious one. So, the owner of a profitable garbage collection company is esteemed.

It's not only what we do for a living but also how we do it that creates our occupational identity. Expertise, productivity, success, and accomplishment all shape this identity. For most people, work is a way to feel that they are contributing and adding some value to society, by either helping others (for example, a social worker), providing a service (a travel agent), or manufacturing a needed product (a factory worker).

Besides this feeling of productivity, our identity is interlaced with our perception of how successful and accomplished we are. This perception is based on a comparison with others in our profession or a determination of how we measure up to internal expectations regarding salary, job promotions, special recognition, and capstone positions.

Sometimes what we do and how we do it aren't in sync, resulting in people in the same profession having different occupational identities. One judge, for example, may not feel as successful as another because he wasn't appointed to a higher court. By the same token, someone in a "lower-caste" profession may have a superior occupational identity to that of someone in a higher-caste profession because he's met his internal expectations. A plumber may feel terrific about his career because he has achieved his goal of earning a six-figure income, being the boss of four other people, and being able to bring his son into his business.

Work involvement is a term psychologists use to describe the degree to which a person identifies psychologically with his or her job and the importance of the job to the person's self-image and self-esteem. Typically, the people with the most work involvement are the ones who have careers rather than jobs. Careers demand commitment, a strategy for "moving up," and a period of training and education before competency is achieved.

If you have a career, money is not the main reason you work—though it's an important benefit. Instead, you derive internal satisfaction from what you do and a strong sense of identification with your profession. Career people value the prestige of their work and the challenges they encounter there. The opportunities for new learning and challenges that are needed in order to complete work assignments keep them stimulated and excited about their occupation.

On the other hand, the person with relatively little work involvement has a job. It's primarily a way to earn a living. Usually within a short period of plying the trade, the person feels proficient and competent. Possibilities for new challenges and advancement are few, and extrinsic factors such as money, fringe benefits, and job security are extremely important. This person's sense of identity frequently is derived from non-work arenas such as family or a volunteer project—maybe as a coach or scout leader.

Again, people in so-called prestigious occupations may have a job mentality. For instance, I know a pediatrician in private practice who saw his work as mostly a way to provide for his family; he lacked the commitment and internal satisfaction necessary for it to be a career in the true sense of the word.

As a general rule, the higher the work involvement, the greater difficulty someone has adjusting to retirement.

Let's say you're dedicated to your career as an investigative journalist and you worked long and hard to achieve a top position with a leading newspaper; you've received awards from various groups for your muckraking as well as continuous recognition from peers. After 40 years, you retire. Suddenly your identity and status have waned. While you may have several satisfying roles in your personal life—spouse, parent, grandparent, amateur gardener—none is as compelling as your identity at work. If your major role is now as a spouse, you're naturally (and perhaps unconsciously) going to contrast it unfavorably with your position as investigative journalist. Your spouse doesn't praise you as much as your peers and editors did. Shopping for groceries together lacks the excitement and discovery of breaking a big story. Going with your spouse to donate blood doesn't instill the same sense of 'doing good' as exposing a conglomerate that's exploiting its workers.

Obviously, these comparisons aren't fair—a marriage provides satisfactions that work can never provide—but from the perspective of a retired person, fairness doesn't enter into it. Some people who have left highly involving careers lack the objectivity to analyze their restructured roles rationally. Instead, they become angry or depressed because that high level of work involvement has been "taken" from them and they haven't found anything to replace it. Since work was a context for having meaningful experiences that provided a sense of accomplishment, leaving work causes stress because of the hardship of replacing that sense of accomplishment.

Roberta was the head of the litigation department in a large law firm. She was clearly a workaholic and spent many hours involved with complex litigation. She liked the "high" while preparing for trial and the "rush" of locking horns with the opposing attorney; she also liked to mentor younger associates and teach them the secrets of the trade. Perhaps just as important was the power and prestige her position gave her. Most of Roberta's friends were either colleagues or clients, and she had no hobbies or interests besides her family. She had been married for 18 years to Bill, a successful psychologist in private practice. His two children from his first marriage were married and living in other states.

Roberta was not prepared for her retirement. Her law firm merged with another, and the atmosphere changed in a way that made it less rewarding for her. Since she was in her late 60s and had enough money, she decided to retire. Shortly thereafter, however, she became depressed and started therapy. During our sessions, she came to realize how much her sense of self-worth was based on the recognition and approval she received at work and how hard it was for her to have a feeling of self-worth without being considered an authority in her field.

Facilitating this realization was Roberta's discovery that her parents had always used tangible accomplishments as a measure of her worth. She recalled that when she was a child, the notion of stopping to smell the roses was frowned upon as a form of laziness. When she recognized that her intelligence, hard work, and mentoring capabilities could be useful outside of the work environment, she rediscovered her sense of self-worth.

Therapy also helped her acknowledge how much she missed her colleagues and how they reflected her value as a person back at her—they were a mirror for her worth. Finally, she was able to approach the impact of her depression on her marriage, and she became much more conscious of her pouting and whining behavior with her husband.

She eventually realized that she was angry with herself for not enjoying her retirement—she had expected to continue to excel as she did in almost every aspect of her life—but instead of facing this anger, she displaced it to Bill. She discovered that she was furious with her husband because he didn't know how to "take care" of her as he did during their working years. Since Bill was a psychotherapist, she expected him to know how to help her with her depression. Expressing her vulnerability, owning the responsibility to take care of her depression rather than putting it on Bill, and asking for the help she needed led to improvements in both her feelings about herself and her marriage.

Life Purpose

Some people are driven to achieve a goal, often sacrificing income, time, and even family life to reach a noble objective. For these people, work provides an opportunity to fulfill their life purpose. Mother Teresa and Albert Schweitzer are two examples of people who were consumed by their life purpose, but others who are not as well known are similarly driven—a scientist who spends the majority of her time in the laboratory looking for a cure for a disease or a teacher who works overtime to enrich the lives of inner-city kids.

When these people are cut off from their life purpose, they are cut off from their reason for being. It's a mistake to think you can turn off a life purpose at will. Still, some people approaching retirement fool themselves into believing that they should no longer tilt at windmills or follow their dreams. Perhaps they feel they are no longer as effective as they once were or they've been pushed aside by others with more youth and energy.

While some people burn out and lose interest in a life purpose, most retain that itch to scratch. In these instances, they must find a way to continue their life work, albeit in a different manner. Sometimes people can continue to pursue their goals on a consulting basis or in a voluntary capacity; they can provide their former associations or organizations with advice and become involved in different ways from when they were full-time employees or leaders. Even if they're working toward this life purpose for less or no money, and even if their roles have been diminished, they still derive great satisfaction from doing what they feel they were meant to do.

Louise was an executive in a charity organization that provided care for seriously ill children. She loved what she did; it was far more than work or even a career. She was childless, and performing her job gave her an opportunity to feel maternal and nurturing. After her retirement, she wisely decided to continue her involvement with the charity in a volunteer role. Not only didn't Louise mind giving up the money and responsibilities that came with her executive job, but also she was relieved to be able to apply herself to the parts of the job she loved and eschew the tasks—such as fund-raising—that she disliked.

If your work helped you pursue a life purpose, and you still are motivated by that purpose upon retiring, find a way to contribute to your cause. If you don't, it's almost inevitable that you—and your marriage—will suffer.

While others can replace the jobs and careers they miss with some other activity or interest, you can't replicate a life purpose by taking up tennis or golf. You can expect to be irritable and even depressed, and your spouse will remark to others that "Pat really started to change for the worse after retirement." As close as you and your spouse may be, the relationship has probably always been equal or even taken a backseat to the life purpose. Throughout the years, there's been an understanding that "the cause" will sometimes take precedence over family activities.

This often is accepted by the family because the purpose is noble rather than mercenary. You can't just cut yourself off from this powerful feeling without negative consequences. Moreover, your spouse may not know how to relate to you when you're not being driven by your life purpose; it's as if you become a different and often less admirable person.

Retirement Satisfaction vs. Adjustment to Retirement

An important 2008 study makes a distinction between adjustment to retirement and retirement satisfaction. While the two concepts are related they are not identical. Yet both are crucial to our understanding of how to best make the shift to retirement.

Retirement satisfaction is primarily related to access to resources. Health, money, and a marital relationship, which are of minor importance to adjustment to retirement, are important to retirement satisfaction. Important factors here are how the individual retired—voluntary vs. involuntary, and from which job, i.e., challenging vs. boring. The greater the intrinsic value of the job, the lower the retirement satisfaction. Thus people who have fulfilling careers will show lower levels of retirement satisfaction.

Individuals who have *careers*, whose self-identity is tied with work, have more challenges for re-establishing and maintaining self-identity in retirement. They often prefer to continue to work rather than deal with a life where this highly meaningful activity is taken from them. For individuals who had *jobs* and saw work merely as a source of income, adjustment to retirement is easier and they are less willing to continue work after retirement unless they need the money. They also tend to have higher levels of retirement satisfaction.

Engagement in volunteer work increases retirement satisfaction. Pre-retirement engagement in volunteer activities has a beneficial effect on adjustment to retirement as well. The non-work identity of the volunteer role provides stability and support as one enters retirement and acts as a bridge between the work and retirement lifestyles. In a 2007 study, individuals who showed more stable patterns of satisfaction were those who had many resources to compensate for the loss of the work role: High self-esteem, being married, having good health, and maintaining non-work activities were factors contributing to their high and relatively stable life satisfaction.

A 2009 study found that the most important predictors of women's retirement satisfaction were self-esteem, mastery, emotional support, and ethnicity. Instrumental support, such as getting help in meal preparation, housework, shopping, and transportation, didn't contribute to retirement satisfaction. Likewise, informational support (receiving information or advice on how to handle difficult circumstance and situations) did not contribute to retirement satisfaction. In this study African-American women were more satisfied in retirement than their Caucasian counterparts.

Here are some other key findings of the study:

- High self-esteem had a positive impact on well-being in retirement by lowering depression and contributing to more participation in activities that fostered feelings of self-worth, e.g., volunteering. Women who adopt multiple roles in retirement experience a greater sense of well-being and higher self-esteem.

- Mastery, having a sense of control over life events and decisions, and the ability to solve problems is important to retirement satisfaction for women as well. This relates primarily to *voluntary* retirement. Women who feel an obligation to retire due to family pressure or extenuating circumstances experience a reduced sense of mastery, thus contributing to negative assessment of retirement and lower psychological well-being. Involuntary retirement is discussed in depth in Chapter 10.

- Emotional support is the only support that contributes to positive retirement satisfaction for women; informational support and instrumental support did not. Since retirement can be a stressful transition involving multiple losses and relationship changes, having a supportive network buffers the stresses of this transition and contributes to greater retirement satisfaction. This finding reinforces the importance of close friends to women's retirement satisfaction.

Retirement adjustment is mostly a psychological process involving a detachment from the social contacts of work. Both the context in which the retirement transition is made and psychological factors help determine retirement adjustment.

While health and financial considerations are important to retirement satisfaction, they are of relatively minor importance in retirement adjustment and play a minor role in explaining differences in why one person adjusts well and one person doesn't.

People struggle to adjust to retirement when they have strong attachment to work and a general disposition to respond with anxiety to changes. Lower feeling of self-efficacy (low confidence in one's ability to deal with changes) and expressed anxiety about consequences of retirement (such as loss of social contacts and status) are related to a difficult adjustment to retirement. These factors, though, are not related to retirement satisfaction.

Another factor that impacts retirement adjustment is how we view retirement. It may be seen as a life period of uncertainty and crisis stemming mainly from loss of work and fear of the great void of unscheduled time. Or we may have a less bleak perception of retirement, viewing it as a liberating experience and as an opportunity to do things that work had precluded. Those who viewed it with uncertainty feared it, while those who viewed it as an opportunity welcomed it and had an easier adjustment to it.

Women have bigger problems with retirement adjustment than men, perhaps because women who work until retirement age and after are motivated and career-focused individuals. For these women, the losses associated with retirement include: loss of identity, social contacts, and social status. These losses are more substantial for women than for men. In addition women, more often than men, retire because their husbands did or want them to do so while they are not fully ready to retire, so their decision is not fully voluntary.

Involuntary departure from work has a negative effect not only to the adjustment to retirement but also on retirement satisfaction. When we have a sense of control or mastery over our life, we find it easier to maintain well-being as a retiree. Not having a say in the timing of retirement challenges our opportunities for self-management. This hampers not only the adjustment to retirement but also has a negative effect on our well-being and quality of life in the long run—even up to six years after retirement.

Pre-retirement concerns about marital conflict suggest that adjustment may be difficult for both partners. Particularly when the marriage is not strong, the prospect of spending more time together can create increased apprehension. When people who are still employed experience adjustment problems, their partner's adjustment is hampered too. Partners play an important role in the retirement decision and it is important that each partner can feel he or she has some control over the decision.

Another way to look at retirement adjustment is by using the concept of *cognitive dissonance*. Cognitive dissonance is an uncomfortable psychological state involving incongruence or disconnect between what one holds to be true and what ones know to be true. In turn, this tension results in attempts to reduce the discomfort by adjusting one's beliefs.

People, who are able to change their views about the importance of work and recognize that retirement is a good thing experience less cognitive dissonance and a smoother transition to retirement. Retirees need to change their reference group—those they compare themselves to—from their colleagues to other retirees. For example, if retired people rate their health against the health of their retired peers rather than their prior work colleagues, they may begin to see themselves as relatively healthy. So an important adaptive mechanism to cope with retirement and avoid cognitive dissonance is to change our frame of reference to reflect our age group and social peers. By doing this, we help maintain positive perceptions and an optimistic outlook.

While the transition to retirement does require adjustment, a healthy level of satisfaction is reached by recognizing that retirement is a process of moving forward into a new stage, not leaving a life behind. Gaining satisfaction in retirement is derived from good health, adequate finances, and a strong marriage. Developing the resources to compensate for loss of a fulfilling career can help ease the transition and provide a beneficial sense of control, and thus, a fuller life.

Exercises:
Evaluating the Meaning of Work and the Difficulty of Letting Go

Whether you are happy with yourself and your marriage in retirement, or whether your marriage is suffering after your own or your spouse's retirement, it's likely that work was a meaningful experience for one or both of you. Letting go of work means being aware of and acknowledging your feelings of loss, talking about them with your spouse, and taking certain actions to replace the meaning that's been subtracted. In order to be able to let go, you first need to achieve awareness of the ways in which work was meaningful to you.

The following exercises will help you assess the meaning of each of the four work elements. In each question, circle the answer that seems to be the closest to your situation.

Structured Time Exercise

1. How many hours did you work during the course of an average week?

    A. 70 or more
    B. Between 45 and 70
    C. Around 40
    D. Fewer than 40

2. How would you characterize your work schedule?

   A. Traditional five-day-a-week routine with weekends off
   B. A mixture of a traditional schedule and a more flexible schedule of days off during the week and work on weekends
   C. A highly flexible schedule in which you could choose the hours you work
   D. No particular schedule; you operated your own business and worked a wide variety of schedules based on business requirements, or you haven't worked consistently or at all (housewife or househusband)

3. During your off hours—vacations, on weekends, and in the evenings—how did you feel?

   A. Restless and anxious—more comfortable at work than when relaxing with friends and family
   B. Experienced mixed emotions about the time off; enjoying being at home and on vacation but also thinking a lot about work
   C. Sometimes wished you could be at work, but mostly could enjoy your time away from the office
   D. Completely relaxed and rarely if ever thought about or wanted to be at work.

If you selected one or more A responses, it's likely that work met a significant need for time structure in your life, and this loss may bear heavily on your retirement. If most of your responses were Bs and Cs, then it may be somewhat of a problem. If your responses were all or mostly Ds, the impact should be negligible.

Social Interaction Exercise

Which of the following statements best characterizes your work relationships? Circle the answer that seems the most appropriate.

   A. The people with whom I worked were my closest friends. Almost all of my socializing involved them. They really understood who I am and appreciated my strengths.

B. I really appreciated the relationships I formed on the job. I felt close to the people with whom I worked, and we socialized away from work. I made equally good friends who had nothing to do with work, and I wouldn't put one type of relationship above the other.

C. I liked the people with whom I worked, and a few became good friends, but most of my close relationships involve extended family, friends I made in school, neighbors, and people involved in activities in which I participate.

D. My work associates were fine, but I didn't develop real friendships and rarely did anything with them after work or on weekends.

Again, an A answer suggests that it will be more difficult to leave work relationships behind and that this may hamper your relationships with your spouse. At the other end of the spectrum, a D answer probably means that the quality of your social interactions will not be affected.

Personal Identity and Status Exercise

Indicate whether or not each of the following statements applies to you. If you no longer work, answer the questions as if you did.

For me, time at work tends to really fly by.

     Yes   No

A great satisfaction in my life comes from my work.

     Yes   No

My approach is often to plan ahead the next day's work activities

     Yes   No

I am very involved personally with my work.

     Yes   No

I've received a number of promotions.

     Yes   No

Through my education, training, and experience, I've achieved a high level of expertise in my field.

Yes   No

The most important things that happen to me are usually related to my work.

Yes   No

I believe it's okay to work long hours if you love your work.

Yes   No

I often think about my work when I'm away from it.

Yes   No

I would probably keep working even if I didn't need the money.

Yes   No

If the majority of the statements apply to you, you had a career and therefore probably derived a great deal of your identity from work. If most of the statements do not apply, you had a job and didn't derive much of your identity from work.

Life Purpose Exercise

Some people know immediately and instinctively if their work revolved around their life purpose, especially if they were in a helping profession such as medicine, social work, or community activism. When people sacrifice money and creature comforts in order to help others, it's usually because they see their work as their destiny.

For others, however, it's more difficult to make this determination. A civil liberties lawyer might have sacrificed income to uphold the rights of disadvantaged individuals, but he might have grown increasingly disenchanted with this mission as his career wound down. Or a computer entrepreneur may believe that his life purpose was to invent a new, better way of computing, and even though he made a lot of money doing it, he might not have made the world a better place.

People in any field may feel that they never came close to achieving a particular life purpose and that, therefore, achieving their life purpose through their work was just a pipe dream.

If you're unsure where you stand, ask yourself the following questions:

Did I have a vision of what I wanted to accomplish in my life?

If yes, did my work enable me to pursue this vision with great commitment and satisfaction?

Would I feel less fulfilled without my work?

If your answer is yes to more than one of these questions, consider yourself lucky, but also consider that this will make your transition to retirement enormously difficult if you separate your life from this purpose.

Now that you have a sense of what work meant to you and the challenges associated with this meaning, let's proceed to the psychological implications of a "life of leisure" and the need to establish goals to add meaning to this phase of your life.

CHAPTER THREE

Finding Your Purpose in Retirement

If work was a meaningful experience for you or your spouse, it's probable that part of this meaning reflected pride of professional achievement and expertise. Getting a promotion or a raise, contributing a breakthrough idea, growing your own business to a certain level—objectives such as these were milestones along the way that marked your career progress and provided a sense of achievement.

When these goals and accomplishments disappear upon retirement, people who did not prepare psychologically feel empty and directionless. These feelings can have a devastating effect on a relationship. Typically, people segue from empty and directionless to depressed or angry, alienating their spouses with the behaviors that these feelings spawn, such as being uncommunicative or argumentative. Or they attempt to live through the spouse, drawing sustenance from the partner's accomplishments rather than their own. Trying to live one's life through another person can ultimately be destructive to the relationship. A goal-less person who spends too much time with his or her spouse can drain the partner's emotional energy.

The remedy is to develop non-work goals that fill your time with meaningful, satisfying, fun, and challenging activities as well as help you fulfill your life purpose. Some of these goals revolve around volunteerism. Others relate to physically and intellectually stimulating activities. All of them will enhance your life and marriage. The hitch is formulating these goals "leisurely."

Leisure time is confusing, and I've found that people do a better job of formulating new goals if they understand the psychological implications of leisure. Before plumbing that psychology, it's useful to review the different stages of retirement, particularly the honeymoon stage, and the critical function of stimulating activities as the ensuing stages of retirement unfold.

The Honeymoon Stage

Retirement is an event, but it is also a multistage process, as described in Atchley's classical 1982 work, "The Process of Retirement." The first stage is *pre-retirement*, the period in which anticipatory attitudes and often subconscious expectations are formed. Then comes the *retirement event*—the specific act of leaving work, usually around the time that the worker is entitled to receive full-retirement benefits. This exit from the labor force is sometimes marked by a celebration and retirement party. The *honeymoon* stage comes next, and in it we experience anywhere from a few months to a year of great joy—a honeymoon period. We relish being able to do what we want when we feel like doing it as well as the freedom from having to be somewhere at a certain time. When the stress of a highly structured, highly demanding work life is removed, many people feel that they can finally relax and enjoy life.

Initially, that's exactly what they do. They start projects around the house: cleaning closets, examining stuff that was in the basement or attic for years, mounting photos in albums or creating a digital gallery of life's special events. Others plow through years of accumulated paperwork and sort out what needs to be discarded. All this cleaning and organizing confers a temporary sense of order and control. When they're not cleaning, sorting, and putting things together, people often set out on long-deferred trips. Sometimes they take elaborate, extended vacations to remote parts of the globe. Other times they are content to go to one special place or to spend more time at a vacation home.

This honeymoon period ends when these projects and trips no longer furnish the same sense of satisfaction they did at first. People who have longed to travel and then do so upon retirement remark that they begin to feel disconnected from family and friends after extended trips. Those who had a long list of home-repair or cleaning projects recount how they finished everything faster than they thought and how the projects turned to drudgery.

Certainly some individuals continue to derive the same satisfaction from home projects and continuous travel, but they're in the minority. For most, the enjoyment decreases, and the disenchantment stage of retirement commences at this point. It is the "letdown" following the honeymoon stage as people realize that they need to reorient themselves.

In order to understand why the honeymoon stage ends, it helps to distinguish between positive experiences that are *pleasurable* and those that are *enjoyable*. The American Psychological Association devoted a special issue of its journal, *American Psychologist* (January 2000), to "Happiness, Excellence, and Optimal Human Functioning." In the introductory article, the authors define pleasure as the good feeling that comes from satisfying homeostatic needs such as hunger, sex, and bodily comfort, while enjoyment is the good feelings people experience when they break the homeostasis—when they do an activity that stretches them beyond what they were. This can be an athletic event, an artistic performance, or a good deed.

Enjoyment rather than pleasure is what leads to long-term happiness. During the honeymoon stage, retirees experience many pleasures that diminish with time; they fade away because they do not require you to stretch beyond what you were before. Given a sustained lack of enjoyment, free time can feel more like a curse than a blessing. Though we have the freedom to choose when and what we want to do, we no longer are particularly interested in exercising that freedom. What we do for entertainment begins to seem frivolous or boring, especially in comparison with meaningful work.

When the honeymoon ends, people who are not psychologically prepared for retirement begin to suffer emotionally, and invariably their personal relationships also begin to deteriorate. A couple who started out relishing the leisure time they shared begins to find it stifling and trivial; it ceases to be a pleasurable experience. In fact, many couples bicker about precisely the things that used to be so much fun. The fur flies over decisions of what movie to see, what trip to take, what museum to visit. It's as if their leisure is mocking them.

Why did a leisure activity that promised to be so enjoyable transform itself into something so mundane? Retirees need to reorient themselves when the honeymoon stage draws to a close and the disenchantment stage starts. This means setting realistic goals and developing satisfying and meaningful routines that will stretch them, resulting in a sense of personal growth.

Happy, meaningful relationships are possible only when you replace meaningful work with multiple-level stimulation and a sense of accomplishment or mastery. That brings us to the three types of stimulation and why they're important in reorienting yourself in retirement.

Physical, Intellectual and Creative Stimulation

Research about intrinsic motivation helps explain why stimulation is so important for a successful retirement. *Intrinsic motivation* is the inherent tendency to seek out novelty and challenge, to extend one's capacity, to explore and learn. *External motivation*, on the other hand, sets goals that are external to the person, such as money or respect. Researchers have found that intrinsic motivation enhances feelings of competence and efficacy, particularly when it is self-determined and autonomous. It is a source of enjoyment and vitality that never wears off, unlike the enjoyment that comes from extrinsic motivation, which fades relatively quickly. Intrinsic motivation, therefore, should be what retirees aim for.

Another way of looking at this involves the notion of "being in the flow"—a term first used by Professor Mihaly Csikszentmihalyi from Claremont Graduate University. Flow is one of the behaviors identified by researchers as a buffer against depression. Between the anxiety of being overwhelmed and stressed and the apathy of being bored lies a zone in which people experience flow.

Flow arises from the engagement in an activity or skill cultivation that requires high levels of concentration, active participation, and perception of the importance of the activity. When we are in the flow, often we can't believe how quickly time has passed while we were absorbed in this highly satisfying behavior. Repetitive jobs in which we are competent and for which we are handsomely compensated, or passively enjoyable entertainment such as watching television, are not flow-inducing activities. Only complex and challenging activities provide the opportunity for flow. Any complex activity that engages one's skills and requires complex thinking and high concentration can be a source of flow, including gardening, knitting, creative writing, handicrafts, music performance, tennis or other sports, chess, and artistic painting.

Getting into the flow of retirement doesn't mean becoming accustomed to a mundane life or learning to "relax." In the best sense of the term, it means pursuing highly engaging and complex activities. By doing so, you're likely to not only find your purpose in retirement but also be a much more enjoyable and empathic companion for your spouse. As we'll see, both members of a couple have to maintain not just the passion in their marriage but also their individual passions for life.

Let's look at the three sources of stimulation that you could pursue and how they can provide you with intrinsic satisfaction as well as be a source for flow.

Physical Stimulation

People seem to lose their spark when separated from meaningful work. It's common for spouses to report that a recently retired husband or wife has become "less vital." While physical activity in and of itself can't replace meaningful work, it can make people feel as though they have not lost their drive and are capable of achieving new goals.

There is an ever-increasing stack of evidence that points to the rejuvenating effects of physical activity and exercise. A combination of cardiovascular and strength exercise helps older adults reduce the risk of osteoporosis, bone fractures, diabetes, and heart attacks, and improves heart and lung functions. Regular physical stimulation even improves brain functions such as memory and cognitive task performance, while reducing the risk of developing Alzheimer's disease. Other favorable changes in brain activity include lowered levels of stress, anxiety, and depression, as well as an increase in better moods and an overall feeling of well-being.

In addition to the above health benefits, you also gain a distinct psychological benefit from remaining (or starting to become) active and fit after retirement. Exercising confers a feeling of vitality. Physical activity can provide competition and goal-setting behaviors that many people—especially type A personalities— require. Retirees who are physically active tend to be more satisfied with their lives. Physical activity helps counter the feeling of uselessness and the image of themselves as old and decrepit.

In some instances, retirees can achieve physical stimulation simply by continuing a sport they pursued while they were working. Many times, however, retirement is an opportunity to achieve a higher goal in a given activity or to try something new. I know retirees who have done everything from trekking the Milford Sound in New Zealand to learning ballroom dancing to taking up scuba diving. Others have become physically active in more prosaic ways, such as going for a daily walk or regularly visiting a health club. In either case, the goal isn't temporary. Exploring an exotic location shouldn't be an end in itself but part of a long-term pattern of activity; you might schedule a trek annually and spend the rest of the year getting in shape for it.

Ruth is a good example of someone who helped herself and her relationship by pursuing physical activity upon retirement. At the age of 64, Ruth began going to the health club every other day. Her husband encouraged her, recognizing that Ruth—a former stockbroker who loved the excitement of the market—was growing increasingly restless and irritable.

After a month of working out, Ruth—who had not been particularly physically active during her career—began feeling "toned" and stronger. The energy she formerly poured into her work she now poured into her body. Her husband noted that her irritability and restlessness disappeared, and that she could better cope with her fears about retirement and aging. Ruth said that she had chalked off retirement as "the beginning of the end," but when she saw her physical self improving rather than declining, she revised her definition. She realized it could be a rejuvenating experience, and this realization made her feel happier. According to her husband, she became a much better companion.

Yolanda and Ralph had worked their entire lives, and a year after they both retired in their late 60s, Yolanda convinced her husband that they should take line dancing lessons. This suggestion was surprising, in that Ralph, who loved dancing, had always complained that Yolanda "would do one slow dance with me and then complain that her feet hurt." In reality, she was shy about dancing in public, feeling that "everyone is looking at me." When they retired, however, Yolanda resolved to take up a new activity that would force her to be physically active and that she might eventually enjoy.

For her, retirement meant giving herself permission to have a new lease on life and to have "adventures." She was also concerned that retirement had harmed her relationship with Ralph, that they weren't laughing as much as they used to or enjoying each other's company the way they once did. Yolanda thought that dance could at least bring some laughter and common pleasure back to the relationship, and their line dancing lessons did that with flying colors. As she said, "When Ralph and I are out there, I feel kind of silly, but it's a good kind of silly. We're good dancers, and we can keep up with people much younger than us."

Engaging in a sport or some other type of activity provides a slew of other benefits that indirectly impact a relationship in positive ways. People report feeling better physically, having more energy, being in a better mood, and making new friends. As a result, they're less apt to be moody or needy and more apt to become better companions.

Intellectual Stimulation

A common fear of recently retired people is that their minds will deteriorate, that without the intellectual challenge of work, they'll become forgetful, boring, and even senile. Whether or not this fear is valid, it impacts relationships.

A man might have berated his wife for forgetting her keys throughout their marriage, but when he calls her on this forgetfulness after retirement, it provokes a heated argument. The recently retired spouse becomes defensive; she is now being accused of something that scares her to death. Or couples find that they have nothing new to say and that most of their conversations rehash the past. An interesting new subject and accompanying new knowledge can give people something to feel excited about and a sense of pride in having learned it. It also gives them a new subject to talk about with their spouses.

Continuous learning, therefore, is a goal that retired people should set for themselves. Learning can take many forms, from the traditional one of attending a class to the less formal one of exploring a subject on your own. Susan and Roger, for instance, had planned a three-month trip to Italy. Both of them knew a smattering of Italian, but as part of their preparation for the trip they enrolled in a Berlitz course together. Today, there are also plenty of online resources for classes ranging from degree programs to literature, even free courses through AARP and MIT's OpenCourseWare program.

Learning, like physical activities, can be accomplished to equal advantage as an individual rather than as a couple. Jamal, an engineer, had always felt inferior because of his lack of knowledge of the humanities. Even though he was successful in his field, he was often embarrassed when someone tossed off an unfamiliar term such as *postmodernism* or referred to a book he'd never read or even heard of. While he was working, Jamal had practically no time for anything outside of his family and his field, but after retirement he became a semiprofessional student, enrolling in classes in literature, architecture, and art.

This pursuit gave an enormous boost to his self-esteem. As Jamal broadened his knowledge, he started to see himself as interesting, educated, and well rounded. He also found that he enjoyed talking with his wife as well as with other people about his newly gained knowledge, and this made him a more stimulating conversationalist.

Some of the best learning experiences that retired people describe don't involve traditional subjects or formal modes of study. Jack, for instance, decided to start studying the meaning of love in various cultures and to read everything he could find about it. Eros had always been a concept that intrigued him, and after he retired, he had time to follow this quirky conceit. What Jack told me was instructive. As much as he enjoyed learning about an interesting subject, he found that his rather esoteric body of knowledge gave him a keen intellectual reward. He also discovered that in social situations, people (including his wife) enjoyed hearing his informed take about a fascinating topic, making him feel proud and pleased with himself.

Creative Stimulation

Giving ourselves permission to do new things that engage the right side of the brain, which regulates our emotions and artistic abilities, and use our creativity after retirement can be the source of much joy. I've known scientists, businesspeople, technicians, and members of the military who always wanted to express themselves artistically but never had the time or energy while they were working. Retirement provides them that venue. For some, it's taking up a long-dormant interest in painting or playing an instrument. For others, it's breaking out into new areas by taking pottery classes, cooking innovative dishes, or writing sonnets.

The objective isn't to get a poem published or become a concert pianist. Rather, it's to gain an outlet for all the creativity that used to be applied to work. Even the most by-the-numbers professions such as accounting and engineering require people to be innovative problem-solvers. At work, people are frequently challenged to find ways to do things better, faster, and cheaper, and this challenge demands creative thinking.

All of us have the needs to think "out of the box" and to push boundaries. Creative endeavors satisfy these needs and make us feel good about ourselves. People are inordinately proud of their creative effort, whether it's an asymmetrical pot or a moderately successful soufflé. It helps us say to ourselves: "I can still produce something uniquely and creatively me; I still have interesting ideas." In summary, when people stop working, they don't have to stop being productive and creative.

A Life of Leisure: Making the Most of It

One of the great things about retirement is that it hands people the leisure to find their purpose in life. Many of us get so caught up in trying to make a living or taking care of the kids that we're deprived of the time and space necessary to discover our purpose.

The word *leisure* comes from the Latin word *licere,* which means "to be allowed." It implies freedom to do what we want and freedom from obligations. We are permitted to choose what we will do during retirement, and what we choose has wide implications for our emotional and psychological well-being as well as the health of our marriages.

The Greek equivalent of the word leisure is *schole*, which is the origin in many languages of the words *school* and *scholar*. According to Plato, schole is the ultimate goal of education—to be liberated from the toil of work and unnecessary labor so that art appreciation and contemplative thinking will take place. Thus, leisure suggests involvement in "higher" activities.

Another component of leisure is the emotional enjoyment derived from a given activity; it's not just a higher-order endeavor. This combination of emotional and intellectual satisfaction is what the leisure ideal should be, along with accompanying feelings of mastery, success, and achievement. Ultimately, leisure's satisfaction is rooted in an awareness of enjoyment coming from the associated experiences of stimulation, competence, and control over one's life.

Leisure activities can be divided into four types:

- Active-social: requires physical effort and takes place in a group, such as a team sport
- Active-isolate: requires physical effort and is done by one person, such as jogging
- Sedentary-social: requires little physical effort and is done in a group setting, such as a book club
- Sedentary-isolate: requires little physical effort and is done by one person, such as reading

Although you may simply pursue a single leisure activity that you enjoyed before retirement, a mixture of the four types is preferable. In research studies, retirees who engage in social and physical activities outside the home in addition to the sedentary and isolated ones report the highest levels of life satisfaction.

While you may not discover your life purpose through reading and sports activities, you may find it through "serious leisure" pursuits that demand skill, attention, and commitment and involve development of demonstrated competence. Challenge and community are often two key elements of serious leisure. Community creates meaningful interaction and integration with others. Many retirees say that what they miss most about work is the social contact and stimulation derived from interacting with people who have a common interest.

Serious leisure, therefore, breaks the homeostasis of retirement, requires you to stretch beyond where you were before, involves different stimulations, and often leads to personal growth. It is usually driven by intrinsic rather than extrinsic motivation and can also induce flow; it offers enjoyment rather than pleasure. Pleasurable activities can and should be mixed with more serious ones. It's the latter that provide the sense of purpose that's so important for retirees.

As noted, leisure activity in retirement is often based on previously established competencies and usually involves a pursuit that was meaningful and satisfying before retirement. Of all the serious leisure activities available, the one that seems best suited for retirees is volunteerism.

Volunteering: Helping Yourself by Helping Others

To a certain extent, physical, intellectual, and creative stimulation can lead to accomplishment and expertise, but many people feel that they need something else in order to be fully engaged. Short of "un-retiring," one of the best ways to feel accomplished and useful is through volunteering.

In the special "happiness" issue of *American Psychologist* of January 2000, researchers found that happy people tend to participate more in community organizations, are more liked by others, are less likely to get divorced, and tend to live longer. They also tend to be less self-focused, more loving, more energetic, and less vulnerable to diseases and premature death.

In a similar way, surveys of volunteers conclude that volunteering enhances life satisfaction and that participation in a volunteer organization is associated with improved levels of functioning, while noticeable declines in functioning are evident among non-volunteers of the same age. Volunteering allows us to be autonomous and to feel in control. When the volunteer activity is for a cause or organization about which we care, this firm commitment and sense of belonging to a social group with like-minded members is a vaccine against depression.

According to the contributors to this special issue on happiness, volunteerism provides a sense of both personal and subjective well-being. *Personal well-being* is optimized when the needs for competence, autonomy, and belonging are satisfied. For example, volunteering to tutor or to help immigrants learn English and adapt to the culture can satisfy all three needs: the tutor is aware of his competence; the act of tutoring expresses his autonomy; and he creates a personal relationship with the person being tutored, satisfying the need for belonging. *Subjective well-being* refers to what people think and how they feel about their lives. It is not what happens to people that determines how happy they are, but how they interpret what happens. When individuals volunteer, they do so with awareness that they have more resources than those who receive their help, and as a result, they feel fortunate about their subjective situation.

People who volunteer after retirement also often have an "outer-directed" component to their relationships with the world. Inner-directed relationships, in which people have no strong attachment to a meaningful cause or purpose, tend to produce insular lives. Research on happiness shows that the more people focus on themselves, the more their connection to others is weakened, and the likelihood of depression rises.

Another way to understand the importance and significance of volunteering is by using Erikson's theory of adult development and Atchely's adjustment stages model of retirement.

Erikson stated that at the last stage of our life generativity—helping and contributing to the well-being of others or to a cause that makes the world a better place—helps prevent "stagnation"—feeling stuck, hopeless, and lost.

According to Erikson generativity, the care and concern for others, is the hallmark of successful maturation.

Atchely's retirement adjustment stages model stated that after the initial honeymoon period comes the disenchantment stage when the retiree feels purposeless. When people experience a high degree of continuity—when they feel the same about themselves post-retirement as they did pre-retirement—this difficult stage becomes shorter. Pre-retirement engagement in volunteer activities has a beneficial effect on adjustment to retirement as well as on retirement satisfaction. As noted earlier, the non-work identity of the volunteer role fosters self-esteem and acts as a bridge between the work role and retirement lifestyle. Thus, volunteering provides an outlet and opportunity for both generativity (Erikson) and continuity (Atchley).

In 2011, the oldest baby boomers turned 65, and can expect to live to age 83, according to *"Reinventing Aging – Baby Boomers and Civic Engagement,"* by Harvard School of Public Health. The U.S. Bureau of Labor Statistics reports that about 33 percent of all boomers volunteer on a regular basis, the highest rate of any generation.

Growing resources for volunteer activity include the Senior Corps (getinvolved.gov) which involves older citizens who use their experience and skills to meet community challenges. Another organization, VolunteerMatch. org is an online service that matches volunteers with various causes where their skills can be used.

It's healthy to devote a portion of your time to something larger than yourself. People who believe they are contributing to society and using their knowledge and skills for a good cause are less likely to get wrapped up in self-doubt and recrimination. They feel like valuable, contributing members of society. The volunteer activity enhances their personal and subjective well-being. Considerable research shows a positive relationship between altruistic behavior and multiple measures of psychological, physical, and social well-being.

A 2010 study found that benefits of volunteering apply even to physically disabled older adults and may even keep us alive longer. Among over 900 American adults 65 and older, physically disabled men and women who volunteered regularly outlived their non-volunteering peers and lived just as long as people without physical disability. Functional limitations were associated with an increased risk of dying *only* among participants who never or almost never volunteered. Although it may be more difficult for older adults with physical limitations to volunteer, they seem to receive important benefits from doing so. Another 2011 study states that when the volunteer activity is motivated by pleasure in helping, it is associated with multiple positive measures such as self-esteem, positive mood, and feelings of self-actualization and life satisfaction. These benefits don't exist when service is driven by sense of internal pressure, duty, and obligation.

Thus, as the Dalai Lama put it, "If you are going to be selfish, be wisely selfish—which means love and serve others, since love and service to others bring rewards to oneself that otherwise would be unachievable."

Volunteering also helps us realize how worthwhile, competent, or even wise we are. It gives us an opportunity to be seen as and feel like a valuable resource. Wisdom, it is often said, comes with age. The retired volunteer has a chance to behave and be perceived as a wise person, a prized trait in our culture.

Most of us can cite some cause or social issue that concerned us and to which we contributed money while we worked. Whether it's cleaning up the environment, helping homeless people, or stamping out a particular disease, after you retire, you have the opportunity to contribute more than money. Most not-for-profit associations and many religious organizations want and need volunteers, and in return you feel productive and needed. You may also find that volunteering helps structure your time and provides new social contacts. In many surveys of volunteers, respondents mention meeting new people, making new friends, and filling time with worthwhile and meaningful activities as some benefits of volunteering .

Formal volunteering can lead to informal volunteering—the non-organizational help that people offer to friends and neighbors, from taking soup to someone who is sick, to baby-sitting for a friend, to doing grocery shopping for a person with a disability.

Formal volunteering can also give people the chance to develop skills that they can apply in a variety of unstructured situations. I know one retired woman who volunteers twice a week for a not-for-profit agency that helps interpret health insurance bills for seniors who are ill. She has used the skills she honed through the activity to help friends and relatives in the same way.

Lewis is a 75-year-old retired businessman who feels strongly about illiteracy and is bilingual in English and Spanish. He serves three days a week at a center where he teaches reading and writing to illiterate adults, most of whom are from Mexico. After doing it for a few weeks, he realized that his mood was much better on his volunteering days. He said, "I jump out of bed and feel so much more energized, productive, and worthy. My day has structure and meaning." Lewis was also surprised at how fond he was of some of the people he tutored and appreciated being invited to their homes as an expression of their gratitude. Over time, he became more informally involved with two individuals and branched into coaching them on work skills. He no longer tutors them but sees them often and considers them friends.

"I get more than I give" is a common statement people make about their volunteer activities. *Altruism*, getting pleasure from giving to others, is one of the coping mechanisms that contributes to psychological well-being and helps strengthen our purpose. Putting something of value in the world that was not there before is personally transforming. By giving back to society, we feel better about ourselves.

A prime example of a volunteer activity that draws on work expertise is that of Cindy, a retired human resources director who donates her time to a center that helps welfare recipients obtain jobs. She uses her human resources knowledge to help clients perform better in interviews. She even enlisted her sister, who was a buyer for a clothing store, to give job applicants suggestions on what to wear.

Some retirees surprise themselves by applying new skills in new ways. When Jeri retired, she decided to learn how to use a computer, so she took a class and became moderately proficient. A few months later, she decided to volunteer at an animal shelter, as animals had always been an issue she cared about. With a limited staff, the shelter didn't have much time to devote to administrative procedures and paperwork, so Jeri put her new computer expertise to good use, experimenting with different programs and compiling and analyzing the shelter's population data.

Jeri was able to document that the shelter was providing care for an extraordinary number of animals with a comparatively small staff. With Jeri's detailed data analysis, the shelter's director was able to obtain additional funding from a foundation that allowed them to improve and increase services. Jeri, of course, received much positive feedback for her efforts. She felt as valued by the shelter as she had been by her former employer and was enormously proud of her contribution to a cause that she championed.

Not everyone feels comfortable volunteering. Some people are rubbed the wrong way by the prospect of doing something for nothing. Others are deterred by what they perceive to be a negative reaction to volunteers; they feel they will be looked down upon by paid staffers. I've found that people usually can get past these misgivings by talking to other retirees who have volunteered. The vast majority have positive things to say, especially those who contribute time to a cause in which they believe and that allows them to develop new skills or capitalize on expertise they developed while working.

While you may already know of many groups in your area that need volunteers and for which you'd be interested in working, you can also check out credoaction.com, the website of Working Assets or volunteer-for-change. com for other possibilities. Several volunteer organizations are designed specifically for retirees or older people, including American Foreign Service

Assn., RSVP— Retired Senior Volunteer Program, SCORE—Service Corps of Retired Executives, the Foster Grandparent Program, and the Senior Companion Program.

Finding the Right Activity

Some people know immediately what volunteer position will give them satisfaction, what leisure activity offers the right level of challenge, or what physical, intellectual, or creative stimulation is appropriate for them and will induce a state of flow. If you haven't prepared yourself psychologically for retirement, however, you may not have any idea what you should pursue. I've seen retired couples bounce from one activity to the next and fail to find the satisfaction they're seeking.

Fights can even result when people can't pinpoint the right activities to occupy their time. When one person hops from activity to activity and finds fault with each one, the spouse accuses, "Nothing satisfies you." With each failure, the "happy" spouse may claim that the partner "doesn't want to like anything."

To avoid this scenario and make a healthy psychological transition to retirement, it helps to determine who you are at your core and what your life purpose really is. Beyond your profession or your role as a parent or spouse, what are your underlying values and interests? A surprising number of people go through their working lives unaware of what these values are. They substitute their work roles for satisfying that deeper, value-based need and thus don't examine what it is that really drives them.

Some individuals are even more uncomfortable facing this question when they retire than when they were working. The analysis raises further questions regarding our mortality and the value and meaning of the lives we're leading. The transition to retirement is often associated with "an anxiety of the end." Because retirement tends to symbolize the beginning of the end, it can make us anxious about confronting the question of who we really are. We may feel that we missed our calling or that our calling was our work and now it's over.

Most people can find a way of fulfilling their personal missions in retirement, but first they must do some self-examination. The following exercises can help you determine your life purpose and identify corresponding leisure activities that support it. When you're connected to this purpose, you'll find that there's a positive spillover to your relationship. When something engages you at the deepest level, you are likely to be happier with yourself and your spouse. Idiosyncrasies of your spouse that used to annoy you now seem trivial and easily ignored. You don't take out your frustrations on your partner, because your frustration level has been ratcheted down.

Another way to think about your life purpose is as a life "passion." If you look closely at that word, you can see that it can be divided into PASS-I-ON— you want to make a difference in the lives of others and leave a memory of yourself and of your uniqueness. Passion means desire; it allows us to be alive and expresses our uniqueness. It comes from deep within; we experience it in the right side of the brain, rather than figuring it out and constructing it logically from the left side.

Bridge Employment

In recent years a new term, bridge employment, appears in the retirement literature. Bridge employment is a transition into part-time, self-employment or temporary work after full-time work ends and permanent retirement starts. The bridge employment can be in the same industry or in a completely different field.

The 2009 American Psychological Association study, "Bridge Employment and Retirees' Health", found that "a suitable type of bridge employment is likely to lead to beneficial effects on retirees' physical and mental health conditions." An added benefit cited was a decrease in health care costs, even after workers move into full retirement.

Additional studies about bridge employment found that relatively young male retirees with higher education who perceived the job market as good, who wanted to have better use of their skills, and had less concern about changes in their benefits, were more likely to engage in bridge employment in a different field. If they wanted to earn more money they were inclined to have same-career bridge employment.

Females usually opted for same-career bridge employment. Employees who have interests outside of work view bridge employment in a different field as an opportunity to pursue new challenges; continuing in the same field was not attractive to them.

Older employees were less inclined to engage in bridge employment of any type, perhaps because they still valued using their current skills. Mentoring programs and allowing them to mentor others might encourage older employees to fulfill their need for generativity and being industrious, contributing to the well-being of others instead of engaging in bridge employment.

Whether because of financial necessity due to an economic crisis or because of a growing awareness of the benefits of bridge employment, we see more resources and opportunities for those who want to pursue this option. Sites like FlexJobs.com have listings for artists, bankers, nurses, marketing professionals and other occupations.

Another possibility is the "encore career" concept, offered by Civic Ventures (encore.org), where colleges and social sector employees work to unleash the potential of boomers as a new workforce for social change. The program trains workers in fields such as the environment, adjunct nursing, and teaching.

Along the same lines, IBM launched a $2 million program that will pay tuition, licensing, and interim salaries for employees who want a bridge to new careers as math and science teachers. Their 'Transition to Teaching' program also joined with the non-profit Partnership for Public Service works on an array of initiatives aimed at recruiting Americans to public service. In 2008, it launched an initiative focused on recruiting older workers, called FedExperience Transitions to Government (ourpublicservice.org).

Entrepreneur.com, on their SecondAct.com site tells the story of John Wood, a former Microsoft executive who quit his job to form a new start-up: Room to Read. It is a non-profit providing books and libraries to people in the world's impoverished areas. He now says he is "working 24/7 with a smile on my face . . ." We may not all have the funds or the energy to build over 12,000 libraries, but new work can bring energy to a new life.

Another entrepreneur, 71 year old Randal Charlton, after a long career buying and selling many businesses, created a business incubator to revitalize Detroit's failing Techtown. Among the project's achievements, Charlton created over 1,800 local jobs, and over 2,200 entrepreneurs graduated from his training programs.

Psychiatrist Judith Broder delayed retirement to create The Soldier's Project, offering free counseling to military veterans and their families. She won the Purpose Prize, an award given to people over 60 who combine their passion and experience for social good, and was a recipient of The Presidential Citizens Medal in 2011.

Benefits of bridge employment include easing the transition, both financially and emotionally, toward full retirement. Best of all, it can open your mind to opportunities to learn something different, and to connect with new people. Maybe all the examples described above will inspire you to find your own bridge employment.

Exercises:
Two Steps to Take Toward Your Life Purpose

The first exercise here is designed to help you identify your life purpose in retirement, and the second will assist you in formulating specific actions to achieve this purpose (or purposes—some people come up with more than one). Both of these steps include a range of questions and activities. You may know your life purpose after answering only one or two questions and require only one action to achieve it, but it's equally possible that more probing is necessary. Therefore, you don't necessarily have to answer all the questions or take all the recommended actions. Choose the ones that are appropriate to your situation, or the ones that make the most sense and "speak to you."

Step 1: Identifying Your Purpose

1. Imagine your grandchild as a grandparent telling his grandchild about you. He remembers that he was present at your 80th birthday party and that it was a wonderful celebration. Think about what guests you want to be present at that celebration. While you should include loved ones, you don't have to be completely realistic: feel free to add teachers from your childhood or friends with whom you've lost touch. Further imagine that many of these people prepared a speech acknowledging you, describing how you have contributed and enriched their lives, as well as all that you have accomplished in your life.

Think about what you would like for them to say about you.

What is it that you want your grandchild to hear, remember, and tell your great-great-grandchild?

In other words, what do you want your legacy to be?

Write down the traits, values, and achievements that you respect and like about yourself and for which you want to be acknowledged. Try to list at least 10 items.

Here's a sample list for guidance:

A great friend
Very generous and kind
No one is more reliable and loyal

Treasures family
Intrepid traveler to exotic places
Great aesthetic taste
A terrific salesperson
Built the first all-female practice
Wrote a bestselling book
Wonderful sense of humor

2. Make a list of all the things (at least 20) that you always wanted to have or do. Don't limit your list to what is actually achievable or even to the realm of possibility. Allow your imagination and wishes free rein. You don't actually have to pursue any of the items on your list, so don't feel constrained by the exercise.

Here are some sample items:

Live in an oceanfront mansion
Complete a triathlon
Travel around the world
Learn to oil paint
Become a psychotherapist
Be profiled in *People* magazine
Become a spiritual leader
Join the Peace Corps

Rate each item you listed on a scale of 1 to 10 (with 10 being the highest) according to the following factor: How much do I want to do or have it?

Now look carefully at the 10 items that received the highest scores and analyze the underlying reason for each choice.

Ask: Why do I want to do this?

What does it mean about me or about who I am that I want to do it?

For instance, you may find that the reason you want to be a psychotherapist is that you want to help others cope with the disappointments and emotional obstacles in their lives. Or your reason for wanting to join the Peace Corps is that from the time your mother admonished you to eat everything on your plate because people were starving in Africa, you wanted to help people less fortunate than yourself. Or you want to paint because you've always wanted to add a bit of beauty to the world.

3. Think about people you like or admire. Write down their names. They can be people you know or knew in the past or individuals you read or heard about. Beside or below each name, list all the qualities the person possesses that you respect.

Now assess whether certain characteristics appear on your list more than once. Characteristics that repeat the most times are generally the ones that are closest to your heart. These represent the qualities you value most and are probably the ones you like and respect in yourself. They express or are related to your purpose and passion in life.

4. Reflect on what it is that you enjoy in different aspects of life. In order to get in touch with your life passion, you need to know what it is that you love. Think in terms of categories such as family, friends, sports, alone, outdoors, indoors, and so on. List as many as you choose. Now consider:

How often do you do each of the things you listed here?

What reasons do you give yourself for not doing them more often?

5. Think of five people to whom you feel close. Arrange to talk with each of them individually, and ask them what talents and traits make you unique. Write down their responses. If certain traits are mentioned by more than one person, determine which ones are similar to each other as well as to your own perception of your talents.

6. Think about situations in which time seemed to fly by.

What were you doing, or who was with you?

Why do you think time passed so quickly?

Were you in a state of flow? If yes, what induced it?

Now think about situations where time seemed to drag or even stop.

What were you doing? Who was with you?

Why do you think it went so slowly?

7. List your skills and competencies. They can be a result of your education, work or life experience, or inherent strengths. Anything from organizational acumen to musical ability to being a good listener is appropriate—don't limit your list to work skills.

The easiest way to find your passion is by relying on the talents you have naturally and the skills you developed around them. The unique blend of your talents and skills is a pointer to your passion and purpose.

8. We all have an inner voice at times that tells us that we are not good enough. It expresses our inadequacies. Likewise, we can all recall times when we felt proud that we were more than good enough or that we made a difference somehow.

Think of three to five situations in which you felt that you were more than good enough.

What did you learn from these situations?

Do they connect with your skills and talents?

Do they match the times you experienced flow?

Can you think of ways to translate them into something you can do regularly that will increase your self-esteem and get you closer to your purpose?

9. Now combine all the lists you've compiled and determine if common themes emerge.

Can you see one overriding purpose or passion?

You may have more than one, though it's unlikely that you have more than three or four. Don't worry if the lists don't mesh perfectly; you'll probably note some inconsistencies. What you're looking for is an overarching purpose or passion.

Here are some examples:

Contributing to my community
Being a good friend
Living a life of adventure
Releasing my creativity

Nurturing others
Learning continuously
Parenting
Helping underprivileged and oppressed people
Teaching

Step 2: Translating Your Purpose into Actions

Your challenge now is to translate your life purpose to behaviors. Essentially, these behaviors are an expression of your purpose or passion. When retirees pursue their passions, they enjoy the last quarter of their lives and are excited and energized about what they're doing, since it conforms with the essence of who they are.

For example, the purpose of being a contributor to the community can take many different forms and be expressed by various behaviors: helping homeless people, being an elder in your church or temple, or serving on the zoning committee of your city or on the board of a start-up theater company.

1. For each purpose or passion you listed, come up with something you can do about it. Next, write a personal statement of your life purpose, using the following techniques to articulate it:

Use a verb to express your purpose, such as teach, serve, help, or create.

Use a noun to designate who or what you want the verb to act upon, such as abused children or homeless families.

Mention the skills or talents you have that will help you accomplish it, such as computer literacy.

Include the result you want to get from this activity, such as to improve the life of people with diabetes.

Assign a time frame for when you will start it and how long it will last, such as next month, for six weeks.

When you put it all together, it might look like this:

My purpose is to better the lives of others in my community by teaching reading to illiterate adults, using my love and knowledge of language as well as my patience, so that they will be able to improve their lives, which will help reduce ignorance and illiteracy in my community. I will start to do it when I come back from my trip in September, and I will do it for at least three months.

2. Share what you've written with your spouse (but don't share it before this point, or you may be too influenced by him or her). Discuss your reactions to your spouse's response, how it fits with what you want for yourself, and how you can support each other in accomplishing these goals.

For example, Kate and Frank were married for 32 years. They raised four children, to whom they are devoted. They lived a modest lifestyle that fit with their modest incomes. Frank was a teacher and worked throughout their marriage, while Kate was a librarian and worked only after the kids left home, to help pay for their college.

Though they thought they knew everything about each other, when they compiled their lists of life goals, they discovered that they each had dreams that the other knew nothing about. Frank's purpose was to do things that are exciting and adventurous, and one of the goals that emerged from this purpose was a desire for a convertible sports car. He had never mentioned it before, since with the kids, car pools, and other family needs, the station wagon and later the minivan seemed like more appropriate choices.

Writing down things he wanted gave Frank the opportunity to express this small but significant dream as well as the awareness that he viewed retirement as his last chance to take care of a personal rather than a family need. Kate was very supportive of Frank's purchase of the car, and together they found the money to buy a used convertible Mustang. They both spoke positively of the fun they had going for drives together.

Frank was equally surprised to find out that Kate's purpose was to travel, and her most compelling goal was to visit Alaska. Like Frank, she had never mentioned this desire, since she felt that the money was needed elsewhere. Again the process worked: They took the trip and felt closer than they had on a vacation in years.

Granted, these one-time actions won't sustain Frank and Kate's marriage through years of retirement. But the individual exercises and the shared discussion enabled them to be more aware of who the other person is and to support each other's efforts to be authentic. In making future choices about volunteering or about physical, intellectual, or creative activities, they now had some guidance for what they should do and how they should do it.

Readjusting the Togetherness-Separation Balance

Chapters 2 and 3 examined the impact of retirement on relationships in the contexts of work involvement and post work life purpose. Becoming aware of how meaningful work was for you and defining equally meaningful goals for yourself in retirement can be a deterrent to personal and marital difficulties. With that grounding, we now delve into the psychological impact of retirement on marriage.

I emphasize the word *psychological*. Some people mistakenly believe that the impact is limited to non-psychological matters, such as travel, grandchildren, and finances. In reality, the impact is not only broader but also deeper. For instance, underlying the subject of how much money you can afford to spend on your vacation is how the relationship dynamic changes when there is no work to go back to after the vacation. This relationship becomes the primary focus of your life, since few, if any, other obligations now have claim to your time, energy, and attention.

The changes in one's roles and identities after retirement are significant stressors on the marriage. As social networks shrink after retirement, the importance of the marriage increases. Due to the increased time spouses spend together and the greater salience of this close relationship, qualities of marital interaction are very important to retirement satisfaction. Generally, marital satisfaction is positively associated with an emotional climate of interaction that is high in positive affect, low in negative affect and physiologically calm even when discussing disagreements.

One way to home in on the psychology at play when the relationship takes center stage is through the concept of differentiation.

The Paradox of Togetherness versus Separation

We all want to have intimacy in our marriage. Every couple engages in an attachment-separation dance during all phases of their relationship to maintain a delicate balance between feeling connected and preserving a sense of individuality. I often see loving couples struggling with this sensitive issue. The marital contract formalizes this struggle, demanding that we put our partner's needs on par with our own. In turn, when we get married we expect our partner to do the same so that our need for attachment and intimacy will be met.

This paradox of wanting to feel connected to each other while retaining a sense of individuality is called *differentiation*, as defined by David Schnarch in his book *Passionate Marriage*. Resolving this paradox allows each partner to function independently and interdependently at the same time. Successful differentiation is the ability to become well-developed individually while still maintaining emotional contact with the partner.

Because differentiated people are able to balance individuality and togetherness, they tend to welcome and maintain intimate contact with others. They are able to take their partners' wishes and priorities into account and accommodate them without feeling as though they have sold themselves out. They are also able to see the merit in their spouses' point of view even if it contradicts or interferes with their own. They create mutuality; they go forward with their own self-development while being concerned about their partners' happiness and well-being. These people understand that sometimes being out of sync with their spouses is normal and they recognize that they will be able to resolve the disagreement without losing their individuality.

Well-differentiated couples hold onto each other and try to make one another feel good. At the same time, they recognize that their partner is a separate individual with competing needs and agendas. This outreach is made out of choice rather than necessity; they don't need their partner's constant approval to make them feel good. They achieve what psychologists refer to as "self-validated intimacy."

When people have little differentiation, their identity is constructed out of a "reflected sense of self"—they need continual contact, validation, and agreement from others, particularly their partner. They create emotional fusion rather than self-validated intimacy. When people are emotionally undifferentiated, their need for togetherness often seems overpowering to their partners. In order for them to feel that they are loved and accepted, their partners often experience a burdensome neediness. Many times, however, the two partners are not equally differentiated or they use different ways of expressing differentiation. Obviously, this gap can cause serious marital problems.

Spouses with a less differentiated self try to change each other, hoping they can cause their partner to adjust ingrained behaviors regarding intimacy and togetherness. At this point, many people struggle with being true to themselves versus pleasing their spouses, with living according to their own values and creating a unique identity versus following the directives of the partner.

Delaying your own individual agenda without losing your integrity is a major marital challenge. For people who want less intimacy and more alone time, requests for more togetherness often feel like a demand for emotional fusion. They frequently express this feeling by such comments as "He's not giving me enough room to breathe." On the other hand, people who don't receive the intimacy that they expect feel lonely and deserted. They often experience too much time alone as a form of rejection by the spouse and sometimes feel abandoned emotionally.

Today, technology sometimes plays a role in this form of isolation. A spouse may get bored and begin spending more time on the computer, resulting in a type of technology-isolation. If time on the computer is seen as a way of avoiding interaction with one's spouse, the relationship suffers. If one spouse is overly absorbed in computer games, or surfing the internet or Googling various subjects for information, it sends a signal of rejection to the other spouse. In other cases, one partner may suddenly experience jealousy over the other's attachment to online companionships.

The lure of social media sites such as Facebook and Twitter can further cause a person to feel socially connected but not within their relationship. The pseudo-online connection with strangers can not replace the real emotional intimacy with the spouse. It is important that the online connections and other isolated computer activities will not be at the expense of emotional intimacy at home.

Various factors impact how we attempt to balance individuality and togetherness. One is our innate tendencies. Some babies are content lying in their cribs for long periods of time, while others start crying almost immediately when they sense that they are alone. Similarly, some toddlers readily entertain themselves, while others constantly demand that someone play with them. As adults, some of us can be perfectly content reading, thinking, or running errands by ourselves, while others can barely tolerate an hour or two of "alone time."

Gender differences also impact our differentiating behaviors, expectations, and comfort zones. Unlike for men, connection and intimacy become part of a woman's identity from an early age. In fact, a woman's moral sense is tied to connection, while a man's moral sense is linked to separation. A woman's need for connection is not a symptom of dependency but rather an expression of her sense of self. Women are encouraged to be empathetic and to "feel as others feel" from the time they're very young, while men are not. As a result, women develop identity and autonomy through connection with others, whereas men do so through disconnection, achievement (which is often perceived to be available only through competition and disconnection), and emotional isolation.

It's important to stress that women do not have less differentiated selves than men; they simply have different strategies for achieving differentiation. Men often produce unnecessary distance in order to avoid "disappearing" in the relationship. They adhere to the stereotype of the rugged, macho, individualist male and mistake being empathetic and supportive with taking on their spouse's feelings. Therefore, a man's struggle to understand and achieve differentiation and self-validated intimacy comes about differently than his partner's. Given the distinct differences between male and female socialization regarding connection, it is no wonder that so many couples flail before they reach a comfort zone.

Gender also dictates in part what is said and what is heard. For most women, what is said has a major impact on their feelings of connectedness and intimacy. For men, words are not as important as physical proximity. It's not that a woman needs to talk all the time, but she does want to know what's going on in her husband's head and heart. It's equally important for her to feel that he cares about what's going on inside of her. Conversation, therefore, is needed in order to achieve closeness. Although it's true that most men simply need physical proximity to feel this sense of closeness, this doesn't mean that men devalue conversations or don't recognize the importance of talking as an integral part of the relationship. It's just that words aren't always at the center of the relationship, and they can be more easily satisfied by non-verbal activities.

For many men, their wives' repeated requests that they express their inner lives and the accompanying full range of feelings—particularly vulnerability, sadness, and fear—become burdensome. In our society, boys are raised and socialized to be "a man," someone who doesn't easily communicate his innermost feelings. When wives request this expression, men are likely to "shut down" in order to protect themselves. This is why women often push for more attachment while men push for more separateness.

Let me introduce you to a typical scenario that many couples have experienced. Carl and Judy—who have been married for 17 years—are sitting in their family room watching a nature program on the Discovery channel. Judy has her head in Carl's lap while Carl is stroking her hair. Judy tries to start a conversation, but Carl is engrossed in the program and answers monosyllabically.

After a short while, Judy gets up, calls a girlfriend, and has a long phone conversation. Carl becomes upset because he feels rejected, and he expresses his feelings by saying some angry and even nasty things to Judy. Judy is surprised and upset as well.

Judy remarks: "For the life of me, I cannot understand why he gets angry when I get on the phone. I want to talk to someone who will talk back to me and cares about what I have to say. I don't take anything away from him. He was not noticing me for a while; we hardly talked or said a word to each other. So, what's the big deal?"

Carl's point of view is that Judy always hassles him for not talking enough to her and for watching too much TV. He counters: "Doesn't she get that I feel close just by sitting next to her? I felt very content when she had her head in my lap—her hair is so soft and smells so nice. She did take something away from me: she spoiled a sweet moment. When she got up to talk to her friend, I felt as if I wasn't enough, as if I can never please her."

In addition to innate individual differences and gender differences, socialization—what we learned or observed as acceptable family behavior while we were growing up—affects how we handle attachment and differentiation. In some families, it is considered rude to close your bedroom door when you want to be alone, while in others it's perfectly acceptable. One couple might have frequently taken separate vacations, while another set always vacationed together and viewed separate vacations as a sign of a weak marriage. In some families, all fun and leisure activities were undertaken together; in other families, Mom and Dad did their own things—he played golf every weekend with his buddies while she visited art galleries with her friends.

As you think about how you and your spouse handle differentiation, don't be too quick to form opinions based on gender or innate tendencies alone. Our family of origin has a tremendous effect on our differentiation too. Our level of differentiation is directly influenced by how well our parents and grandparents succeeded in becoming well-developed individuals. Differentiation transcends generations because it is partly about boundaries. In some families, intense emotional bonds may impede a member's development, forcing them to avoid family interactions by geographical distance. In other situations, there is little room to individuate—become your own person—when parents live vicariously through their children. Often, when people choose their spouses, they choose someone whose family used different, or even opposite, ways of coping with emotional fusion. Socialization can loom large, and its impact is sometimes complex to unravel.

Joe and Maria had been married for three years when they sought the help of a therapist. Maria grew up in a large Italian family, and her social needs were met by her cousins. Her parents never left home for any extended period without being accompanied by at least one family member. Maria does not remember ever being by herself for long without having a relative drop by or call. Being alone translated into "People don't care about you." She learned that blood is thicker than water and that only friendships within the family count. While it was acceptable to have work relationships, the family culture made it clear that those associations were not deep or meaningful.

Joe grew up in a completely different environment. His father was in the army, so the family moved a lot, and his father was absent for weeks at a time. His mother, who raised him and his brother by herself, was an outgoing person and quickly developed friendships wherever they moved. She was not close with her own parents. Her mother died when she was young, and her father remarried and had two children with his new wife, to whom she did not feel very connected. Joe rarely saw his grandfather; most contacts—at holidays and birthdays—were by telephone and felt cold and empty.

When Joe and Maria married, Joe loved the warmth of her family. Granted, he sometimes was taken aback when her mother would open their door unexpectedly with her own key to their house, but the family's love, acceptance, and inclusion were too important to him to raise a complaint. Likewise, once when Joe told Maria that he wanted to play basketball after work with some friends, she was surprised and couldn't understand why going to the health club with her didn't suffice. But since Maria didn't want to make a big deal about it and could rationalize that it might further his career, since he was playing with people from work, she did not express her dismay.

As long as Joe and Maria lived close to her family, their differences regarding how they handled conflicts between individuality and connectedness, as well as the different ways in which they tried to achieve differentiation and deal with emotional fusion, remained largely dormant. When Joe received a promotion, however, they were forced to move away, and that's when the problems began.

Maria was lonely; she missed her family and did not know how to develop new and meaningful friendships. She became much more dependent on Joe and resented any time he wanted for himself outside of work. The basketball nights that previously were acceptable now felt like betrayal. Joe said he was suffocating and that, as much as he loved Maria, he could not give her all that she wanted from him. He also felt that he didn't have enough space to himself and that she was always "talking at him."

Maria perceived herself as a nag and shut off from her husband. The crisis that brought them to therapy came when he said he wanted to join some college friends whom he hadn't seen for a while on a ski trip.

In therapy, they learned how individual socialization and family background shaped their views about togetherness—and about the importance of differentiation. They realized the impact of the different messages they had learned from their family of origin. Joe's family stressed staying detached as a way to decrease the pain of losing a loved one. Conversely, Maria's family taught her to emphasize and rely on family bonds as a way to protect against a foreign and unfamiliar environment.

Joe was finally able to see that Maria wasn't as outgoing as he and his mother were, and Maria came to recognize that Joe's wish to participate in activities without her didn't mean he loved her any less. He understood the reason for her greater need to be with him, and Maria came to understand that Joe's wish to engage in an activity without her did not mean that she was failing to fulfill his need for friendship. As their communication and disclosure helped them realize that intimacy does not always mean sameness, they were able to grow. Therapy also helped them develop a more differentiated self and come closer to achieving self-validated intimacy in which the other spouse's preferences were on par with their own. They stopped criticizing each other and not only resolved the argument about the ski trip, which was the initial reason for their marital therapy, but also achieved a much deeper and more important balance as well.

Sexual Intimacy

The elderly remain sexually active and interested in sexuality all their lives even if this activity and interest is less than when they were younger. Older adults have the desire to feel close, affectionate and intimate with a loving partner. Mutual caressing is enjoyable and satisfying at all ages.

Older adults who have sexual relations benefit from an important source of reinforcement and pleasure that helps preserve psychological and physical well-being and indirectly reduces various physical and mental problems. We also know about specific sex-related changes that occur with age—changes that every retired couple should know about so they understand what's "normal" and can adjust their minds and their bodies accordingly.

For instance, we know that age decreases the intensity, frequency and quality of sexual response. It also decreases sexual desire, arousal and the frequency of sexual fantasies. Aging also leads to more conservative attitudes about sexuality. Despite these developments, sexual activity among the elderly does not need to stop, only to be altered. Aging individuals remain sexual beings in spite of the physiological changes. 23 percent of women and 55 percent of men age 60-80 report sexual satisfaction either by penetration or mutual caresses. However, there were also a considerable number of people (29 percent of women and 12 percent of men) who report no sexual satisfaction.

Here are some facts people need to be aware of:

Physiological changes linked with aging in men:

- As men age, their testosterone levels get lower.
- The lower testosterone levels affect many sexual responses:

  - Causes the penis to be less hard (but sufficient for penetration)
  - The ejaculation is less powerful with a decrease in the ejaculatory need, i.e., men do not always feel the need to ejaculate during sexual relations.
  - Erections take more time to occur, needs more direct stimulation, are more difficult to obtain, are infrequent and cannot be maintained for as long.
  - The refractory period—the duration following ejaculation before a new erection can occur—is much longer, from a few minutes in a male aged 17 to at least 24 hours in a 70-year-old man.

- Men should not interpret these changes as the equivalent of impotence. If they do, they are likely to develop feelings of failure, become nervous about sex and even avoid sex altogether. Older men should also be aware that the listed changes can be caused or accelerated by certain medicines. For example some anti-Parkinson drugs cause impotence as a side effect; drugs for hypertension diminish sexual desire and erectile capacity. However, if men are aware of and accept these physiological changes they can continue having sexual relations all their lives.-

Now let's look at the female side of the coin.

Physiological changes linked with aging in women:

- The diminished estrogen levels cause menopause with symptoms of hot flashes, insomnia, fatigue, sensory difficulties, bladder or urethra irritation during intercourse and incontinence.

- It also causes thinning of the vaginal walls, decrease in vaginal lubrication, shrinkage of the width and length of the vagina and a loss of elasticity.
- These changes in the vagina can increase the vulnerability to infections and provoke pain during penetration and intercourse.

As in men, the intensity and duration of sexual responses also diminish with age; it takes longer to reach orgasm, direct stimulation of the clitoris is often needed, and the contraction-orgasm is less intense. However, unlike men, women's ability to have multiple orgasms remains the same and their refractory period does not extend.

Regular sexual activities can help delay or reduce the physiological effects of menopause. Women who have sexual intercourse once to twice a week before, during, and after menopause seem to have less decline in their ability to lubricate, have a good muscular tone and less sexual dysfunction. Similarly, Menopause can be linked with psychological difficulties, such as being less attractive due to weight gain, less firm breasts, and hair loss. The psychological as well as the physiological changes often cause diminished sexual desire and fewer sexual fantasies. The lack of lubrication can cause pain during sexual activities and lead to dyspareunia or vaginismus in some cases. The combination of longer time in reaching orgasm and a partner's erectile difficulties can bring about a loss of sexual interest or even avoidance of sexual activities. Nonetheless, women like men can remain sexually active all their lives, as long as they are willing to understand these changes, ask their partner to caress them longer, use lubricant creams, do Kegel exercises to increase vaginal muscle tone and try new sexual positions that cause less pain.

Psychological factors linked with sex life decline and aging:

Sexually active individuals over age 70 are those with a more positive attitude towards aging and sexuality. They do not adhere to social taboos and attitudes towards sexuality among the elderly; for instance, the beliefs that if one is interested in sex as an elder he is a dirty old man. These beliefs can have a negative impact on sexuality and marital satisfaction.

When full-time work is removed from the marital equation, the marriage itself assumes greater importance for couples and impacts sexual satisfaction. Because retirement diminishes social contact (due in part to loss of some or all work relationships), marital satisfaction and attention to relationship factors become more important. Positive feelings toward the partner affect sexual satisfaction more than erectile and lubrication capabilities. Women's satisfaction with their sexual relations is more strongly linked with their marital satisfaction than with their age. Similarly, menopause or gynecological problems impacted the frequency of sex much less than marital satisfaction and attitudes toward sexuality.

Indeed, a 2010 Canadian study found that older couples with high levels of marital satisfaction presented values twice as high as those with low levels of marital satisfaction on sexual variables (sexual desire, activity, communication, satisfaction and orgasm) and presented much less psychological distress (depressive symptoms, anxiety, irritability, and cognitive problems). These finding were true for both genders. Thus, a link exists between lack of marital satisfaction and depression. In this study, lower levels of marital satisfaction and sexual satisfaction predicted psychological distress for both men and women. Lack of marital satisfaction was the variable that contributed the most to psychological distress among elder couples. Unsatisfying marital relationships—often couples with a high degree of conflict—have a detrimental effect on sexual functioning and exacerbate psychological distress. Frequently, the sources of marital dissatisfaction were unfulfilling sexual relations, communication difficulties, and conflicts regarding time spent together.

As mentioned earlier, acceptance of the physiological changes and not misinterpreting these changes as sexual dysfunction, enables men to reduce performance anxiety and the resulting marital tension. In the same way spouses must face various health problems that may affect the quality of their sex life as well as every aspect of the marital relationship.

Findings from a recent study provide fresh insights about sexuality among retirees. The first finding is that men age 55 and older are more sensitive to the decline in the physical appearance of their partners than vice versa. The more that the partner has changed physically, the more likely the man is to mention loss of interest in sex. It seems that men today are still impacted by sexist cultural values about beauty.

The second finding is that the cessation of sexual activity in couples who are age 55 and older is more attributable to the man than the woman. This finding is compatible with other studies about sexual activity among younger couples. While women report less sexual interest and activity than men, both men and women see the end of sexual activity as the men's doing at all ages, including the elderly.

The more unresolved issues that block you from being authentic with your partner, the more they intrude during sex. In other words, the more you ignore discussing crucial subjects with your partner or hide your feelings about these topics, the more difficult it will be to have a satisfying sex life. It's stressful being physically close to someone from whom you feel emotionally distant, and this makes it harder to fully enjoy sex.

Therefore, great sexual pleasure and intimacy is possible in the later years when people are well-differentiated and have developed a mature sense of self—the absolute requirement for achieving intimacy with a partner.

Only when you feel "at home" inside yourself do you have a good place to invite your partner to visit. When the meaning of the sexual experience agrees with who you are, the quality and depth of your connection with your partner can reach new sexual heights. Passion and desire for your spouse contribute to your total stimulation, and you express this feeling through your sexual behaviors.

Developing strategies to face the physiological changes in the sexual function linked with age is an important task for retired and older couples to achieve in order to continue and enjoy high levels of marital satisfaction. Intervention programs for the elderly and retirees should focus on communication, and improving the quality of sex life. Remember, too, that despite the conventional wisdom, *Sexuality does not equal penetration.* Hugging each other, massages, sensual baths, manual or oral caresses and other similar activities can bring physical intimacy that satisfies intense emotional needs without fear of failure or discomfort.

Better sex later in life often is a matter of attitude adjustment. When retirees discard misconceptions and negative attitudes regarding sexuality in older age, they often experience better sexual relationships. Finding ways to avoid boredom due to repetition and monotony during sexual activity help a lot too. For example, using new positions, having sexual activity at different times of the day, to mention a few.

Many older couples report that they have the best sex ever and reach levels of stimulation and satisfaction that they were not aware were possible when they were younger. In spite of the lower biological drive that comes with aging, older adults can broaden the repertoire of sexual interactions, find new ways to engage the partner, lengthen the duration of their encounters, and increase pleasure. For them sex becomes an opportunity to experience their partner completely, rather than a way to only feel their partner physically.

I remember a couple I worked with who went on a trip to Paris to celebrate their retirement and the progress of their relationship as a result of their therapy with me. When they came back and I asked them about their trip (it was their first visit to Paris), they shyly said that they saw very little of this beautiful city. They had so much fun and joy in their hotel room, discovering each other in new ways, that they spent very little time outside their bed; they'll have to go back if they want to see the sights of Paris. For them it was a second honeymoon, only much more intense and pleasurable than their first one.

Retirement allows couples to take the time to enjoy and even focus on this aspect of their life—to have a second honeymoon. Retired couples who mature and develop differentiated selves also enjoy self-validated intimacy with a never-ending desire for their spouse. Like the desire for wisdom, the desire for your partner does not diminish with age or disappear once your body is wrinkled. It grows with time, and enjoying sex to its fullest pleasurable potential is a reality many retired couples experience.

Stages in the Intimacy Pattern

After a few years of marriage, most couples settle into a mutually acceptable pattern of togetherness-separation and sexual intimacy; it's a pattern that allows both people to meet their need for intimacy without losing their individuality. Differentiation, however, is not a singular event that couples deal with and resolve once and for all. It's a process that keeps on changing as a couple's lifestyle and circumstances change.

Couples go through four major life stages that impact an established intimacy pattern and can make an acceptable pattern unacceptable. Let's look at each stage.

Stage One: Before Children

At this stage, couples start to address expectations about intimacy, emotional and physical space, and leisure time. Here the intimacy pattern is established in four areas.

First, a decision must be made about how much leisure time a couple spends together. Most newly married couples spend the majority of their discretionary time together. A consistent finding in research on family behavior is that husbands and wives who share leisure time tend to be much more satisfied with their marriage than those who do not. Furthermore, the more time allocated to joint participation in mutually satisfying leisure activities, the more special the relationship becomes and the greater the couple's attachment.

Naturally, people also spend some leisure time away from each other, with friends and family members. Again, they negotiate how much time away is acceptable. Once a week playing poker with college friends may be okay for one couple but too much for another, for whom once a month may be the preferred balance.

In addition to the amount of leisure time away from each other, partners also must come to terms with personal autonomy and freedom to pursue their own agendas. In other words, they must decide if the only acceptable activities are those enjoyed by both partners. Questions that need to be addressed could include whether or not it is okay for one spouse to pursue an activity that the other dislikes or disapproves of, or whether or not one partner can veto or disallow the other from taking part in certain activities.

In some relationships there is enough differentiation and personal space for such activities to occur, while in others it is totally unacceptable. Similarly, some men and women would find it intolerable for a spouse to regularly have lunch with a single friend of the opposite sex; others wouldn't give it a second thought. Often negotiations are needed in order to resolve such disputes and differences. It is in the best interest of the relationship if these differences are discussed and negotiated.

The second area in which the intimacy pattern is established concerns how much daily contact is required as a statement of connection and bonding. Some couples call each other a few times a day while they are at work, and others don't talk with each other at all during the workday. Some couples feel comfortable spending an evening at home engaging in separate activities, while other couples expect a mutual activity to take place when they're in the same physical space.

Doing almost everything together may feel normal to one person but suffocating to another. Developing a viable pattern through negotiation is usually necessary to resolve differences. As a general rule, women are more likely to interpret higher levels of time spent alone as a rejection or lack of concern on the part of their husbands, and they pressure the man to adjust his differentiation in an attachment direction.

Third, self-disclosure and emotional support must be determined at this stage. Sharing what happened during the workday, bolstering each other, and giving advice on how to handle a difficult boss or colleague are common at this stage, when both spouses are often working. What needs to be negotiated is the degree of detail. Some people feel that they need to disclose every nuance and feeling, while others are less expansive and submit only the bottom line. Similarly, people must decide whether they will share just the facts or also their feelings and reactions to events.

The fourth area is sex. Couples develop a sexual pattern which involves several aspects: frequency—how often sex occurs; timing—when sex occurs; location—where sex occurs; and duration— length of sexual intimacy. Other issues that need to be addressed are sexual positions, who initiates sex, and does sex occur when one is upset or tired.

The pattern of marital communication and intimacy that is developed at this early stage sets the tone for what comes later. Typically, women expect more sharing and support than their husbands do; they want to feel that their partners are equally interested in their thoughts, feelings, and reactions; men expect more sex than their wives and often experience frequent sex as a sign of interest and love.

Stage Two: Child Raising

Adjustments to the pattern that developed earlier are usually necessary here because of the demands that come with the child-raising years. Spontaneous and exciting conversations, activities, and even sex become less frequent as children dominate everyone's time and thoughts.

As a result of all this, people often perceive matters of intimacy and emotional space in very different terms. The presence of children significantly alters the way husbands and wives relate to each other, and changes usually occur in all four aspects of intimacy that were established in the first stage.

The amount of time available for marital leisure activities away from home declines, or at least becomes more difficult to arrange, as couples do not want (or cannot afford) to leave the baby with a sitter and go out regularly. Thus, changes occur in the pattern of acceptable boundaries for leisure activities without the spouse.

For instance, John's all-night poker games were fine before the first child was born, but now his wife, Mary, objects to these games on the basis that child-care responsibilities need to be shared. On the other hand, Steve used to be irritated when Shari went to dance class twice a week after work, but after having a baby, Steve thinks it's a good idea because Shari is eager to get back in shape and also needs some time to pursue an activity without the baby in tow. Research confirms my clinical observations that after children are born, both men and women report a substantial increase in the amount of time they spend doing activities alone or with someone other than the spouse.

Perceptions that one does "not have enough free time anymore" increase markedly during childbearing years. "Alone time" becomes a desirable commodity, especially among couples in which both people work outside of the home. For primary caregivers, the desire to spend time together as a couple is heightened after they have children because they've spent all day with children and they long for some adult conversation.

Marital communication, too, undergoes significant changes during this stage. Having those wonderful heart-to-heart conversations becomes harder, since much of what is discussed now has to do with diaper services, car pools, homework, parent-teacher conferences, which college to send the child to, and the like. As family obligations increase and flexibility and spontaneity decrease, couples experience higher levels of daily stress and less ability to meet expectations for companionship and emotional and sexual intimacy. Similarly, as child-centered leisure time activities increase and adult-centered activities decrease, marital satisfaction can also sag.

Stage Three: Empty Nest

When their children leave home, couples need to make another adjustment to the individuality-connectedness balance. The void left by the kids' departure needs to be filled, and the pressure on the couple's intimacy intensifies. While some couples enjoy the opportunity to spend more time together and discover new things about each other, other couples who are less differentiated realize that they've grown apart and that the kids were a major force that kept them together. Some couples reconceptualize their relationships, often devoting more time to shared leisure activities. Others continue the pattern that developed during the parenting years of parallel activities done alone.

During this stage, couples often need to adjust the amount of physical space that they give to each other. For example, Ronald used to spend most of his evenings talking with his young adult children, helping his son with homework and mentoring his daughter, who still lived at home and worked in his field. His wife, Patty, who had a higher level of differentiation than Ronald, used to spend her evenings reading and talking on the phone with her friends and her parents. While Ronald was fine with Patty's reading in the den during the parenting years, he became resentful of her being "away from him" after the kids left. He felt lonely and emotionally abandoned by her; the physical distance between them was too much for his comfort level.

Patty was oblivious to Ronald's feelings and unaware that this was the reason he became so grouchy after the kids left. Since sex role stereotypes impede men from openly sharing feelings of sadness, vulnerability, and abandonment, they often express these feelings through anger, confusing their wives.

True to form, Ronald did not express his abandonment but started to criticize Patty's cooking, housekeeping, and "excessive talking." She was hurt and surprised by this turnabout because, as she saw it, "For 20 years, my cooking, housekeeping, and conversation were fine; I can't understand what changed." Her sister-in-law, who is a therapist and "knows" her brother, suggested to Patty that she change her evening routine and increase the amount of time she spent with Ronald.

Within a few weeks, Ronald stopped his stream of criticisms. Only after they reconnected and restored the attachment balance was Ronald able to get in touch with his feelings and share.

Sensitivity, good communication, and a willingness to negotiate and make adjustments often smooth over these rough spots in marriages that have good foundations and aren't pelted by excessive resentment and chronic problems with intimacy. As child-care obligations diminish and household management becomes less complex, couples need to find new topics to talk about. Showing more interest in each other's work and having more discussions of a personal nature are two ways communication often evolves at this stage.

The decreased complexity of everyday living puts pressure on both people to increase their sexual intimacy and emotional communication. If communication was difficult in the first stage and was not improved to a comfortable level before the kids arrived, it is likely that it will again become a hindrance.

Stage Four: Retirement

Retirement affects marital solidarity. However the effects are subtle and complex. The retirement experience is different for wives and husbands and has different consequences for each partner. As in the previous stages, couples must again revise the rules on which their relationship is based. During this stage, partners spend much more time together than they ever did before.

On the positive side, increased time together gives partners the opportunity to do things with and for each other that might have been neglected in the past. The example in the previous chapter about Frank and Kate buying the sports car and visiting Alaska represents a positive development.

On the negative side, retirement strips away all the excuses and rationalizations that hampered togetherness. In the past, you could always point to the demands of the kids as the reason you didn't spend much time together, take lots of trips, have frequent sex, or express feelings. Similarly, work kept you and your spouse apart and provided each person with ample space to do his or her thing. Among many couples during the child-raising years, an unspoken pact often exists: She will give second place to his emotional needs in favor of the children's needs, and he will give first priority to his work, so her needs also come second. Retirement then exposes the disappointment that couples feel about not having their intimacy expectations met.

As noted earlier, simply spending more time together during retirement can exacerbate what were previously ignored idiosyncrasies or minor irritations; a spouse's heretofore mildly dismaying habit becomes almost intolerable. Suddenly Carla notices how Sergio always interrupts others before they finish speaking, and Sergio realizes that Carla can't stop herself from telling the same joke repeatedly, often to the same audience.

Several studies document that after retiring, men frequently become more concerned with interpersonal relationships, particularly with their wives. As he spends more time at home he shifts his main focus from his work to his wife. On one hand, it makes the relationship more equal in power, and in turn, some women become more instrumental and assertive. On the other hand, many wives find that the husband's greater focus on her means loss of her autonomy in running the household as well as of any privacy she enjoyed during work hours when she was home alone (if she was a homemaker) or the contact with work colleagues (if she was employed outside the home). Other wives start to resent having less time to devote to activities and relationships outside the marriage. Of course, if the increased involvement of the husband results in deeper sharing and more intimacy, the wife often welcomes the change. But if it reduces her privacy, autonomy, and intimacy with friends and colleagues without compensatory emotional intimacy, she feels controlled and resentful.

A friend of mine once confided with good humor that her recently retired husband had quizzed her about what she'd been doing that morning when she had come home later than he expected. She told him that after going to the health club for an aerobics class, she ran a few typical errands—going to the cleaner, picking up some milk, and so on. She was amazed that he was at all interested in such mundane matters that she'd routinely taken care of throughout the marriage. It also amused her that he was impressed by how well organized and efficient she was. The exchange highlighted for both of them how unaware her husband was of all the little details and errands she handled during their marriage in addition to her work.

She told him that while his wanting to know such details was fine this time, making such sharing a regular pattern of their interaction was totally unacceptable to her. It made her feel that her husband was becoming too intrusive and controlling; failing to leave her enough space to be herself.

Another couple, Harriet and Larry, were married 42 years when Larry retired after selling his business, where Harriet worked part-time. She had a pattern of talking with her daughter and her close friend almost every morning before she went to work, which was one to two hours after Larry left.

After Larry's retirement, when these morning phone calls occurred, he would pick up the other extension and listen to her conversations. Harriet steamed at this invasion of her privacy, which surprised Larry. He felt he had the right to know what was going on with his daughter and grandchildren. And he couldn't understand why Harriet made such a big deal about conversations with her friend, since she'd share the information with him later anyway.

Before retirement, this behavior had never created dissension. Larry was seldom at home in the morning, and when calls came in the evening, they usually were from mutual friends, and being on the phone together made the conversation more efficient: it was easier to decide which restaurant to go to or which movie to see. Now they had to negotiate new boundaries regarding privacy.

In addition, because retired people can no longer experience their autonomy and self-worth at work or through professional accomplishments, they become more sensitive to how the partner "controls" them and intrudes on their space. This catalyzes the need for conversations and negotiations on this subject.

Resolving Differentiation Issues in Retirement:

A Story With a Happy Ending

Having been married for 37 years, Trudy came to therapy because she was depressed. Bud, her husband, had been a successful partner in a large and prestigious consulting company before he retired, and he worked demanding hours and traveled a great deal. Trudy, who was a teacher before her three children were born, had stopped teaching and raised the children almost as a single mother, since Bud was away so much.

Though part of her liked having this autonomy and freedom, she was lonely much of the time while Bud worked, and Trudy's expectations for togetherness weren't being fulfilled. When Bud was in town, he was so tired from work pressures that she refrained from expressing her dissatisfaction.

Throughout their years together, they had a wonderful sex life, and this was the arena where most of their bonding occurred. Because they always had a great time on vacations, Trudy assumed and hoped that when Bud retired, this was what their life would be like all the time.

Those hopes were soon dashed. After the brief honeymoon phase of retirement, Trudy began to feel lonely again. She noticed that Bud could be with her for hours and not say a word, or that he would be involved in a book and hardly respond to her attempts to connect with him.

When she expressed her resentment to Bud, he was shocked and confused. As a contemplative, introverted person, he felt that they were connecting more than they ever had in the past but that she just couldn't get enough togetherness. Trudy interpreted his refusal to be more attentive as a sign that she was not sufficiently interesting and that he didn't care for her as much as she had thought. She felt that all her patience during the previous 37 years was in vain and that the Shangri-La she'd anticipated would never appear. The difference in their differentiation level became much more obvious and they had no explanations for it. Therefore, it's no surprise that their wonderful sex became less wonderful and less frequent. Because of this, Trudy became depressed and sought counseling.

When Bud joined the therapy sessions, he was able to express both his fear of "losing himself" if he became more involved with Trudy and his perception of her as controlling and invasive. He said that throughout their marriage, he saw her as being too anxious about how their children and grandchildren were doing. He often felt that she wanted him to be similarly anxious; she would get angry with him when he disagreed with her or was not as anxious as she was. Bud felt as if the only way to please her was for him to mirror her moods, which he was unwilling to do.

Work gave him the opportunity to be distant and disconnected during their marriage, and now he no longer had this "excuse." As a result, when she would talk about the grandchildren or other topics about which he didn't share her feelings, he wouldn't answer because he found it futile to disagree with her. Similarly, he avoided the frequent sex they used to have because (unconsciously) he wanted to preserve his physical individuality.

It became clear to me, and I made it obvious to them, that they needed to learn about differentiation and self-validated intimacy so that there would be space for their differences. In particular, Trudy had to accept Bud's opposing viewpoints without criticizing him and feeling angry. Over time, Trudy was able to perceive the difference between listening and agreeing. In addition, she realized that Bud's need to have some time and space for himself had little to do with how much he loved her. Instead, it was his attempt to rebalance the differentiation scale. The more Trudy was able to tolerate his opposing opinions, the more Bud shared his thoughts and feelings with her.

After a few weeks, Trudy's depression eased up, their marital satisfaction increased, and they felt closer than they ever had. In addition, their sex life reached new heights. They learned how to adjust to the impact of retirement on their individuality and togetherness and strike an appropriate balance.

The increased time together forced Trudy and Bud to confront and repair a weak spot in their marriage that had remained hidden for a long time. The successful resolution that happened in short-term therapy made a profound difference in the quality of their relationship.

Exercises:
Assessing Your
Togetherness-Separation Balance

Couples establish a differentiation pattern throughout marriage, and it's important to be aware of that pattern in order to deal with its manifestations in retirement. Here are three simple assessment steps that will foster this awareness.

1. Identify how your attitudes and behaviors and those of your spouse regarding individuality versus togetherness were shaped by the following three factors:

- Gender. Men typically achieve closeness by virtue of being in the same space as their wives, while women typically require a verbal exchange.
  Do you follow these traditional patterns in your marriage?
  Does the female partner usually push for more sharing and togetherness, while the male wants more separation?

- Innate tendencies. Some people are naturally introverted and quiet, while others are more extroverted and want frequent and continuous verbal contact.
  What are your innate tendencies as compared to those of your spouse?

- Socialization. While this component is more complex than the others, and not always easily assessed without the help of a professional, you probably can make a good guess based on your upbringing.
  Did you grow up in the type of family in which everyone always did things together, or one in which people went their separate ways?

Based on these three variables, do you recognize major differences in how you and your spouse have been impacted?

Is it fair to say that you and your spouse have significantly different mind-sets regarding individuality versus togetherness?

2. Your responses to the following questions will aid in determining past similarities or differences related to intimacy:

Over the years, how satisfied were you with the amount of leisure time you and your spouse spent together?

Do you wish you had shared more time together, or do you feel that you did not have enough time to do the things that you enjoyed?

Do you feel that you were the one who suggested doing things together, or the one who felt guilty and pressured to do more than was comfortable for you?

How satisfying is your shared time as a couple compared to leisure time you spend with other people?

How satisfied are you with the amount and quality of your alone time at home while your spouse is in the house?

Do you feel that you generally have enough physical space to do what you want, or do you feel that you are often interrupted and unable to pursue your own agenda?

How satisfied are you with the amount and quality of self-disclosure and sharing of emotional topics that happen between you and your spouse?

Would you say that your spouse generally understands your feelings?

Do you feel that there are enough opportunities for each of you to share and be listened to, or that it is often a one-way conversation in which you hear but are not listened to (or the opposite—that you share but do not receive emotional feedback)?

After you've answered how you feel, repeat the process, this time trying to predict how your spouse would respond. Ask your spouse to do the same exercise. At this point, you should compare responses. Remember that you and your spouse probably have different subjective realities, and this is perfectly normal. Your goal isn't to agree on the past and on whether both of you were satisfied, but to discuss and discover what is going to be mutually satisfying for both of you now.

3. Examine how your and your spouse's attitudes and behaviors were impacted in the first three stages of marriage, adapting the questions to match your particular circumstances. Write down your responses without trying to predict your partner's answers, and ask him or her to do the same.

Before Children

Do you feel that in the first stage of marriage, you achieved a good and satisfying balance between the time you spent together and the time you spent alone or with other people or in other activities?

Were the depth and content of your conversations with your spouse satisfying?

Were there things that bothered one or both of you from the beginning?

If yes, did you reach some accord on them?

If you were able to resolve your conflicts, how did they get resolved, and how satisfied were you with the outcome?

Child Raising

Once you had kids, did either of you find that the balance shifted in an unsatisfactory direction?

Did either of you become angry or resentful that there was too much or not enough togetherness?

Did you feel during that time that something else frequently took priority over what you wanted?

Were work demands or children's needs overwhelming, not leaving you enough time to follow your own agenda?

Empty Nest

How did the balance change when your kids left home?

Did you spend more time together?

If so, how satisfying was it?

Did you feel that you had adequate amounts of emotional interaction with your spouse as well as alone time without too many interruptions while your spouse was at home?

Were there plenty of opportunities to spend time with other people and without your spouse?

Was there any change in your sexual behavior?

If yes, how satisfying was it?

If your relationship was affected by one or more of these life stages, consider how it was affected. Did the changes that came with each stage create a particular type of problem or situation?

If so, did it get resolved successfully, and how did you accomplish that?

Or was it swept under the carpet without a mutually agreeable adjustment?

Identifying what that problem or situation was helps isolate the vulnerable areas in your marriage that may become even more sensitive in retirement. The festering problems of earlier stages can intensify during the retirement stage. Recognizing the origin of these problems by reviewing your intimacy history can help you better address them.

Signs of Imbalance: A List of Identifying Questions

Differentiation difficulties can manifest themselves in a wide variety of ways, as we'll see in the ensuing chapters. You'll find that your problem solving is facilitated when you ferret out the cause of the problems. When you understand why you're having skirmishes about housework or money, you can confront the deeper causes, and this approach will help create permanent solutions.

The following list of questions reflects the common symptoms of relationship imbalance. Affirmative answers signal an imbalance in the relationship.

Measuring the frequency and intensity of the feelings and beliefs represented by these questions is important. In retirement as well as in earlier life stages, all of us experience some dissatisfaction with the separation–togetherness balance. In retirement, however, these feelings and beliefs can become pervasive and have negative repercussions for the relationship. When answering these questions, evaluate how often or how intensely you experience the specific item. The pattern of your answers to the questions here should give you a sense of the frequency and intensity of any feelings of dissatisfaction that apply to you.

1. How often do you feel emotionally disconnected from your spouse?

Always   Often   Seldom   Never

2. Does it seem that you and your spouse rarely have meaningful, rewarding conversations?

Always   Often   Seldom   Never

3. How often do you think of ways to get out of the house and escape spending additional time with your spouse?

Always   Often   Seldom   Never

4. Do hours or even days go by during which you feel as if your spouse is a roommate rather than a partner?

Always   Often   Seldom   Never

5. Do you find yourself in a rage when your spouse makes requests that formerly wouldn't have angered you?

Always   Often   Seldom   Never

6. Do you react to some of your spouse's actions or words in a way that seems extreme or even irrational?

Always   Often   Seldom   Never

7. Do you find yourself longing to have a regular break from your partner?

Always   Often   Seldom   Never

8. How often do you feel as if you're being "crowded," that your spouse is intruding in your personal space?

Always   Often   Seldom   Never

9. Do you feel that your spouse no longer loves you, or loves you less?

Always   Often   Seldom   Never

10. Do you feel as if your spouse is trying to control your life?

Always   Often   Seldom   Never

11. Do you feel that over the years, the two of you have drifted apart?

Always   Often   Seldom   Never

12. Do you feel that because of being with your partner you are losing your own identity?

Always   Often   Seldom   Never

13. Do you feel that in order to please your spouse you have to give up your own agenda?

Always   Often   Seldom   Never

14. Do you fantasize about getting a divorce from your partner, or even about his or her death?

Always   Often   Seldom   Never

If you answer "Often" or "Always" to many of the questions here, it is likely that the intimacy problem in your marriage is intense, and you need to take action for the health of your relationship.

The Psychological Meaning of Money

For many people who plan for retirement, finances are a major concern. Typically, they express the following worries:

- If we both live another 30 years, will we have enough money?
- Will we have to make lifestyle changes in order to survive on the money we've saved?
- Do we have the money to take the trips we always wanted and do all the other things we planned?

These are all practical questions, but there is a psychological side to money that people planning for retirement should also consider. Money carries a range of emotional connotations based on family values, early experience, and cultural background. In some families, money matters are discussed openly, and kids are aware when things are tight. In other houses, the topic is taboo. Some families have a history of financial stability, while others jockey between rags and riches.

Someone who suffered a family financial crisis during childhood, such as being evicted, will have a money mind-set different from that of someone who didn't experience any turmoil. In fact, our first memory of money—losing a quarter that Mom gave us to buy milk, versus receiving a quarter from Uncle Otis to buy a treat at the candy store—can have a pronounced effect years later.

The culture in which we grow up, too, affects our relationship to money. In some families, the cultural norm is to be humble about their affluence, while that of others is to flaunt their wealth. Most of us are unaware of how these factors influence our behaviors regarding money as adults.

Possessing sufficient financial resources can represent autonomy, personal independence, and self-esteem. It may also convey power, success, and status. In relationships, money is often associated with love; giving money or material gifts is a sign of affection. In relationships, however, money can turn into a symbol of control over others. The person who has more is likely to dominate decision making about how the money is going to be spent.

In American culture, money tends to be a private and intimate subject. People are more likely to talk about their sex lives before they'll disclose their income or financial assets. Since money symbolizes worth, competence, and prestige, people are shy about it and often have emotional conflicts related to the subject. For example, shame or guilt can accompany both having money and the lack of it.

The mighty dollar, therefore, can have an impact on people and relationships that goes beyond its purchasing power. Understanding your own and your spouse's psychological money styles and related financial concerns, and how they've been affected by retirement, can help ease the tension and arguments that often surface at this stage.

How Retirement Increases Money's Psychological Impact

The financial reality for most people in retirement is that paychecks stop and reliance on savings begins. Therefore, when retirement approaches, all the psychological ramifications of money intensify and can change the couple's relationship dynamic.

Many people enter this stage with a lifelong concern or fear about not having enough money for old age. Decisions and behaviors hinge on this apprehension, which often is reflected by a constant need to save, to defer enjoyable but expensive activities, or to meticulously calculate one's pension and other projected savings. Such people don't ask, "How much is enough?" Earlier in life, they might have bought a less costly house or less expensive cars. As they age, they are likely to grow more frugal.

Having enough money becomes a way to cope with the fear of dying. It's both a psychological defense against the inevitability of death and a way to achieve immortality. "If I have enough money, I'll be able to live longer" is the irrational thought and the persuasive theme that runs through the person's subconscious. For many people in this category, the more rational part of this fear is that they will be remembered for the money they will leave after they die rather than for being themselves.

Other subconscious fears include:

- **Fear of dependency.** "If I have enough money, I'll be able to buy services or afford a good nursing home so that I will not have to depend on my family in case I'm sick or weak."
- **Fear of abandonment.** "If I don't have enough money, they (friends, neighbors, and even family members) will abandon me. They will not be interested in me if I can no longer buy them presents or continue to participate in the activities they like to do."
- **Fear of the unknown.** Some people view life as being full of unpleasant surprises that they have to be ready to handle. Because the future is unpredictable, it is important to have "enough money" to cover whatever unexpected expenses the future springs on us.

Many middle-class people are fortunate enough to retire with sufficient funds to maintain a comfortable lifestyle. Nevertheless, for those who wallow in psychological fears about not having enough, this financial reality is insufficient to overcome their growing anxiety in retirement. As a result, maladaptive behaviors emerge, from shopping only where a senior citizen discount is offered to refusing to buy a needed article because there is not a coupon for it.

In addition to subconscious fears, the values one holds regarding retirement and aging have a great influence on how financial matters in retirement will be handled. In our culture, many people suffer from "ageism"—a belief that the older you become, the more senile, sick, dependent, and useless you become. It's also true that plenty of people perceive being old as synonymous with wisdom, experience, and nurturing. Likewise, when it comes to retirement, there are those who view retirement as a well-deserved and hard-earned reward for years of productivity, a time to enjoy newfound leisure and to seek interesting activities. For others, it's the beginning of old age and all of the negative implications that go along with it. For still others, retirement represents something in-between, a time of both rewards and dread.

People who look on retirement as a time for deserved and earned enjoyment will be more willing to spend money on fun as well as satisfying and meaningful activities. Of course, conflicts can arise if the spouse does not share that vision. On the other hand, people who view retirement as a waiting period for death, a time of loss and constriction, will tend to be frugal and deny themselves the enjoyment that money can bring. In extreme cases, this frugality can make marriage a living hell for the mate, especially one who has a "can't-take-it-with-you" approach to life.

Thus, the attitudes people have about retirement and aging combine with their psychological attitudes about money to impact the marriage in new ways after retirement. Arguments in which blame is assigned ("You're spending all our money!") or in which pleasures are denied (a much-anticipated trip is canceled because the stock market took a dive and "we don't have enough money") eat away at marriages when there is no consensus on these matters between husband and wife.

The next section outlines some of the specific money-related problems that pock the surface of marriages when both people retire.

Upsetting the Money Balance

All marriages have to reach a balance regarding how money is handled. When neither partner is aware of what money means to each of them from a psychological standpoint, conflicts and power struggles become the norm.

Most marriages that last develop a balanced pattern regarding money. Even so, as retirement approaches, the balance may be thrown off. Financial conflicts that were settled early on can resurface. Disagreements that existed before retirement might have been expressed as taste difference and been passed over lightly. Now, with more time spent together and with cash in shorter supply, these arguments often intensify and take on financial overtones.

Debates over daily and relatively small expenses can reach fever pitch; what begins as a disagreement over whether to go to a bargain movie theater versus a more convenient but expensive one dissolves into vicious name-calling. One spouse usually is in favor of cutting back to conserve funds, while the other maintains that now is the time to spend because it's the last opportunity to enjoy it.

Following are a few common situations that illustrate how retirement can foster money-based conflicts:

- Joan and Richard rarely if ever quarreled about money during their marriage. Less than a year after they retired, however, Richard began accusing Joan of being a spendthrift. Though Joan was certain that her spending patterns hadn't changed, Richard perceived that she was squandering money on what he termed "frivolous things." Such accusations invariably followed a dip in his stock portfolio.

When Richard retired, he became his own stockbroker and managed the portfolio himself. This was a coping mechanism for him, a way to still feel financially involved and in control. Unfortunately, when the value of his investments took a dip, he felt out of control and became angry with his wife. His criticisms were an ineffective attempt to regain control by shifting the "blame" for the negative financial situation from himself to his wife. Joan in turn felt resentful of his accusations, and a rift developed in their relationship.

- Though Noel and Gina had a decent amount of money saved when Noel retired, they began living as if they were one step away from the poorhouse. For Gina, this reaction wasn't far out of character; throughout their marriage, she had been the conservative one, always cautioning against overspending. Now she was even more pessimistic about their future, certain that one unwarranted expenditure might tip the scales against them.

  For his part, Noel had more or less removed himself from the family's financial affairs while he worked, letting his wife handle the finances because he believed that her frugality qualified her for this responsibility. That posture changed after he retired; he became much more aware of how much things cost because he did more of the shopping, and Gina's anxieties rubbed off on him.

  Pretty soon, Noel and Gina were denying themselves many of the activities they enjoyed, such as going out to dinner and taking trips to see their children and grandchildren. As the quality of their life declined, Noel became depressed. Though he was accustomed to relying on Gina when it came to financial decisions, part of him resented the fact that her fiscal policy prevented him from enjoying certain things in life. Even worse, her frugality made him feel that he was a failure as a breadwinner. He became increasingly withdrawn, and their marriage suffered.

- While Vince pursued a high-pressure, time-consuming career as a consultant, he spent relatively little on himself. After he stopped working, though, he found that he enjoyed buying all sorts of things. During the first year of retirement, he bought himself a luxury automobile and surprised his wife, Rose, with a trip to Japan. Though Rose was alarmed by these two major purchases, she initially wrote them off as isolated occurrences.

  To her dismay, during the second year, Vince began spending

even more, and when he purchased a summer home over her protests, she was furious. She had always considered her husband a prudent, non-materialistic man, and now he had changed dramatically. She was uncomfortable with his willingness to spend freely, and she found herself growing more distant from him.

While most of us are aware that money is a central retirement question, the psychology underneath that question generally escapes us. As the three foregoing situations demonstrate, retirement can have a profound effect on our attitudes and behaviors regarding personal worth. On the most basic level, if you were in the habit of defining who you are as a person by your level of income, what is your worth in retirement? If your marriage was based on certain expensive lifestyle choices, what happens to your relationship when you can no longer afford these same choices? Or what happens if one of you suddenly *perceives* that you can't afford to maintain the same lifestyle and the other is convinced that you can?

The psychology of money in retirement is complex, and to understand what all is involved, it helps to be familiar with the following subjects:

- Values about money
- Gender, money, and marital satisfaction earning and handling money
- Money styles

Values About Money

There are those people who believe in doing things in the easiest way possible, even if it will cost more. To others, the name of the game is to do things in the cheapest way possible, even if it means more work. You may be perfectly willing to spend $25 on a taxi to take you to the airport, while another person in the same financial situation opts to spend $2 on public transportation that is less convenient. Some people were raised to believe that waste is a sin; Gina in the previous example is one. They view it as "wasteful" to buy something that they'll use only once, or to pay full retail price in an upscale store. You may willingly spend $50,000 on a luxury car and not see it as wasteful at all, whereas someone in a better financial situation than yours will go for a less expensive model.

The values sustaining these choices can be deep-rooted and culturally based. Certain ethnic groups with a history of privation and persecutions view money as a means of safety and security. In the past, it has helped them escape oppression and even death. Money is a way to buy passage to freedom or to bribe someone into helping them get away. Even if such threats are no longer realistic and money is plentiful, their collective subconscious still fears some unexpected disaster, and they continue to be extraordinarily frugal. Richard, for instance, came from a family of Vietnamese refugees who had to bribe their way to safety.

Given this background, it's not surprising that his heart raced and his nerves rattled whenever he lost money on his stock portfolio.

In you're like most people, the values that underlie your money-mindset can be inferred from how you treated your children's allowances. Did you give your kids an allowance that was contingent on doing chores around the house, or was it handed over no-strings-attached? People in the former category believe that there are no free rides, and children were paid only if they contributed to the common good. If you're in the latter group, you felt that your kids deserved a certain amount of money to meet their basic needs; that it was their due as your children and your responsibility to pay them as a parent, even if they did no chores. Thus, the underlying value here is entitlement—one is expected to have and spend money in the same way that one is able to breathe and move about. In the former situation there is no such assumption.

If you and your spouse have different values about money, retirement, and aging, or if you're unclear about these values, then retirement may add heat to tensions that simmered during the work years. Because a steady income no longer exists, one partner's wasteful ways will seem dangerous to the other. Because retirement is a time to enjoy what one has earned, one spouse's frugality will be incredibly irksome to the other: "You can't take it with you," the sufferer will think.

These types of arguments can be fierce. It's important to remember that the real conflict is not just about money; it's about values. To you, your spouse seems reckless and materialistic; to your spouse, you seem to be placing a higher priority on saving than on enjoying meaningful experiences together. Nine times out often, people's arguments about money aren't about whether they can afford something—there is usually enough money to pay for whatever product or service is in question—rather, the arguments are about underlying values that conflict and become a power struggle.

When you retire, you need to be conscious of both your and your spouse's values related to money, retirement, and aging and to be sensitive to the general life fears that may affect these values. Any differences between you and your spouse during your working years will probably be a more frequent source of arguments after retirement. You can restrict the damage that these rifts cause by talking about the base issues rather than having the same circular arguments ("We've retired; we are on a fixed income and can't spend money the way we used to...").

Instead, talk about the feelings that gave rise to the money debate. Why is one person so frugal? Did she grow up poor? Is she terrified of ending up in an awful county home for senior citizens as her Aunt Sally did? What psychological meaning does a specific expense hold? How does spending money in a pricey restaurant make someone feel about who he is? Getting to the deeper meanings and expressing them will dissipate much of the relationship-wrecking tension.

Gender, Money, and Marital Satisfaction

Recent decades have brought substantial changes in beliefs about the role of women regarding work and their financial contributions to the family. Yet, despite this revision, society continues to view men as the primary family breadwinners. Our society also tends to equate money with success and power. Therefore, moneymaking is often connected to masculinity, and men generally have less conflict about it. It provides them with a means to be a caretaker. Men who achieve financial success are frequently viewed as the best "catches" in the marriage market. When it comes to selecting mates, research indicates that women rank earning power as the most important factor, while men place priority on beauty.

Certainly, there are many couples in which both men and women bring home money, and sometimes the woman earns more than the man. Nonetheless, many women, even those with successful careers, still allow their husbands to make most or even all of the important financial decisions. In fact, a significant percentage of women still agree with sex role stereotypes stemming from a patriarchal society, acceding to the concept that men are inherently better at handling money.

These assumptions may be traced to the fact that many women retiring now grew up in a household in which the father made and controlled all the money. In the '40s and '50s, children were taught that it is the man's responsibility to make money and to decide how it should be spent. Therefore, women hold an unconscious belief that making and handling money is unfeminine. They expect their money to derive from a relationship with a man rather than from their own efforts. It has been said that men can be unsexed by financial failure, while women can be unsexed by financial success. The outcome is that many successful women hand over their money (and power) to their husbands, as their mothers and grandmothers did.

Studies from the 1950s and '60s generally supported the proposition that socioeconomic rewards such as income, education, and occupational prestige increase the likelihood of marital satisfaction and stability. However, more recent studies yield inconsistent results and generally are not supportive of this premise. They show that when income meets one's expectations, regardless of the amount, or when the husband is perceived as a successful provider, marital satisfaction is maintained.

Therefore, relatively poor couples can be as happily married as wealthy ones if their income meets their expectations. People who are not materialistic, believe in simplifying their lives, and are satisfied living in a modest home, for instance, often have happy marriages. When it comes to marital satisfaction, the stability of a man's income plays a feature role: how regularly a husband brings home a paycheck matters more than how much he earns. Bringing in a steady paycheck means that he fulfills the expectation of being a stable provider to his family.

Research about financial power and marital satisfaction also reveals that the least stable and least happy marriages are wife-dominant; the greater the wife's earning relative to the husband's, the more likely divorce will ensue. Researchers attribute the lower satisfaction among these couples to the lack of role congruency and the departure from cultural norms. Husbands in these situations sometimes respond by withdrawing even further from family involvement, while wives try to force their husbands to respond, be more involved, and take a stronger leadership role in the family. The more he withdraws, the more she tries to force his involvement.

The highest level of marital satisfaction was found among egalitarian couples. In modern companionships, equality between spouses is an important dynamic. Congruency with this norm, as opposed to that of the masculine financial power base, was shown to contribute to marital satisfaction. These couples typically engage in two-way discussions regarding financial matters, using reward and positive reinforcement to influence each other's behavior rather than coercion and manipulation. Use of positive comments to influence each other's decisions and maintenance of an equal power structure characterized the most satisfied couples.

In short, if financial expectations are met, and if there is a sharing of responsibilities and power regarding financial decisions, marital satisfaction tends to be high. Couples who can talk reasonably and supportively about their finances will probably have better marriages.

Money and Marriage in Retirement

Keep in mind that, even when there has been power sharing and good communication about financial matters throughout the marriage, retirement can tear away at that cohesion. For one thing, many men can't readily accept the absence of a paycheck in their lives. Consciously or not, they ask themselves: "Who am I if I no longer am making financial contributions?"

As a result, a man who gave his wife great autonomy to make financial decisions when he worked becomes a micromanager in retirement. He asks her questions such as "Why did you buy that brand of bread when it wasn't on sale?" In essence, this type of question becomes a coping mechanism; he feels that he is still controlling his financial destiny because he is controlling his wife's spending decisions. As you can imagine, these controlling behaviors drive many women crazy and ripple the fabric of the relationship.

Women also can change their attitudes toward and behaviors about money after retirement. Many women become acutely aware at this point that they are likely to outlive their husbands and need to be knowledgeable about and involved in financial matters. Added to that, some homemakers are uncomfortable seeing their husbands in the role of non-moneymaking retiree; they find this posture less attractive. Women who have retired often become more interested in participating in their household's financial decisions, decisions they might have ignored while they were working. A woman who asserts herself in this manner can easily create conflict, particularly if her husband, who had made most of the financial decisions for years, views this assertiveness as criticism of his financial wisdom or as lack of trust.

The opposite situation is another possible source of conflict: the man may request that his wife become more involved in financial decisions, fearing that she will be unable to take care of herself if he should become sick or die. This request can anger a woman who perceives involvement in financial matters as unfeminine, or she may feel that her husband wants to abdicate his role and is no longer interested in "taking care" of her.

On the positive front, retirement can be an opportunity to switch from traditional gender roles regarding money to more egalitarian ones. It's possible that the husband has always hated being the financial decision maker and that the wife has always felt left out because she was responsible only for the household bills. Retirement provides a chance to try out new roles; he can cede the major money decisions to her, or they can participate equally in intellectually challenging decisions such as investments.

Couples need to be cognizant of what their feelings are in this regard and to communicate them honestly. They should talk about:

- How not bringing home a paycheck makes them feel about themselves and each other.
- How gender roles related to money affected them during their working years.
- The financial decision-making patterns that developed during their marriage.
- Whether they should make changes in these patterns during retirement.

After retirement, both men and women need to be reassured that they are still valued and respected and that they still have an integral role in the marriage. Just as important, couples should agree that it's okay to question each other about investments or expenses. Couples must also find a way to maintain a sense of autonomy for each partner. For instance, problems can emerge when couples who used to have separate checking accounts or credit cards decide after retirement to consolidate and have only one joint account. As they become more aware of each other's expenditures, arguments can erupt.

Make a pact with your spouse to talk about money matters in a calm and open manner. You increase the odds of making a smooth retirement transition if you discuss the impact of gender roles and maintain autonomy, fairness, and equality in financial concerns.

Earning and Handling Money

Many psychological factors influence a person's ability to earn and manage money successfully. Parental attitudes about money—its perceived abundance or scarcity, its priority, the ease of dispatching financial matters, the ability to talk openly about money— shape children's own attitudes and actions. This parental influence is complex, which is why two siblings may have markedly different reactions to growing up poor: one may choose to continue the pattern and forsake material things to become a missionary, while the other may become a wealthy entrepreneur.

The wish to have more money or less money than one's parents is integral to understanding the relationship between personality and money. For some people, making more money than one's parents is perceived as an act of disloyalty that can cause shame.

Dan, for instance, was the first man in his family to graduate from college. His wife worked full-time while he worked part-time and went to school. When he graduated, they were able to buy a house in a much better part of town than where his family lived. This caused Dan much discomfort. He knew that in his first job out of school, he made as much money as his dad made after many years of experience and that in a relatively short time he made more than his dad ever did. Dan declared his salary and the cost of their home as classified information and continued to feel a sense of guilt about these achievements.

On the other hand, earning more money than one's parents is seen by some as an act of love, validation, and pride. Donna was born to parents that were immigrants from Turkey. Her father was a factory worker, and her mother was a cleaning lady. Both parents worked hard and paid for Donna's nursing school. When she graduated, got a job as a nurse anesthesiologist, and began to earn more money than either of her parents ever did, all three of them felt tremendous pride. Her professional and financial success validated their hard life and selfless care.

Money-related idiosyncrasies take many forms. Some people are inhibited by the prospect of financial success. It is as if something stops them from working and earning money up to their potential or from being taken seriously as a mature and powerful adult. They may do very well when working for someone else but fail on their own. Sometimes this is because they need the father-figure boss to watch over them, and they labor under a subconscious taboo of surpassing this boss by making more money or being more successful.

Similarly, low self-esteem causes some people to believe that another person's needs matter more than their own. There are people who keep detailed financial records at work and vigilantly meet all obligations to the company's creditors while bouncing their personal checks. It is as if they do not owe themselves the obligation to look after their own finances, since they feel valuable only insofar as they are connected to someone else.

Some individuals have addictions to money. I've known people who earn millions annually yet still compulsively acquire more wealth. They seem to want to become "all-powerful," to beat some unclear competition, defend against vulnerability, or even achieve a form of immortality.

Given the diversity of ways in which we relate to money and how they impact our personality, it's no wonder that retirement can color our perceptions of ourselves as individuals. When you've spent 50 years addictively making more and more money, you may not be able to get that monkey off your back without experiencing grueling withdrawal symptoms. In the same way, if you've always had a boss who has served as a father figure, when you become boss-less, you naturally feel a sense of great loss. The depression you feel may not be from a loss of work as much as a loss of the "father." The person who was responsible for giving you your money is no longer in your daily life.

Relationships can bend or break under the strain of this transition. People can become withdrawn, depressed, antagonistic, or confused when their established relationship to income is taken from them—even when it's relinquished voluntarily.

You need to think about what your earning power meant to you during your work life. The abruptness of the shift—from making money to not making money—can be traumatic. If you are afraid of it, you probably should consider finding a way to make this transition less sudden. Getting a part-time job, implementing a phased retirement, and doing consulting work are just a few possibilities.

Money Styles

People possess distinct psychological styles relative to money. Edward Hallowell and William Grace described four money styles with which you should be familiar:

1. *Assemblers* are the least ambivalent in their love of money. They are aggressive in getting it and the least guilty in having it. The predominant meanings of money to assemblers are power, freedom, and self-esteem. These people often enjoy little of their wealth—they own modest homes, take short vacations, and have simple habits. Because spending money for pleasure is not the goal, these people and their families often do not get to enjoy the fruits of their labor. The goal is to increase the amount of money in order to purchase self-esteem, rather than to spend it.

2. *Spenders* are the most fun-loving money types. For them, money means action and freedom. They want and expect that there will always be enough of it. In this group we see the over-spender and the gambler. Not being able to spend means loss or failure, since the person is unable to be active or free.

3. *Under-involved* types tend to sidestep money questions and feel anxious about finances. Some can't be bothered with mundane money matters and have trouble finding time to devote to them. Others are uncomfortable when they need to handle money matters

because they're afraid of exposing their financial incompetence. Under-involved people may also be pessimistic. To them, money is a burden, and there is little to be gained by spending time on it; they believe that no financial plan will be successful, and so it's not worth the bother. Others in this group see money as something "dirty." Handling money translates into lowering oneself and jeopardizing one's integrity. Also in this category are women who have been raised with "old-fashioned" values and want to be taken care of by a man.

4. **Skeptics** favor conservative approaches and are often mistrustful about money matters. For them, money means security and control, and thus they are frequently risk averse. Living in a constant state of worry about money, they fret about not having enough. Everything gets translated into money, and the skeptic worrier becomes a sort of fiscal hypochondriac. It follows that this type is frequently miserly. To part with money is to part with more than dollars; they're parting with a sense of security and control.

Retirement affects exemplars of each of these styles somewhat differently, but as a general rule, one of two things is likely to happen:

- A style becomes more extreme (e.g., the skeptic becomes even more miserly).
- An almost opposite style emerges (e.g., the skeptic starts spending freely).

I've also found that certain style-specific patterns emerge in retirement. See if any of the following patterns characterize you or your spouse's behaviors:

- Retirement justifies for the skeptics and the under-involved that their approach to money is correct and often reinforces frugal behaviors. Skeptics become even more conservative, frugal, and cautious. The under-involved withdraw even more from money matters, rationalizing that there is less need now than in the past to focus on goals such as saving for the future or making long term investments. Paradoxically, they worry about money more than ever because they no longer have a steady income to help ease their anxiety and mistrust.

- Assemblers often turn to new defensive behaviors to compensate for no longer making money. They have depended on accumulating possessions as a way to combat feelings of inadequacy. Having lost the coping mechanism of assembling because of retirement, they may become depressed. They may also become over-spenders; this is a counter-phobic reaction, meant to demonstrate that there is no need for caution. Vince—who purchased a luxury car and a summer home over Rose's objections— is a good example. The bumper sticker "I'm spending my child's inheritance" reflects the attitude of some assemblers; they want to make up for lost time and spend before it's too late. There are also assemblers who switch to an under-involved style in retirement, readily handing off financial responsibilities to someone else, even though their lives had centered around gathering their money.

- Spenders who have to reduce their spending at retirement as funds become limited may experience emotional flux, since they can't be as active and free as they were when they were working. Some spenders develop a coping mechanism of cutting back on expenditures far beyond what is necessary. They make a radical swing from spending freely to saving for a rainy day.

You need to know what your style is, as well as the style of your spouse, and, if possible, anticipate how retirement will affect it. While most people are not style absolutes and instead have characteristics that represent a mixture of the four, a person's psychological approach to money tends to reflect one style more than the others. Think about where you fall. Ask your spouse, children, and close friends to characterize your style. If you've already retired, you can expect your particular style either to be more intense or to have been exchanged with an opposing style.

In many instances, financial planners neglect to consider-psychological factors affecting money and retirement savings. Typically, the only psychological factor they take into consideration regarding saving and financial decisions is the individual's risk level tolerance. They could offer much better advice, however, if they would factor into their assessment money styles, values about money, and other components of the psychology of money mentioned in this chapter. In addition they ought to assess both spouses psychological relationship to money, instead of only the husband's (even if the wife was not employed). They will be in a much better position to offer couples a plan that is based on each spouse's psychological monetary needs and includes marital differences and dynamics without spousal power struggles around money.

Similarly, recent research found that self-rated financial knowledge is positively related to feeling prepared for retirement and to proactive retirement savings and behaviors. In other words, when people perceive themselves as being informed about money issues, they tend to do a better job of retirement financial planning (in fact, perception is just as important in this regard as actual knowledge). Of course, those who have more positive values about money and for whom money is not a taboo subject would likely be more willing to learn and be involved in these financial decisions than those who have negative feelings and fears.

Financial planners are also unaware of another important factor related to retirement saving—having a future oriented disposition. Individuals who are future oriented tend to save for retirement and make retirement plans. People who are not future oriented, have fears and worries about the future (often the under-involved and skeptics described earlier) are least prepared for retirement, and don't engage in retirement planning. Thus, financial planners could provide more suitable planning if they were to change their "one program fits all" and tailor their approach to their customers based on their personality, psychological characteristics and marital dynamics.

Whether or not you're using a financial planner, you should take responsibility for knowing your psychological relationship to money as well as that of your spouse. Retirement is a new phase of life, bringing challenges that often are expressed in monetary terms. To enjoy your money after retirement, you need to be attentive to the emotional meanings that financial matters carry for both you and your spouse. This knowledge comes through open and continuous dialogue.

Exercises:
Understanding Your Psychology of Money

The following questions should be answered by each spouse separately to give you the greatest psychological insight about your money issues. After you both are through, discuss your responses. There are no right or wrong answers here. What's important is to become aware of your past patterns and find a pattern that will meet both your needs.

Write down the first answer that enters your mind after you read each question.

1. I consider myself financially successful.

     True   False

2. Depending on your response to the preceding question, explain why you consider yourself financially successful or what would have to happen for you to consider yourself so.

_____

_____

_____

_____

_____

_____

3. Before retirement, what percentage of the family income did you bring in?

_____

Are you pleased with this percentage, or do you wish it had been different? (If the latter, specify in what way.)

_____

_____

_____

_____

4. Do you feel that your spouse sees you as financially successful

     Yes   No

Explain what makes you feel this way.

_____

_____

_____

For me, money means:

Power
       1. Strongly Agree   2. Agree   3.Neutral
          4. Disagree   5. Strongly Disagree

Control
       1. Strongly Agree   2. Agree   3.Neutral
          4. Disagree   5. Strongly Disagree

Security
       1. Strongly Agree   2. Agree   3.Neutral
          4. Disagree   5. Strongly Disagree

Love
       1. Strongly Agree   2. Agree   3.Neutral
          4. Disagree   5. Strongly Disagree

Independence
       1. Strongly Agree   2. Agree   3.Neutral
          4. Disagree   5. Strongly Disagree

Success
       1. Strongly Agree   2. Agree   3.Neutral
          4. Disagree   5. Strongly Disagree

Corruption
       1. Strongly Agree   2. Agree   3.Neutral
          4. Disagree   5. Strongly Disagree

6. This series of questions pertains to values:

For me, waste is morally wrong.
      True   False

I prefer to do things in the fastest or most efficient way possible rather than the cheapest one.

     True   False

In retirement, it is more important to enjoy life than to save money.

     True   False

Growing up in my family, I expected conflicts about money.

     True   False

If so, what was the nature of those conflicts?

_____

_____

_____

_____

In my family today, I often have conflicts about money with my spouse.

     True   False

If so, what is the nature of these conflicts?

_____

_____

_____

In my family today, financial matters are not openly discussed.

     True   False

When it comes to money, I generally feel that what I have is not enough.

     True   False

Given your answers, can you identify your values relative to money?

When you compare responses, try to determine if your spouse's values fit yours. These questions should help you understand the roots of disagreements you may have about money.

7. This series pertains to attitudes toward gender:

Money matters are generally more masculine than feminine.

     True   False

In most marriages, men should handle financial decisions.

     True   False

In most marriages, both spouses should handle money, regardless of who earns it.

     True   False

I prefer to handle money by myself rather than with my spouse.

     True   False

I sometimes have to hide expenses or other monetary information from my spouse.

     True   False

If so, why do you do it?

_____

_____

_____

In your family, who handles the money: you, your spouse, or both?

In your family, who makes the financial decisions: you, your spouse, or both?

Are you pleased with how financial decisions are made in your family, or would you like to make a change in the process?

If you wanted to make a change in the financial decision-making process, would your spouse be likely to agree?

     Yes   No

Given your answers, does it appear that you and your spouse agree about who should handle the money?

When you compare responses, note how similar your expectations are and whether either of you is influenced by gender stereotypes in any way.

8. This series pertains to personality and money style:

I see myself as financially responsible and organized.

     True   False

I see my spouse as financially responsible and organized.

     True   False

I like the way my spouse handles money.

     True   False

If not, what don't you like?

_____

_____

_____

● When it comes to money, which of the following feelings do you experience (indicate all that apply):

☐ power   ☐ pessimism
☐ freedom   ☐ oppression
☐ pride   ☐ futility
☐ competence   ☐ shame
☐ anxiety   ☐ guilt
☐ insecurity

- Rate yourself as closer to one of the extremes in each of the following pairs:

  ☐ saver   ☐ spender
  ☐ frugal   ☐ generous
  ☐ bargain hunter   ☐ extravagant spender
  ☐ serious about money   ☐ cavalier about money
  ☐ enjoy managing finances   ☐ hate managing finances

- Now rate your spouse in those same categories:

  ☐ saver   ☐ spender
  ☐ frugal   ☐ generous
  ☐ bargain hunter   ☐ extravagant spender
  ☐ serious about money   ☐ cavalier about money
  ☐ enjoy managing finances   ☐ hate managing finances

Given your answers, can you tell which money style—Assembler, Spender, Under-involved, Skeptic—best describes you and your spouse?

When you compare responses, note how much agreement exists between the two of you about your money styles.

9. The last series pertains to changes after retirement:

After retirement, did you notice a change in your own financial attitudes and behaviors?

     Yes   No

How much agreement is there in post-retirement between you and your spouse about your individual money styles:

     None   Some   Total

Did you notice a change in your spouse's financial attitudes and behavior after retirement?

     Yes   No

Do you like it?

_____

_____

_____

_____

The more agreement and compatibility there is here between you and your spouse, the better the chance that money matters won't harm the relationship in retirement. Where you disagree, look for ways you can compromise. Most times, all it takes is a little movement on the parts of both spouses—he is willing to spend a little more on creature comforts, she is willing to spend a little less (or vice-versa)—to reach common, mutually acceptable ground.

CHAPTER SIX

The Household Arena

Compared with the preceding discourses on finances and relationship patterns, the topic of housework may seem trivial. After all, how many marriages end because of a dispute over who does the dishes? More to the point, how much bearing can retirement have on the division of household responsibilities and disputes about who does what?

The answer is that retirement has a formidable impact, and marriages can suffer from the cumulative tension of household disagreements.

Marital Dynamics and Housework

On their most basic level, buying groceries, washing dishes, picking up clothes from the dry cleaner, shoveling snow, and preparing income tax forms are daily, weekly, or seasonal chores that need to be done so that the household functions properly—but these and similar duties also have meanings that verge beyond the mundane. They can express caring: cooking your spouse's favorite meal or buying your spouse's favorite flowers, for example, says, "I know what you love, and you are important to me, so I do the chore with you in mind." They can express control: you may know that your spouse prefers that you clear the dishes immediately after dinner, but you let them sit, even though you have nothing else to do and you realize that your inaction is irritating to your spouse. Doing chores around the house means also that you contribute your share to the overall functioning of the family, rather than expecting that everything will be done for you by your spouse.

Given this "baggage," it's evident why battles royal about housework are commonplace. Often what people fight about is not the specific task but its symbolic meaning of caring, control, and contributing one's fair share to the household.

My own experiences as a marital therapist and as a researcher as well as other sociological and psychological studies have shown that housework has a direct bearing on marital satisfaction. In the same way that sex role stereotypes and perceptions of equity determine the impact of money on marriage, they also determine the impact of housework on marriage.

Most housework chores are still considered the woman's domain according to traditional sex role stereotypes. Cooking, dusting, sewing buttons, and similar tasks that often need to be performed daily are perceived as "feminine" chores. Perceived masculine chores, on the other hand, include lawn mowing, snow shoveling, and car maintenance, which tend to be weekly or seasonal needs. Research indicates that among the majority of couples, women do most of the housework regardless of their employment situation. Even women who are highly career oriented and spend many hours at their profession still put more time into housework than do their husbands.

Typically, women view their husbands' participation in household work as an expression of love, support, and appreciation; the man's efforts are seen as easing the woman's load rather than as a necessary contribution to the upkeep. When couples share this traditional view, women tend to derive personal and marital happiness from their perception that their husbands are contributing their fair share (regardless of the amount of domestic work they do).

Thus, what's important is the wife's perception rather than the actual amount of housework the husband does. This perception helps women feel that they are being taken care of instead of having to take care of everyone and everything themselves. Overall, women whose husbands make appreciable contributions to domestic work are less depressed and enjoy happier marriages.

At the other end of the spectrum, women who are dissatisfied with their husbands' contributions to domestic work feel that their husbands are not supportive of them and are making great demands on their time and energy. Therefore, they feel dissatisfied with the marriage.

Much depends on the individuals' beliefs about gender and marital roles. Studies of perceptions of equity, relative to the distribution of domestic work, document that women who hold more egalitarian views of marital roles expect increased participation from their mates in domestic work. In many instances, men feel uncomfortable doing chores that they consider feminine and resist doing anything that makes them feel unmanly or henpecked. Men in these situations are likely to report feeling unsupported by their wives.

Husbands who hold more traditional views of gender roles may want to please their wives in the housework areas but also feel resentful about what they have to do to achieve that goal.

Gender roles thus affect how much and what tasks people are willing to do. When the spouses' expectations do not match, both individuals derive less satisfaction from the marriage.

Research, Retirement, and Housework

Over time, the majority of couples establish a division of housework that both partners consider fair, or at least something they can both live with. Then retirement comes along and can upset this division.

Many studies repeatedly show that among most couples, only slight changes occur in housework responsibilities after retirement. There are no significant changes in domestic masculine chores, which tend to be done by husbands, e.g., yard work, home repairs. Retired men increase their participation in domestic work, although this increase does not appreciably reduce the amount of work their wives perform as it mostly increases men's performance of masculine chores.

Because these tasks usually aren't performed by women, the husband's increased participation doesn't reduce the wife's workload. In most instances, men refrain from or participate only sporadically in the daily traditional feminine chores such as cooking and cleaning up after meals or doing laundry.

Also, some women report an increased amount of time devoted to domestic work because their husbands are now home for lunch, and they prepare this meal and clean up afterward.

A significant number of retired men don't do any housework at all, continuing a pattern from their working years. In general, the basic divisions of household tasks remain intact during retirement, with women continuing to do most of the domestic work. And women spend more time than men on these chores: 20 hours per week for women versus 8 hours for men.

Researchers emphasize that these findings represent only the current crop of retirees, who were largely raised with traditional male and female roles. As more dual-career couples start to retire, particularly those who had to develop less segregated family roles while they worked, the division of domestic work after retirement is likely to be more equal in terms of time, less sex-segregated, and based more on skills and preferences.

Strong sex-typing among men seems to handicap their adjustment to retirement. Older or retired men who are more involved in domestic work were found to have higher self-esteem and an enhanced sense of psychological well-being. These men reported feeling useful when they shared housework. It also gave them an opportunity to express love, companionship, and support in their relationship.

An interesting point that emerges from the research is that each spouse's sense of purpose, productivity, and identity after retirement affects his or her perception of a fair division of domestic labor. Some men, especially those who hold more egalitarian views of men's and women's roles, find that performing housework is a good way to re-create one's identity after retirement. For them, housework becomes a welcome outlet for their time and energy.

This does not imply that egalitarian men who are retired take pleasure or find meaning in scouring a toilet, but they do develop hobbies and interests from housework, such as gourmet cooking or carpentry. It gives them a means to be productive, engage in new activities, and develop new expertise. Some men are also motivated by the money they save by doing chores themselves rather than hiring others as they did in the past.

Other men who hold more traditional views feel that housework is incompatible with their sense of masculinity and try to preserve the status quo. For this group, increased participation in domestic work is humiliating and uncomfortable. If a man has to help his wife with a domestic task, he sees it as "doing her a favor." Typically, he'll excuse himself from further involvement by claiming incompetence. As one such man quipped, "When it comes to the kitchen, I'm a religious cook: I make burnt offerings."

In retirement, some women expect that because they and their spouses have an equal amount of free time, a more equal division of housework will ensue. This is particularly true for women who hold more egalitarian views of gender roles and those who are disenchanted with the routine aspect of housework. They say, "I did it for so many years; now it is your turn to pitch in." They welcome having their husbands take over, relieved to be able to surrender control of the house.

Other women see a change in the previous division of labor as an intrusion into their sphere of influence or encroachment on their autonomy. In some studies where men showed increased involvement in feminine or general household tasks, retired women report that they resent their husbands' participation in housework and perceive it as an invasion of "their domain." This can be a potential source for marital tension if the husband impinges on the wife's territory without her agreement and/or they have different expectations about their role in key aspects of family life. These results were true for both homemakers and women with careers.

Domestic work contributes to women's sense of self-worth after retirement; it makes them feel productive and useful. Of course, there are homemakers who look forward to their husbands' participation in cooking, cleaning, gardening, and the like, seeing it as an opportunity to enjoy life together.

Clearly, retirement has a concerted and varying impact on both men's and women's ideas about household work. Because of this, couples need to renegotiate the division of domestic work according to values, preferences, and skills. Renegotiation should also take into account previous housework patterns as well as gender role expectations.

To facilitate this renegotiation, keep in mind that involvement in domestic work can ease the transition to retirement. Participation in these chores can boost both men's and women's self-esteem. When both spouses contribute their fair share, the payoff is often increased marital satisfaction and togetherness.

The ability to maintain comfortable communication even when dealing with the stress of marital problems and disagreements is an important aspect of a good marital dynamic. This aspect of the relationship becomes a very important contributor to the quality and satisfaction with retirement as spouses need to re-negotiate many aspects of their lives that were previously settled. As stated earlier in this book, almost all couples report less marital enjoyment and a decline in marital vitality after retirement. The impact of a woman's retirement on the dyadic unit is as strong as that of a man's retirement.

A 2003 study found that the emotional quality of marital interaction greatly impacts retirement satisfaction. The ability of husbands to remain physiologically calm and relaxed while discussing marital conflicts is an important contributor to retirement satisfaction (above and beyond its contribution to marital satisfaction). For wives, the emotional qualities of the marital interaction had no impact on retirement satisfaction. Husbands who were relaxed while discussing disagreements prior to retirement had a higher retirement satisfaction. Men who were able to negotiate marital conflict while staying relatively calm and exhibiting positive behaviors and feelings were happier in their marriage and more satisfied in life after retirement. This suggests that comfort and competence in marital communication, as expressed by maintaining an emotional even keel, reflects trust and mutual respect between spouses that helps in the transition to retirement.

Potential Scenarios

To identify how retirement is impacting your housework and relationship dynamic, it's useful to look at the most common scenarios and see which may be relevant to you.

Scenario One

Neither partner wants or expects any changes in their established pre-retirement division of domestic work. Marital satisfaction will remain constant in this situation.

> Marsha was a homemaker who enjoyed her role and loved to cook. When her husband, Leonard, retired, it meant more work for her; she made breakfast and lunch for him, cleaned up afterward, and tidied up the inevitable messes he made with his various carpentry projects. None of this bothered Marsha, since she had always enjoyed cooking and tolerated cleaning. Besides, she was happy to have her husband home and even happier that he enjoyed his carpentry hobby as much as or more than he had enjoyed work. While she still did the lion's share of the housework, Marsha didn't expect or want Leonard to contribute in this area. As a result, housework dynamics had no impact on their relationship.

Scenario Two

Both partners want and expect greater participation in household chores from the spouse who participated less prior to retirement. This should result in increased marital satisfaction.

> We can use the example of Matthew and Abe, a gay couple, who retired at the same time. Since Matthew used to travel a lot with his job, Abe was responsible for almost 100 percent of the domestic work. He did not particularly like doing housework but accepted that there was no alternative. Matthew appreciated his partner's willingness to take on these tasks and acknowledged the inequity.
>
> After retirement, Matthew accepted that it was now his turn to handle housework duties. He asked Abe which chores

he particularly disliked and relieved him of them by assuming full responsibility for all grocery shopping, laundry, and cleaning tasks. Abe continued to cook because he enjoyed it. Abe appreciated Matthew's contribution, while Matthew liked feeling useful. Both felt proud of the mutual respect they exhibited, and their relationship was even better in retirement than it was when they were working.

Scenario Three

She expects more domestic participation from him, but he resists and resents having to comply. The likely outcome here is increased conflict and decreased marital satisfaction; some compromise is needed to restore the balance in the relationship.

Bruce and Shirley had a stable marriage but also had frequent fights about housework. Shirley felt that she was doing too much and wanted Bruce to participate more. Bruce had grown up in a Hispanic family in which men's participation in domestic chores was ridiculed and men who did housework were seen as wimpy.

After retirement, Bruce expected that the couple's division of domestic tasks would remain status quo, and he was surprised when Shirley demanded a big change. In the past, when her "bitching" about his unwillingness to pitch in escalated, he would do a few chores to placate her and then quickly revert to form. To his chagrin, he found that this ploy no longer was effective.

Shirley viewed her husband's attitude and actions as "unfair." She interpreted them as meaning that he didn't care about her, took her for granted, and didn't appreciate the contributions she made to their household. Throughout their marriage, Shirley would seethe with resentment when they both returned from work at about the same time and, while she slaved over the stove, he would flop down in front of the television.

Bruce rationalized his behavior by claiming that his work was more physically demanding and that he needed to rest more than Shirley did. This made Shirley feel as if she were the maid and Bruce were the master. When this behavior continued after retirement, Shirley was adamant that he needed to participate in domestic chores.

After negotiation, Bruce agreed to come to the kitchen

while she cooked and keep her company rather than watching the tube. While this was not the outcome she wanted—she expected that they would both cook and clean up together—this compromise created a balance she could tolerate. She no longer felt humiliated and demeaned by his behavior. In addition, Bruce made sure to thank her frequently for the chores she did.

With his increased awareness of Shirley's feelings, Bruce began to see how repetitive, time-consuming, and mundane housework chores could be, and he gradually became more willing to help. At first, he did some grocery shopping "for her." Then he started to use his shopping trips to buy her little items that he knew she liked. Showing her affection in this manner helped ease her anger and disappointment.

While Shirley continued to shoulder the bulk of the work, and the new pattern that they developed did not match the picture she'd hoped for—a much more equal division of family labor, a model her parents had established for her—it was still better than before. As a result, much of the tension, resentment, and hostility was diffused, and the balance in their marriage was restored.

Scenario Four

He wants to increase his participation in housework, but she is against it. As in the previous scenario, increased conflict and decreased marital satisfaction are likely, and compromise will be necessary.

Todd, a high-level production manager, was eager to help his wife with the housework after he retired. At first, Doris, who was an advertising executive and had also just retired, welcomed his help and the opportunity for them to do more things together. Unfortunately, Todd began applying the same rigid quality-control standards he'd used at work to his chores at home, which Doris resented. She started to resist and refuse his suggestions.

Because Doris felt that she was being controlled and that her autonomy was at risk, they started to fight much more often. Their marital satisfaction decreased, but they weren't clear why their relationship had taken such an argumentative turn. The final straw was when Doris returned from her tennis game and discovered that Todd had arranged the contents of their pantry in alphabetical order. Todd was shocked by her angry reaction;

he'd thought she would be pleased by his organizational efforts.

Because her reaction was explosive and their fighting had already increased to an uncomfortable level, they decided to seek marital therapy. During the sessions, they shared their feelings. Doris relayed that she was stung by Todd's implicit criticism that she was poorly organized and inefficient. She added that his increased involvement in housework and frequent suggestions for improvement just fed her resentment. Finally, a deeper issue emerged: she perceived Todd as overly rigid and controlling, trying to get her to do things his way. When she did things her way, he criticized her for being disorganized. As an example, she had organized the pantry in a way that made sense to her— by item: vegetables, soups, etc.—rather than according to his alphabetical scheme.

Throughout their marriage, this deeper issue lay dormant between them. While they both were working, however, Doris had sufficient space to do things her way at work, where she was recognized and appreciated. During this time, she was able to tolerate his criticism, domineering attitude, and suggestions for how she might improve. After retirement, not only did his criticism become more frequent and pointed, but also she no longer had her work satisfaction to sustain her. Their fighting increased, and their decision to seek therapy probably saved their marriage as it helped them understand the different styles they each used with regard to efficacy and organization. By finally addressing this unresolved issue and finding a way to accept and appreciate their differences, they were able to become more intimate.

Through Doris's disclosure, Todd realized that the subconscious motive for his criticisms was to secure validation from her that would increase his self-esteem. When he grasped that he was having the opposite effect on his wife, he agreed that he needed to become more easygoing and flexible.

Todd shifted his efficiency mind-set to more appropriate areas, volunteering at a soup kitchen and joining the board of the temple. Housework ceased to be a crucible in their marriage, and the underlying tension between them that had persisted through the years was finally addressed and resolved, resulting in a much more satisfying relationship for both of them.

How and When:
Setting the Terms for Household Chores

Many times, the power struggle over household chores encompasses not only who does what but also how and when it's done. When the traditional situation exists—housework is largely a woman's domain—the typical conflict is set off by the husband's not doing these tasks according to the wife's specifications.

The how and when of housework, of course, is not the crux. As is the case with power struggles in other areas of family life— which movie to see, which restaurant to go to—the conflict is rarely about the specific activity. Rather, it's about the symbolic meaning of the activity.

Each partner in the conflict wants to feel important; each wants the other to acknowledge his or her status by being considerate, approving, and willing to change an objectionable behavior. Whatever the conflict is about becomes a symbol of one's importance in the relationship. An argument over how and when a spouse clears the table is symbolic of an individual's standing in the relationship. Arguments about housework can also express criticism for certain characteristics, such as being too slow, too superficial, or too disorganized.

Consider the example of Linda and Ken. Linda wanted Ken to take a greater role in housework after they retired, and he gladly acceded, since he always liked to cook and found doing the dishes "therapeutic." They agreed that whoever was not doing the cooking would be responsible for the cleaning, and that at least twice a week Ken would cook.

The problem was that Linda micromanaged Ken. She remonstrated with him when he didn't put foodstuffs back in the cupboard immediately after he finished using them, as she did when she cooked, or when he failed to sponge up spills right after they happened, which made them harder to clean. She also commented that he used too many pots and pans, announcing that the kitchen looked as if a tornado had blown through it when he was finished preparing a meal.

Ken resented her "suggestions" and exploded when she reminded him to put items away. Linda resented having to clean up his mess, and the fact that he cooked a nice meal didn't ameliorate her resentment. From her point of view, the benefit she received from his cooking was lessened by the extra cleaning she had to do. Their fights became more frequent and bitter, and behind the words, they were about power, control, and autonomy.

In counseling, Ken and Linda were able to confront the real meaning of their fights. Ken explained that he felt that Linda was trying to control him with all her "suggestions" to put things away and by not letting him cook in his less-organized way. Furthermore, he believed her attitude was a continuation of her lack of approval of him throughout their marriage; she had found him disorganized in many other areas of their life. Ultimately, Ken was able to see that her suggestions were not meant to be controlling as much as they were to lighten her cleanup load.

After the underlying feelings were expressed, they were able to stop the power struggle and reach a compromise that was mutually satisfying. Linda agreed to stop correcting Ken and to let him do things on his terms when he cooked, and Ken agreed to put things away when he was done so that Linda's only responsibility would be washing the dishes.

Counseling helped them separate a general difference they had with regard to organization from the specific acts of cooking and cleaning. While the broader difference remained, they were able to achieve consensus about the specific arena of the kitchen so that the style difference was no longer disruptive to their marriage.

Variations on this housework theme abound. Eddy, for instance, was an engineer who retired at age 67 when his company was bought. Since he was bored and somewhat depressed and purposeless, he followed his wife, Candy, around, wanting her company but at the same time observing her way of doing the housework. He offered her many suggestions that he felt would make her work easier and faster. Candy found his commentary to be critical and disapproving. When Eddy became angry with her for not following his "useful advice," she became depressed and withdrew from him.

With their marriage in jeopardy, they tried therapy. After a few sessions, Candy clearly communicated that she was upset about how much Eddy focused on her after he retired. She felt that he wasn't giving her enough space and that she had become a "project" like the ones he used to attack so diligently when he was working. While he was surprised to hear how much she resented his housework advice, he acknowledged that he had been feeling "empty" since he retired and that focusing on Candy doing her household chores distracted him from this awful feeling—one he didn't want to face.

During the next few months, Eddy made an effort to give Candy more space and to allow her to do housework in peace. He also began searching for other activities that would fill his time and give him the same satisfaction that work once provided. Thus, the initial fight over housework that brought them to therapy helped Eddy realize that he had been psychologically unprepared for retirement. By taking responsibility for himself, he not only improved his mental health but also preserved his marriage.

Exercises:
Understanding Your Housework Dynamics

To remedy retirement-induced conflicts about domestic work, use
the following exercises to understand the real issues at stake and
to negotiate a more equitable arrangement. As you consider your
responses, be aware that people often overestimate their own housework
contributions but underestimate the spouse's contributions. Both
you and your spouse should answer each of the following questions
without any input from the other. When you've both completed the
questionnaire, discuss your answers.

General Division of Housework

1. How much time, in an average week, do you spend on various
housework chores?

2. How much time, in an average week, do you estimate that your
spouse spends doing housework?

3. How do you feel about this division: do you think it is fair?

4. What do you like about this division, and what would you like to
change?

5. Do you feel appreciated for the domestic chores you do, or are they
being taken for granted?

6. Do you appreciate your spouse's contribution to the domestic work,
and, if so, do you express your appreciation?

7. Do you feel criticized by your spouse over domestic work? If so, how
does it make you feel?

8. Do you disapprove of the way your spouse does certain chores, and, if
so, do you express your disapproval?

9. Do you use doing chores as a way to show affection for your spouse,
and, if so, how?

10. When it comes to housework, I feel: (check all that apply)

☐ appreciated for what I do ☐ competent
☐ bored by the repetitiveness ☐ taken for granted
☐ productive ☐ mostly inept

☐ creative and challenged   ☐ willing to contribute a fair share
☐ entitled, bitter   ☐ used and taken advantage of
☐ open to learn new skills   ☐ wasteful of my time and skills

Changes in Division of Housework and Retirement

The following questions are designed to help you analyze your housework conflicts, resolve your differences, and establish an equitable division of labor after retirement.

1. After retirement, did you notice any changes in the division of domestic work?

- If so, what were the changes?
- Why do you think they happened?
- How do you feel about them?

2. Instead of expressing housework conflicts or resentments "in the moment" (and often in an angry way), it's preferable for spouses to make time to discuss them. With this in mind, write a paragraph describing how you would like to change the division of labor in general or with regard to a specific chore. You should also communicate how you feel, to help explain why you want a given change.

Here is how this paragraph might read:

> "Please come with me to do the grocery shopping, since it takes less time to do it together, and it's more fun and less boring. I feel that our division of tasks is unbalanced, and it makes me feel as if you're not doing your fair share now that you have the time to pitch in more."

3. Rate each of the chores in the following table by the four categories as shown:

1. Gender association—Masculine, Feminine, or Androgynous trait (M, F, or A)

2. Your like or dislike of the activity (use a 1–5 scale: 1=love, 2=like, 3=neutral, 4=dislike, 5=hate)

3. Your comfort level—Competent/comfortable or Inept/uncomfortable (C or I)

4. Whether it should be performed by you or your spouse, or someone should be hired to do it (F=Family, H=Hire)

Task	Gender M-F-A	Like/Dislike 1-5	Competent / Inept	Family / Hire
Clearing after meals				
Washing dishes				
Cleaning kitchen				
Vacuuming				
Washing floors				
Tidying				
Scrubbing bathroom				
Dusting				
Grocery shopping				
Laundry				
Ironing				
Mending clothes				
Yard work				
Outside work & repairs				
Home repairs				
Car maintenance				
Paying bills				
Keeping financial records				
Taking out garbage				
Writing thank-you notes				
Buying presents for friends & family				

Use your realization that you see certain tasks as gender related or that you feel inept doing them to explain to your spouse why you resist doing the chore.

4. For each task in the preceding table, indicate if any changes have occurred after retirement. Specifically, have you or your spouse taken over responsibility for the task from the other person?
Are there more conflicts over the task?

If there are, can you figure out what the conflict is really about (what it symbolizes)?

Once you and your spouse have compared responses, review the list of chores and do the following:

- Trade—take on the tasks that your partner hates the most and exchange them with those you hate (or at which you feel incompetent).
- Identify chores that neither of you enjoy doing and agree to hire or employ someone else to do them.
- Identify chores that may prove to be enjoyable when done as a couple, and work out your approach.

CHAPTER SEVEN

Friendship

Retirement's impact on friendships may not be as immediately obvious as that of some of the other areas we've covered. Nevertheless, while the linkages are subtle on the surface, they are important from a psychological perspective.

Just as retirement can change the relationship between a married couple, so too can it change a couple's (or each individual's) relationships with friends. For starters, retirement can create an economic gap between friends that is often difficult to bridge. Suddenly one couple has to watch expenses and can't do all the things with another couple that they used to do.

It can also highlight a friendship imbalance within the marriage. A man whose friendships were primarily work related may bristle at his wife's circle of friends because his dropped away when he retired, while hers remained. Or a woman may object to her husband's transferring the energy he used to pour into work into developing social relationships; instead of spending his increased free time with her, he's engaged in widening his circle of companions to compensate for the loss of his work associates.

Before analyzing the possible scenarios, let's start by shedding light on the essence of friendship and its social and psychological relevance.

A Voluntary Relationship

My experience with clients is consistent with research findings that interaction and intimacy with friends is psychologically important. Since friendship is a voluntary relationship, as opposed to relationships with parents or siblings, people sometimes attach greater emotional and psychological value to it. We cannot choose our relatives, but we can choose our friends; friendship, therefore, contributes much to our psychological well-being. Unlike with family relationships, friendship's voluntary nature largely avoids feelings of obligation. We don't feel compelled to do things with and for friends; it's much more elective.

In many cultures—but especially in this country—friendships tend to be homogeneous. We are most likely to form friendships with people of the same sex who are similar to us in age and social class. The relationship between friends also is based on equality, not on authority, patronage, or any other hierarchy.

Most of us enjoy different levels of intimacy with our friends. A friend can be a college roommate whom we don't see much but to whom we still feel close, a person with whom we regularly share our personal feelings and deepest thoughts, or someone with whom we share only superficial information but whom we trust to take care of our pets and mail while we're away. As a general rule, women have more and deeper friendships than men, as evidenced by the content of their conversation as well as by its acknowledged importance to their well-being. For their part, men may have many collegial relationships with subordinates, bosses, and peers.

During certain times of our lives—adolescence being the most obvious one—friendship is central to our psychological wellbeing. Though it may take a backseat during other times, friendship figures prominently in the lives of most people and confers a number of benefits, including:

- *Belonging:* Friendship conveys a sense of membership, of the availability of others to whom we can turn in times of need. Loneliness is so devastating precisely because we lack this sense of membership and inclusion.
- *Assistance:* Friends help with tasks that are too difficult for us to do on our own, such as moving to a new home, fixing a broken appliance, or producing a great recipe for guacamole.
- *Social integration:* Friendship sets up a sounding board for our opinions and reactions, and it helps us assess the appropriateness of our reactions to the events of the world. Often the interaction with friends helps us maintain our contact with society at large.
- *Helping others:* Being a friend gives us the chance to feel good about ourselves by doing good things for people we care about. Being useful, giving advice, or performing a service in a way that "makes a difference" increases our sense of self-worth.
- *Disclosure:* Intimate friendships allow us to express our deep feelings, concerns, opinions, and values. They give us permission to say what

we really think, with the assumption that we'll be understood and accepted.

- *Support and reassurance:* When we have doubts about what course to follow, friends validate and support our dealings with the world. When friends agree with us about the ways in which things should be done—what matters and what can be ignored—we feel more confident and reassured. This support also affirms that other people care about us and value who we are. Rightly or wrongly, some people measure their worth by the number of friends they have or the prestige factor of these friends (such as a CEO or doctor). The implication is that because these people like, trust, and value us, we must be worthwhile. Clinically depressed individuals often see themselves as having lost their sense of self-worth and lacking many or any friends.

These benefits help sustain us, not just when we're working but also when we retire. As we'll see, some of these benefits are diminished or even eliminated upon retirement. First, we need to establish the different approaches to and manifestations of friendship, beginning with gender differences.

Gender Differences and Friendship

Both men and women gain from the benefits of belonging, assistance in social integration, and helping others. Men, however, are much less likely to receive the benefit of self-disclosure or of emotional support and reassurance.

Again, research documents what I have seen in my practice: women have more friendships than men, and the content, depth, and intensity are more personal. In one study, two-thirds of the men surveyed said they did not have a best friend, while three-fourths of the women identified one.

Among married couples, more men than women named the spouse as a best friend, most trusted confidante, and the one to whom they would most likely turn in any crisis. Married women, on the other hand, did not uniformly name the spouse as best friend or the person to whom they'd turn in emotional distress. While some women did confer this status on the husband, it was never exclusively his as was most often the case among men.

Most married women identified at least one trusted friend, and many identified several. They also reported relying on these non-spousal friends for emotional support, such as during conflicts with their husbands or in-laws, as well as for physical support, such as picking their children up during an emergency. Women also spoke passionately about how these friendships improved the quality of their lives.

Generally, woman-to-woman friendships are based on shared intimacies, self-disclosure, empathy, and emotional support. In contrast, man-to-man friendships are emotionally controlled and designed to fit men's perceptions of "manly" behavior; men play sports together, discuss and share tips on home repair, investments, work, and travel. Though they may also have intellectual discussions about topics of mutual interest, they rarely disclose personal problems, emotional difficulties, or feelings. Women thus often have more well-rounded relationships than men, integrating activities and intellectual discussions and exchanging information with personal disclosures.

Obviously, some of these gender differences are evolving. The growing number of men's groups in which participants are prompted to share their innermost feelings have encouraged men to move away from the strong, silent stereotype.

A key point here is the fact that men often find it easiest to start friendships in work environments or with work-related contacts such as customers or suppliers. Because these associates know them through their business accomplishments and because they've met tough challenges together, men feel closer to them. The hitch is that these relationships usually don't lead to self-disclosure, partially because of fears of negative work repercussions. Someone may believe: "If they know how bad I feel about my marriage, they will assume that I am vulnerable, may think less of me, and won't include me in important projects."

Thus, if men do have close friends with whom they share their vulnerabilities, the parties probably don't work together anymore. Women, whether homemakers or employed, still make many of their friends through their children—meeting other mothers through school or play group activities—as well as at work.

Friendship Styles

Everyone accumulates friends in life, but the type and number depends to a great extent on one's personality and view of both the importance and purpose of friendship. While combinations and changes do occur throughout the life span, most people lean toward one of three principal friendship styles:

- *Discerning style:* These folks choose their friends carefully, resulting in their having relatively few true friends to whom they feel very committed. Discerners believe that friends are like family and not easily replaceable; they are quick to draw a sharp distinction between friends and mere acquaintances. Discerners feel at ease with friends and believe that their friends know them for who they are. While they don't always see these friends often, when they meet, they are always able to pick up where they left off. Typically, this style of friendship leads to long-term relationships with people they met when they were young—in school, in the neighborhood, on athletic teams, and so on. In fact, many discerners don't believe that they can make friends after adolescence or early adulthood. They need the experience of their formative years and the history in which they shared life's ups and downs as a bond.

- *Independent style:* Independents make friends throughout their lives, using the circumstances of their lives to meet and interact with people with whom friendships develop. These friendships are often more casual than those established by discerners and evolve out of whatever work or leisure activity that brought them together. Independents tend to value the relationship over the person, making a specific person eminently replaceable. For them, having close friends with whom they share their intimate feelings is not a priority, and they shy away from obligations associated with friendship. Consequently, their conversations usually revolve around topics such as movies, golf, or current events but remain impersonal and unemotional.

- *Acquisitive style:* This style is a blend of the previous two. Here we see people who continue to acquire new friends throughout their lives, but they're also likely to hold on to at least some of their previous friends as their situations change. They view friends as irreplaceable, and they and their friends are available for each other in times of need as well as for leisure activities.

These three different styles affect the workings of the marital machinery. If one spouse has a discerning style and the other has an independent style, they will have problems agreeing on what is important. He may want to be friends with the Zanes because they enjoy personal and meaningful conversations, which she views as serious and too heavy. She wants to be friends with the Andersons because they're more lively and fun—though they're not interested in anything beyond a superficial relationship—which feels like a waste of time to him.

Friendship Tensions Within a Marriage

It's clear that gender and style differences can spawn relationship problems in a marriage. As noted earlier, men are often dependent on their wives as best friends, and women frequently recoil from being the husband's singular source of emotional support. Moreover, if a woman has close relationships with friends, the husband can be jealous, especially if he suspects that she is disclosing privileged information. It's common for couples to negotiate disclosure of private information throughout their marriages, grappling over whether it's appropriate for the woman to tell her friends about sexual intimacies, financial problems, and other sensitive topics.

Most couples also have to negotiate stances on mixed-gender friendships. Although having close friends of the opposite sex may seem natural to one spouse, the other may have strong reservations, feeling jealous, threatened, or even betrayed by the prospect.

While it may be okay for a woman to complain about her husband to another woman, it may not be okay when she expresses the same complaint to a male friend. You may feel vulnerable if your spouse often has dinner with a close friend of the opposite sex and discloses personal information. Or let's say both friends are attorneys who met in law school; she gives him constructive feedback and advice about legal issues, while his wife, who is in a different profession, feels that she can never be as helpful or valued because she lacks the specific expertise of his female friend. After retirement, these gender-based tensions can intensify and create more relationship strain, since retirement often exacerbates one's insecurities.

Another potentially troublesome area is the intensity of various friendships. Commonly, husbands and wives distinguish between his, her, and our friends. In many marriages, women have a set of friends whom the men rarely see, and men have a group of work colleagues whom the women don't know well. It's easy for either spouse to be perturbed by the other's "private" friends. Just as readily, the friends they have in common can lead to tensions, since it's rare that two couples all like each other equally. Invariably, husband A will be rubbed the wrong way by wife/husband B, or wife B will dislike wife/husband A.

Different friendship styles and personalities also can be an interference. If a warm, socially involved extrovert is married to an intellectually curious introvert, it's almost a given that their friends will be different. Hackles are raised if each person doesn't give the other room to form his or her own type of friendships. Along these same lines, if one spouse has a discerning style and the other has an acquisitive style, a middle ground must be found so that the discerner doesn't feel overwhelmed by the other's friends and the acquisitive one doesn't feel that the spouse hardly ever contributes to their social circle.

In therapy sessions that I conduct, a frequent goal is to help clients realize how important it is for married people to have one-on-one friendships as well as couple-to-couple relationships. Even if a man doesn't understand why his wife needs to spend so much time with her friends and why their mutual friends aren't enough for her, as they may be for him, he should allow enough "space" in the relationship for her to develop and participate in her own friendships because they are essential to her happiness and psychological well-being. The following story illustrates the value of having a large variety of friends.

During a therapy session, Stuart complained, "I can't understand why Jennifer has so many friends and how she has the energy for all of them. I wish she would give me more attention instead of spreading it among all these people." Jennifer, his wife of 12 years, had a ready answer—as she detailed for us:

"It's very important for me to have different kinds of friends. Each one represents a different aspect of myself. I have the *soul mates*—Tracy and Stacy—with whom I can share everything. When Stuart and I have a fight, when I screw up at work, or when I don't know how to handle my daughter or any other difficult and sensitive situation, they're there for me. I don't see them as often as I would like, as we don't live nearby and we are all so busy, but they are always close in my heart. I know that if I'll call at two a.m., they'll be there for me, supporting and caring.

"Then I have what I call the *children's friends*—friends I met when I was pregnant with Jessica. I see them often and do many activities with them that revolve around the children. We depend on each other for baby-sitting, and we give each other advice and helpful information, but I don't have the emotional intimacy with them that I have with Stacy and Tracy. At first, I was disappointed that I don't have the same closeness with Dina, Rosa, and Sharon, but I learned to accept and appreciate the fun and companionship they offer me.

"In a similar category of fun and companionship, I have my *work friends*—Julie, Rita, and Joel. We support each other in work-related matters. Joel and Rita don't work with me anymore, but I make the effort to continue to see them. Since they don't have children, I rarely talk with them about child care or domestic issues. Nevertheless, I value this comradeship and do not want to give it up.

"Now come my *history friends*. These are my high school friends and people I grew up with in my neighborhood. We share a history together that I don't have with the other three groups of friends. They know about my alcoholic father, and I know all about their family problems. We used to run away to each other's houses when things were really bad. Even though I know I'm in a different socioeconomic situation now—being a lawyer, living in a big house, while they stayed in the old neighborhood—I get mad when Stuart challenges me about what I have in common with them. It's as if he wants me to give up my roots.

"The last group is our *couple friends*, most of whom are from 'Stuart's side'—people he met through his work and, before that, at school when he was getting his M.B.A. Since he has an objection to most of my friends, we don't go out much with couples from 'my side.'

"He feels uncomfortable with my soul mates, since they know everything about him, and not being sure how much they've told their husbands, he prefers not to socialize with them. He doesn't like the husbands of my 'children's friends.' My work friends are no good either; Julie's husband is too old, Rita is unmarried, and Joel makes Stuart nuts because he's a single, handsome guy. As often as I tell him that there is nothing romantic between us, he still feels jealous or threatened. So, since it's important for us that we have people to go out with to a movie or a restaurant on a Saturday night, we go with his friends, but that doesn't mean they're sufficient for my friendship needs, even though they are for Stuart's."

Jennifer has an acquisitive style of friendship. She has many friends from different areas of her life, and each one is significant and important to her in a specific way. There is little interaction among the different groups. The soul mates do not interact with the work group or the history group. Likewise, the couple friends have little in common with the other groups. However, each group holds importance for her, and she is unwilling to stop seeing any of them.

Though they are clearly irritated by it, Jennifer and Stuart tolerate this unwieldy friendship situation. Even so, you can probably infer how little it would take to push the tension level up another notch. As we'll see, retirement can do this pushing.

Why Friendship Takes on Increased Importance After Retirement

People who engage in social and recreational activities improve their odds of having a happy, satisfying retirement. Good friendships go hand in hand with such activities, offering opportunities for meaningful attachments, social integration, competence, and entertainment. Sharing leisure activities with friends is associated with less loneliness, anxiety, and personal angst, and more positive feelings about aging.

A 2010 study found that social support before and during times of adversity, like retirement, promotes resilience and easier adaptation. Social capital, i.e., having friends, access to good quality social relationships and integration in the community helps individuals to become more resilient and cope better with the challenges of old age and retirement. Similarly a 2009 study of retired women found that having friends who provided emotional support was the only support that contributed to retirement satisfaction. Informational support (giving advice) and instrumental support (helping with chores) did not contribute to retirement satisfaction.

Since retirement can be a stressful transition involving multiple losses and relationship changes, having a supportive network buffers the stressors of this transition and contributes to greater retirement satisfaction. This finding reinforces the importance of friends to women's retirement satisfaction.

Another relevant study found that for both men and women, having friends and seeing themselves as good friends to others, prior to retirement, facilitated adjusting to retirement. Positive identity as a friend contributed to self-esteem and provided a bridge to more involvement with friends after retirement. With more time for socialization, people capitalized on friendships formed while they were still working and carried them over into retirement.

Since friendship is a voluntary relationship, friends confirm our independence and worth in a way that family members can't. Friends spend time together and provide support of their own volition because they enjoy each other's company. Relatives, whether they like each other or not, often feel obliged to interact with each other. Thus, when it comes to morale, friends are instrumental; friendship is integral to self-esteem.

Moreover, I have found that the happiest and healthiest retirees are those who have both "old," pre-retirement, friends and "new," post-retirement, friends. For many retirees, maintaining strong relationships with people who knew them when they were employed is a necessity. Whether these are work colleagues or simply non-work friends from the past, they carry with them the knowledge of the individual's career achievements. The sense is that these friends from their past know them more completely or as "whole" people, whereas individuals with whom they've become friends after retirement know only part of them, limiting the friendship to a certain degree.

So, if there's a model to hold up for friendships after retirement, it's one in which people maintain close relationships with at least one person from their past and at the same time form new friendships. A practical strategy is to develop a new social network to replace the one that existed in the workplace. I've found that all retirees, regardless of gender, friendship style, or personality, benefit when they engage in activities that help them integrate into a social network. This is especially true for acquisitive extrovert types, who are loath to leave their work friends behind and confront a social vacuum in their lives.

Beyond the social benefits, self-disclosure with friends that expresses caring and intimacy is as important psychologically after retirement as it is before. The ability to develop intimacy is one of the major developmental tasks of life. Emotional intimacy and close companionship are the most common types of social support provided by older adult friends. Loneliness is a major cause of depression throughout life and can be all the more troubling for retirees. The companionship that friendship provides later in life can serve as a shield against this threat. Studies have validated that having "confidants" promotes post-retirement adjustment and is associated with psychological well-being. The healthiest and happiest seniors tend to have at least one close personal friendship.

Related to this theme is the fact that retirees are often more willing to share negative feelings and experiences of self-doubt than they were before retirement. As retirees become aware of the aging process that they are going through and cultural stigmas about old age, they need and want to air these feelings.

Thus, in many ways and for many individuals, retirement makes friendship even more important psychologically than it was in the working years. Friendship wards off feelings of isolation and loneliness and fosters attachment and social integration, conveying that one is valued, competent, and useful. It provides a peer group of people in a similar life stage and experiencing similar changes. In addition, sharing leisure activities with friends helps create a more positive attitude about aging and life after retirement and helps maintain retirees' connections with the larger society.

Friendship and Marriage after Retirement

Friends are fundamental to a balanced marriage. Individually and as couples, they offer the support, social integration, and other virtues that all of us require to a greater or lesser extent. Though the friendship requirements in any marriage vary, just about every marriage benefits from continuous interaction with friends.

Retirement can intrude by robbing one or both people of friends. Perhaps the most common pattern I've encountered is that of a man losing touch with his work friends while his wife (who might or might not have worked) maintains relationships with a solid core of other women. When these men have relied heavily on their wives as best friends all their working lives, they often find themselves feeling isolated and depressed after retirement. In fact, one study shows that among retired married men who commit suicide, the majority had relied solely on their spouses for social interaction.

The American Foundation for Suicide Prevention indicates the rate of suicide in males over age 65 is seven times that of females who are over 65, as recently as 2008. In part, this is because women are more likely than men to have stronger social supports, to feel that their relationships are deterrents to suicide, and to seek psychiatric and medical intervention, which may contribute to their lower rate of completed suicide.

In less extreme cases, the man becomes resentful and jealous of his wife's friends. Women, in turn, become vexed by spouses who seem unable or unwilling to make friends on their own or to reestablish relationships with work colleagues. This erosion can weaken a marriage that has thrived for years. In addition, any unresolved conflicts that lay dormant while work and children were taking the spouses' time and energy are more likely to be roused after retirement. Unfortunately, interaction with friends is often an arena where these differences spring up.

Take the case of Josh and Martha. After retiring, they moved to Chicago, where their children and grandchildren live. Martha had been a university professor and had a few friends in Atlanta, where they'd lived for the last 20 years and where she grew up. Josh, who is extroverted and outgoing, had been a senior partner in an international consulting company and had many work-related friendships. They'd had a stable and happy marriage for 30 years, but a few months after moving into their new downtown condo, they started to feel bored and lonely. Spending time with the children and grandchildren was great, but it was not enough.

When they planned for their retirement, it never occurred to them to consider how important friends were for their individual well-being as well as for their marital balance. Josh wanted to visit museums and libraries, take classes, and go on architectural tours. He expected Martha to accompany him in all of these activities, which he hoped would also provide the chance for them to meet new people and develop new friendships. He was disappointed to discover that Martha, who was not nearly as outgoing as he, wanted to stay at home and read all the books she'd never had time for and raise orchids, her passionate hobby; she did not want to be "running around all over town." Martha had a hard time understanding Josh's loneliness and resisted the pressure he was putting on her, implying that she was not being a good spouse because she wouldn't join him in his activities.

In the past, when they lived in Atlanta, Josh did a lot of these activities with friends and consequently relied much less on Martha to be his companion. Also, many of his activities were related to work, so Martha didn't have to join him. Her discerning style of friendship allowed her to be satisfied with seeing her old friends and talking with them on the phone. Josh, on the contrary, relied on her to support him in developing new friendships.

Their fighting increased to an unbearable level, and their son, after unsuccessfully trying to help them, referred them to me. In therapy it became evident that both were bewildered as to what to do. In all their years together, they never had a situation in which their needs were so far apart. In addition, they'd never realized how different their attitudes were toward social contacts and friendships.

Martha divulged how hurt she was by Josh's accusing her of not being a supportive wife, given that for so many years she had attended many work functions with him and had often entertained his friends in their home. Josh explained how abandoned he felt by her and how much he relied on her intellect and "southern charm" to bring couples into their social circle.

Since they both had been regular churchgoers, and Martha felt comfortable in this environment, I suggested that they become more active in church. Following another suggestion, Josh started to volunteer with an organization that helps AIDS patients cope with different health and bureaucratic organizations. This combined a worthwhile activity with the opportunity to meet new people in a setting where Martha's presence was not expected. Some of the other volunteers eventually became friends of the couple, while Josh also developed one-on-one relationships there. In addition, he became a board member in their church, which led to other satisfying relationships. His participation in these organizations and involvement with new friends reduced the pressure on Martha, and their marriage returned to form.

Volunteering can be a good way for retirees to feel better about themselves by making life better for others. It confers the benefits of contributing to a good cause and feeling productive as well as meeting other people and establishing new friendships.

The next example features a lesbian couple, but its message about friendship and retirement is universal. Sueann and Ingrid were in a monogamous relationship for more than 25 years. They first met at work, where Sueann was the principal and Ingrid was a teacher.

Ingrid is extroverted, vivacious, and fun-loving and has many friends in whom she confides and to whom she feels attached. She has an acquisitive friendship style and has maintained close ties with friends from both school and work. Not leaving the area where she grew up made it easy for her to stay in close touch with these people.

Sueann is more introverted and serious; she has a discerning style. She has only two close friends who knew about her being a lesbian when she was a young adult, and they provided her with support, but they now live more than a thousand miles away. Sueann suffered social isolation while she grew up, due to her sexual preference and introverted personality. She moved to the Midwest when she was offered the principal position at a good school, and she did not develop any significant friendships from that point on.

As long as both women worked, the difference in their friendship needs and styles never created static. Sueann frequently had administrative duties that occupied her evenings, such as meetings with other school district principals and the superintendent. This gave Ingrid sufficient time to socialize with her friends as well as a legitimate explanation for why Sueann was often absent from these social events.

They retired at the same time, and that's when the trouble began. Ingrid wanted to continue her close relationships with all her friends, but this made Sueann feel neglected, abandoned, and increasingly jealous of the attention Ingrid gave to others. The fact that she was older and less attractive than Ingrid also made her insecure about their future together. Sueann wanted them to take classes together, join book clubs, and immerse themselves in other intellectual activities, while Ingrid preferred playing cards, going to movies and restaurants, and other less cerebral pursuits.

They started to fight on a daily basis about whom Ingrid could see, what she would tell them, and how much time she would spend away from their apartment. Ingrid felt that Sueann was micromanaging her and that she wanted her to be as isolated as she was. She was angry that Sueann was forcing her to choose between two things she valued, and she didn't understand why Sueann was upset when she learned that Ingrid had confided in her friends about the problems in their relationship.

Through therapy and specific behavioral changes, Sueann and Ingrid were able to save their relationship. One of the best outcomes was that Sueann recognized that, despite her discerning style, she required some interaction with the outside world. By becoming involved in community work and using her considerable administrative skills, she quickly developed a core of acquaintances who made her less dependent on Ingrid. She also was able to stop trying to censor what Ingrid said and did.

In reciprocation, Ingrid agreed that she would specifically include Sueann in more of her activities—and Sueann agreed to participate. Ingrid also began making an effort to work on their relationship rather than taking it for granted; she renewed her commitment to Sueann as the most important person in her life.

Obstacles to Keeping the Friends You Had Before Retirement

When people stop working, they often leave behind not only a job but also an astonishingly rich network of bosses, subordinates, peers, customers, clients, and others whom they suddenly stop seeing regularly. Without a work-related commitment, retirees sometimes feel disconnected from former business friends. There's an awkwardness and sense of separateness that grows more acute as time goes by; situations change, and contact becomes less frequent.

While it may seem easy enough to maintain one's work contacts, doing so often requires overcoming some obstacles. Recognizing the following ones and making a conscious effort to maneuver around them will help preserve valuable friendships.

Obstacle 1: Less Commonality

If you stop working, and your friend remains employed, you may find that your relationship weakens. You may feel that your friend values you less because you're no longer in the workforce, and you then withdraw from further interactions because you're less comfortable in his or her presence.

People who are not well prepared psychologically for retirement— who go into it with misconceptions and do not develop new activities and interests—often are hit hard by ambiguity about their self-worth and lack of purpose. If you're awash in these negative feelings, it's harder to retain your identity. Because some people believe they're somehow different and less valuable in retirement, they assume that their work friends will no longer enjoy being with them.

For instance, Marcus was not particularly outgoing even during his career and didn't have many close friends, partly because he was uncomfortable with intimacy and partly because of his limited social skills. He had a few colleagues with whom he sometimes played golf, but mostly he interacted with his children and grandchildren; he also spent a great deal of time watching television. He considered his wife, Ginny, his closest and only true friend.

Ginny did most of her socializing on her own. She had several good friends at work whom she saw regularly, and they helped her avoid feeling alone during the many times Marcus worked long hours or traveled. They had very few friendships with couples: at most, they might go out with another couple once a month on a Saturday night.

After Marcus retired, he was reluctant to develop new social ties or try new activities. He clung desperately to Ginny and expected her to stay at home with him as she did while they both worked, adjusting her schedule to fit his. Marcus also felt abandoned by his colleagues, even though he'd never had close relationships with them. Since Marcus did not perceive the distinction between colleague and true friend, he felt betrayed.

Within a year after retiring, Marcus became depressed and angry. Ginny bore the brunt of these feelings but didn't know how to help him. Arguments erupted over minor incidents. One day Marcus became furious when Ginny told him she was going to have dinner with some work friends; he had anticipated that they'd stay home and watch a television show together. Ginny lashed out at her husband for all the time he watched television, though that wasn't the real problem. As she said to Marcus when they began therapy, "Maybe you wouldn't feel so lonely and needy if you'd stop watching television and start making an effort to meet other people."

But Marcus was blocked. He had convinced himself that none of his work colleagues would be interested in golfing with him anymore and that they would accept his invitation only out of charity, if at all. "Why don't they ever call me?" he asked. It took months of therapy before Marcus would even consider taking the risk of calling a colleague.

He finally made the call once he realized that while they no longer had work in common, they shared a passion for golf, which is what had brought them together in the first place. With a push from Ginny—who clearly communicated to Marcus that his isolating behavior was suffocating her—he began to reestablish contact with old work acquaintances. While he didn't form emotionally binding relationships with them, he did renew his social life, which probably saved his marriage.

Obstacle 2: Less Money

Reduced income can become a divisive factor when the gap between friends' net worth is significant. The Smiths and the Millers, who had been good friends for more than 30 years, learned this lesson.

Jonathan Smith and Herbert Miller had been roommates in law school and stayed close after each of them married. Their wives, Tiffany and Leslie, liked each other, and their children were also close and got together frequently. Tiffany Smith came from a wealthy family, and the Smiths were consequently in a better financial position than the Millers, but this never affected the friendship during their working years—Tiffany was a part-time librarian, and Leslie was an accountant. The four of them used to go to the opera, dinners, and theater and also vacationed together in Hawaii and Aspen. Herbert traveled a lot for work, so they tried to arrange vacations to coincide with his various trips, and he used his frequent-flyer miles to defray expenses.

After both couples retired, the Smiths suggested various ideas for trips that the Millers felt were prohibitively expensive. Adding to the Millers' financial load, they were helping support Leslie's mother, who had Alzheimer's disease and was now in a nursing home. While the Smiths generously offered the Millers the use of their home in Aspen, Herbert and Leslie were peeved that their friends didn't show more sensitivity to their financial situation. "We don't have a trust fund to fall back on," Leslie groused to Herbert one evening. They slowly began doing less with the Smiths, in part because they couldn't afford it and in part because of bitterness.

The Smiths felt rejected, hurt, and puzzled. They couldn't understand what they had done to cause the rift. The Millers didn't feel comfortable disclosing their financial problems to the Smiths, so the impasse remained.

Leslie, who was a client of mine, obviously missed Tiffany; she cried in one session when she talked about her friend and how much she had appreciated her warmth and support. Just as significantly, she felt that not seeing the Smiths impacted the quality of her marriage. She and Herbert were not having as much fun, and none of their other friends provided the companionship and enjoyment that Tiffany and Jonathan did. I suggested that she bring her husband into the therapy sessions so that he could share his feelings about the situation.

It turned out that Herbert missed Jonathan as much as Leslie missed Tiffany, if not more so. His discerning friendship style impeded him from developing meaningful new relationships, so he had no other friend to whom he could turn when Jonathan was not part of their circle. In addition, he confessed that he worried that his wife would blame him indirectly for the breakup with the Smiths, that she'd feel that he was not a good provider.

Once they had cleared the air between them, and Herbert felt reassured that Leslie perceived him as a successful provider, we agreed that they should make contact with Jonathan and Tiffany and invite them to a therapy session. The Smiths agreed to join Herbert and Leslie in what turned out to be a highly emotional session. "We were hurt that you stopped calling," said the Smiths. "We felt that we couldn't keep up with you," said the Millers.

Both couples communicated how much they valued each other and asserted that they wanted to resume the friendship. The Smiths helped matters by acknowledging that they were well aware that the combination of retirement and the cost of the nursing home made it hard on the Millers. They said that they wanted to offer to help defray the cost of vacations but were concerned that such an offer might offend them.

After some discussion, the Millers and Smiths were able to settle on financial guidelines for the relationship: The Millers promised to be open about not being able to afford a given activity, and the Smiths promised to be more sensitive to their friends' needs. They renewed their commitment to maintaining the friendship, which helped put the relationship back on track.

The key to avoiding or overcoming this obstacle is communicating openly and continuously with friends about financial difficulties. Unfortunately, our culture is marked by a reluctance to talk about money with anyone outside of the family. This inhibition can be detrimental to friendships when two couples retire and one pair has to tighten the purse strings. The other pair may misunderstand why their friends say they can't go on vacation or to a nice restaurant. For the newly "frugal" couple, the situation breeds hostility and discomfort. By refusing to make money a forbidden subject, we minimize these misunderstandings.

Obstacle 3: Migration

After retiring, couples frequently sell their residences and move. Some want to be closer to grandchildren; others want to settle in a nicer climate or exchange suburban for city living. The move can be a matter of miles or across the country, or even to another continent. Whatever the circumstances, the result is that friends get left behind. In the reverse situation, the problem isn't that a couple moves but that their friends decide to depart for Florida, leaving them stuck without friends in the same cold climate. More than one retired couple bemoans feeling "deserted" by friends.

For instance, Walter and Michael shared medical offices for many years, and they and their families were good friends. The two men retired and sold their practices at the same time.

Michael and his wife, Laura, began spending most of the fall and winter in Arizona to be near their adult children. When they returned in the warm weather, they found it difficult to resume their friendship with Walter and his wife, Sheila. During their absence, Walter and Sheila had become good friends with two other couples, and Michael and Laura realized that they had lost their position as the people Walter and Sheila always called to do things with. This made them feel excluded, as if they were being "punished" for wanting to be with their children and grandchildren.

Over time, they saw each other less and less, and the friendship waned. What eased the hurt for Michael and Laura was the recognition that they had made new friends in Arizona.

While migration is a common hindrance to friendship, it doesn't have to be. Certainly being physically distant for a good part of the year can cramp relationships or reduce the closeness that friends feel toward each other, but there are many ways of keeping in touch, especially in the age of E-mail. Plus, if couples can get beyond the disappointment of the geographic separation and recognize the valid reasons for relocating, the move is less likely to impair the friendship. At the same time, people probably would be wise not to depend on the friendship in the same way they did when they were geographically close. It's not disloyal to form new friendships when it's impossible to see old friends regularly.

Obstacle 4: Fear of Dependency

A large percentage of retired people move closer to their adult children. This move, however, isn't always motivated only by a desire to see more of the kids or grandkids. Fear of dependency often propels retirees halfway across the country; concerned about declining health, they want to be close to people who can help take care of them if they become infirm. While no one sees being dependent on one's children as desirable, it's nonetheless common.

At the same time, being dependent on friends is deemed neither desirable nor acceptable by most people. Retirees do not feel comfortable depending on friends who are the same age and who may also experience health problems in the coming years.

Thus, younger family members provide "insurance" that friends cannot offer.

That said, moving away from friends to be with adult children may create unnecessary rifts with friends. I've found that people with discerning and even acquisitive friendship styles—those who feel that friends are like family and are not easily replaceable— are often terribly upset by these moves. Therefore, plans and preparations for retirement should always take into account the importance of friends to one's well-being.

A closely related issue here is reciprocity. Even retirees who don't move may retreat from friendships because they "don't want to become a burden." Perhaps they have a chronic illness, and their friends have prepared meals for them or driven them when they weren't able to drive themselves. Pride prevents them from continuing what they feel has become a one-sided relationship, and they withdraw from the friendship. Even though they make this decision voluntarily, they often rue the consequences. Again, people with discerning and acquisitive friendship styles suffer the most when they struggle to replace the friends they've cut out of their lives.

Exercises:
Assessing the Impact of Friendship on Your Marriage

Relationships often wilt in retirement because couples have different expectations about and needs for friendship. The following questions will help you determine how you and your spouse compare in these areas.

1. Make a list of all of your friends. Beside each name, note whether this friendship was recently acquired versus lifelong, and "individual" versus "couple." If you listed any friends with whom you no longer are in touch, record the cause of the split.
   Did a specific incident end the relationship, or did it just fade?

Name Recent/Lifelong Mine/Ours Still in contact with

_____

_____

_____

2. Now list your five closest friends and answer the following questions about each of them:

What is your friend's age and sex?

Where did you meet this person, and how long have you known him or her?

How often do you have contact with this friend, and by what method—in person, telephone, letter, email?

Which of your other friends does this friend know?

3. Rate the feelings you get from each of the five friends on your previous list by indicating a degree of high, medium, or low for the following characteristics:

	High	Medium	Low
Sense of companionship			
Equality and reciprocity			
Enjoyment and fun			
Ability to confide			
Giving help			
Receiving help			
Diversity of interactions			
Respect, trust, and acceptance			
Being understood and "known"			
Loyalty, commitment, and consistency			

4. Look back on your answers to the previous questions and reflect on the following:

Homogeneity: are your friends the same sex as you and similar to you in age and socioeconomic bracket?

Setting: in what settings do you seem to find friends; how much effort do you put into establishing and maintaining the friendship?

Network: do your friends know each other and form a network, or are your friendships individual?

Duration: do you have both short- and long-term friends?

Interaction: how often do you connect with your friends?

5. Based on the number and duration of your friendships, do you think that the discerning, independent, or acquisitive style best describes you?

6. Repeat questions 1 through 5 from the point of view of your spouse, or ask your spouse to complete them. Then discuss the following questions together:

- Are there differences in friendship patterns between the two of you?
- If you see differences, do some of them conform to the information about gender differences outlined in this chapter?
- If you had or have arguments about friends in your marriage, can you see them in a new light now?
- Are you more willing to compromise and accommodate the other person's friendship needs?

7. In planning your retirement, did you consider its impact on your friendships, and did you take into account the psychological importance of friends to your life satisfaction? Answer the following questions in this regard:

What changes happened in your friendships after retirement.

In what ways did your feelings about certain friends change; do you feel as valued and appreciated by them as you did before you retired?

Do you feel abandoned by some friends?

Did you or friends move to a new residence?

If so, did the move affect your friendship?

Is there a financial difference between you and your friends that is having an impact now?

If so, how prepared were you for these changes?

How well are you coping with them?

How open are you to developing new friendships?

CHAPTER EIGHT

Family Matters

When people retire, their relationships with children, grandchildren, and other family members can be affected, a little or a lot, and for better or worse. While retirement frees a couple to spend more time with family members, it also can produce stress and conflict if the spouses aren't in sync about how much time should be spent with the kinfolk. Retirement can stoke the coals of family-related tensions between a husband and wife as well as forge brand-new ones.

It's a mistake to assume that everyone welcomes retirement as an opportunity to spend as much time as possible with offspring. While most people certainly want to dedicate some of their newfound time to family members, the desired amount varies with the individual, as does the priority assigned. One spouse may not want to forgo certain activities that retirement has made possible in order to attend a cousin's wedding out of state or see a grandchild's class play, while the partner ranks all other retirement activities as secondary to family doings.

This chapter exposes how relationships with four specific family groups—grandchildren, adult children, parents, and others (siblings, nieces and nephews, and so on)—can affect a marriage. We'll also see how inheritance can stir up its own special set of problems.

Grandchildren

Approximately 75 percent of Americans over age 65 are grand-parents. Among people over 65 with adult children, more than 90 percent are grandparents. Although relatively little research has been undertaken on changes in grandparenting relationships after retirement, what is known suggests that the grandparenting role can be paramount to older adults in general and to retirees in particular.

Being a grandparent is central to some people's self-image, and it becomes even more meaningful for them in retirement. In a sense, it helps them feel useful, productive, and needed, just as work did. Finding a new purpose in life is often mandatory for people who want to maintain solid relationships at this stage of life, and some can find that purpose in grandparenting.

The grandparent experience contributes to both the psychological well-being and psychological development of older adults. The sense that life is good after retirement may be strengthened by the bond that develops with a young person who looks up to the elder and who is treated in a special way by that elder. Such a relationship also lets grandparents enjoy the grandchild's youthful vitality and, by extension, keeps them plugged in to a rapidly changing world and to what is considered "hip."

Remember that development doesn't have to stop as one ages. The grandparent role is complementary to the process, since it often demands evolving new ways of caring, expressing affection, sharing wisdom, and staying young at heart. People who continue their development often not only are happier with their own lives but also provide more intellectually and emotionally stimulating companionship for their spouses.

Many grandparents remark that they have better and more fulfilling relationships with their grandchildren than they had with their own children when they were the same age. Grandparents can provide unconditional love, acceptance, and support for their grandkids in ways they couldn't always as parents. Because their self-esteem is less tied to their grandchildren's behaviors and achievements than to those of their own children, they don't become upset with every misstep or failure. Thirty years ago, when a couple's own child came home from college with long hair, they freaked out; today when their grandchild shows up with fluorescent green hair, it's easier to laugh about it and philosophize, "This too shall pass." Having a long-term perspective of development makes them more tolerant and less inclined to worry.

In fact, it's a common tendency for grandparents to indulge grandchildren and treat them leniently. This behavior pattern can make for a strong relationship that skips a generation, but an all too common by-product is conflicts with other family members as well as one's spouse.

Kevin, a successful 42-year-old executive in a Fortune 100 company, was in therapy to improve his general life satisfaction, get in touch with his feelings, and understand why his third marriage was crumbling, as another wife was threatening to leave him. He also had to work through his ambivalence about his own father's relationship with Jesse, Kevin's adolescent son. This relationship had become closer after his father, Will, retired from his oncology practice.

While Kevin was happy that his father and Jesse were more in touch, he was disturbed by several repercussions from their relationship. Both Will and Jesse were accomplished chess players, and they spent much time together playing, discussing maneuvers, and attending tournaments.

From an "inner-child" standpoint, Kevin was angry that his father was spending more time with Jesse and paying more attention to him than he ever had done with Kevin. Kevin had always felt that his father's work came first and that the sick patients were more important to his dad than he was. He also thought that his father was disappointed that he hadn't wanted to go to medical school.

Kevin never shared these ruminations with his dad, but at times he would hurl sarcastic and even mean-spirited remarks that hurt his father and made Kevin embarrassed and ashamed at his own abrasiveness. When Jesse announced that he was thinking about following in his grandfather's footsteps and becoming a doctor, Kevin's pain intensified.

To add to Kevin's discomfiture, his father, in spending more time with Jesse, was spending less time with Kevin's mother, Jessica. On more than one occasion, Jessica complained to Kevin that his father seemed to throw all the energy he used to devote to his practice into thinking up new things he could do with Jesse.

Though she considered her husband's relationship with their grandchild positive, Jessica, who had no interest in chess, prickled at being left alone when Jesse and Will went off on their chess outings. She also pointed out that Will had missed their last anniversary in order to take Jesse to a tournament in Europe. As much as she wanted to talk to her husband about what she believed was a serious problem in their marriage, she saw no way of doing so without coming off sounding petty and absurdly jealous of her own grandchild.

After Kevin had been in therapy for a while, I asked him to bring in his father so that he could express his feelings to Will. At the first session, Will said that his relationship with all his grandchildren and particularly with Jesse was central to his self-esteem. After retiring, this role helped him still feel important and useful, and he enjoyed being the repository of family history and wisdom. Later, Will shared his regrets about the way he had led his life and his neglect of Kevin. He acknowledged how much he'd relied on his work to enhance his self-esteem and how that behavior continued a pattern that his own father had set of not being involved with his son. He also admitted that he had learned much from Kevin about being a good father and that his son had served as a role model for him in his relationship with Jesse.

Furthermore, observing Kevin's fathering behavior made him realize that by focusing on his career he neglected and abdicated his role as father in favor of his profession. In some way Will hoped that by being devoted to Jesse he was "making it up" to Kevin and was surprised to hear that it was having the opposite effect. After additional probing, Will conceded that in some way, of which he was not consciously aware, his giving to Jesse was giving to his own inner child who felt neglected. Nurturing Jesse helped him heal his own inner wounds.

Kevin had never seen his father so open and honest about his failings as both a father and a person, and that willingness to expose his vulnerability to his son went a long way toward repairing the rift between them. Just as important, Will vowed to strike a balance between the time he spent with Jason and his other grandchildren and the time he spent with his wife. He was shocked to hear that Jessica felt left out because of all the energy and emotion he invested in Jesse, and he became more attuned to his wife's emotional needs. He had assumed that she wanted him to spend as much time as possible with Jesse, since she had always been on him to do more things with Kevin when he was growing up. Now he realized that, ever since retiring, he was relying too heavily on his grandson and sharing too little with his wife.

Shining a spotlight on the marital bond between Jessica and Will helped Kevin see how much he'd subconsciously expected each of his marriages to be like that of his parents and expected his wife-to-be like his mother: she would sacrifice her wishes and needs in favor of his. The awareness he gained helped him adjust his perspective on relationships, and he gradually improved his marriage.

When Grandparenting Styles and Expectations Clash

Being a grandparent can bring couples closer together rather than wedge them further apart. Some of my clients have commented that being a grandparent has allowed them to experience feelings similar to those they had when their children were young. When spouses obtain mutual enjoyment from grandparenting, their marital relationship can be greatly enriched.

Problems crop up, however, when the grandparenting roles and styles don't match. Being a grandparent can convey a variety of psychological meanings and benefits to the individual, which include the following:

- *Immortality:* Grandparents will be remembered after they are gone when they help perpetuate the clan by providing advice and assistance to descendants.
- *Valued elder:* In this role, people are responsible for passing on important family and cultural traditions as well as the wisdom of experience.
- *Reliving the past:* Many people enjoy seeing their grandchildren doing and feeling the things they did and felt as children; they also enjoy seeing themselves in the role played by their own grandparents.
- *Structure:* Grandparents who help their adult children by baby-sitting at a certain time each week or by joining the family on regular outings may appreciate having some of their time structured in this way. Attending a child's performance in a concert or play, at which the grandparents' presence is wanted and noticed, brings satisfaction for all parties.
- *Social contact:* Taking the grandkids to the park, sharing in their activities, or showing off their photos offers the opportunity to meet and bond with other people.

Not only can a husband and wife derive different psychological satisfaction from being grandparents, but also they can perform this role in different ways. Here are some of the common grandparenting styles:

- *Formal:* In this role, the grandparent is interested in the grandchild, provides occasional treats, but doesn't invest large amounts of time in grandparenting or offer child-rearing advice to parents. A clear distinction is made between the role of parent and grandparent.
- *Surrogate parent:* Here there is no clear distinction between parent and grandparent. Typically, a grandparent—usually a grandmother—takes care of the grandchild, particularly if both parents are employed.
- *Fun seeker:* This style is marked by an informal, playful relationship between grandparent and grandchild. When they interact, it is often around games and other fun activities. This type of grandparent is a "buddy" to the child.
- *Resource:* This grandparent dispenses wisdom, teaches skills, helps with homework, and so on. Grandfathers often take on this style.

- *Distant:* This style is characterized by a distance between grandparent and grandchild, one that often goes beyond geographical distance. The grandparent sees the grandchild infrequently, usually on holidays or other special occasions, and there isn't much emotional warmth.
- *Safe haven:* This style is characterized by warmth, closeness and emotional support. Again, regardless of geographical distance, the grandparent's adoration, unconditional love and approval contributes to the development of a secure self in the grandchild.

Style differences are often reflected by the degree of influence the grandparent has over the grandchild's life and the extent to which the grandparent is involved and provides services. For instance, here are five combinations:

- *Influential:* The grandparent has considerable influence and also performs a lot of "chores" for the child.
- *Supportive:* The grandparent does many things for the child but is not particularly influential.
- *Authoritative:* While this grandparent may not participate much in the daily life of the grandchild, his or her ideas and decisions carry a lot of weight.
- *Passive:* While unlikely to be very involved or have much influence, this grandparent makes an effort to see the grandchild on a frequent and regular basis.
- *Detached:* Similar to passive, but contact is less frequent. After retirement, incompatible approaches to grandparenting can disturb a couple's relationship, as the following case exemplifies.

Carol and Victor retired at about the same time from their professions; Carol was an architect, and Victor was an accountant. Their daughter Sybil, along with her husband and three young children, lived in the same suburb as they did and needed help with child care. Carol volunteered her services after she retired and began baby-sitting for the kids three days a week. Sybil and her husband were trying to save money to buy a larger house, and Carol's baby-sitting would help them reduce one recurring expense.

Carol loved the time she spent with her grandchildren and indulged them in ways in which she had never been indulged as a child. Carol not only felt useful when she was taking care of the children but also was able to be creative, frequently helping them with projects. In addition, she performed many housecleaning chores for her daughter's family while she was there—doing laundry, putting toys away—since this was never Sybil's strength.

Psychologically, grandparenting was at the core of Carol's self-image. She was a surrogate parent who was also very influential in her grandchildren's lives.

Carol expected Victor to fulfill the grandparenting role in the same way she did. She believed that he felt similarly about grand-parenting and therefore would participate and share the chores with her. Victor, however, had another orientation. His own grandparents died when he was a baby. He could barely remember them, and as a result, the role of grandparenting was not fundamental to his identity as a retiree.

Victor was a passive grandparent who wanted little influence and wasn't particularly interested in frequently interacting with his grandchildren. He had a more formal grandparenting style than Carol's and wanted to limit his involvement to sharing holidays and other special occasions or helping out only when the children were sick. He quickly became discontented with the large blocks of time Carol spent at their daughter's house and with her exhaustion on her "off" days. At 68, all that housecleaning and baby-sitting took its toll, and Carol just wanted to stay home and relax when she wasn't with her grandchildren. Victor, on the other hand, wanted to do things with their friends and travel more, and Carol's resistance angered him.

Their fighting escalated. Carol took Victor's formal style to mean that he didn't care about her—if he did, he obviously would have recognized how meaningful being with the grandchildren was to her and would have participated more. Victor felt that she was neglecting him.

In truth, the clash of their grandparenting styles stemmed from conflicts that had been kept under control while they worked; retirement raised the lid. For instance, Victor had been critical of how lenient Carol was in raising Sybil. That old conflict now bubbled to the surface because he believed that his daughter was taking advantage of his wife and that Carol was spoiling her grandchildren even worse than she'd spoiled Sybil. So, when Carol would complain about how tired she was, Victor expressed no empathy. In turn, Carol looked on her husband as selfish and uncaring in thinking more about his enjoyment and leisure than about helping their family. The gulf between them increased to the point that they felt like strangers.

When they started marital therapy, the goal was to save their marriage, which was in imminent danger of failing. The sessions gave them a forum to come to terms with not only the immediate wrangles over grandparenting styles but also more potent problems. Carol aired her concern about the lack of emotional closeness between them during the entire marriage and especially in the previous few years before they retired. Through this process, she came to realize that her surrogate mothering helped her compensate for the waning intimacy in her marriage and avoid dwelling on her sadness because they had drifted apart.

During the exchange, Victor expressed relief to discover that Carol was not angry with him for being "a poor provider." In his mind, if he had made more money, they could have helped Sybil buy the bigger house that she needed for her family, and then Carol wouldn't have to work so hard. He slowly conceded and overcame his difficulty showing emotions and learned how to better communicate how much he loves and needs Carol. Carol said she could see that at times she was overindulgent and that, as much as her daughter and grandchildren needed her, her husband needed her too. Now that the closeness between Victor and her was at the highest level ever, she wanted to manage her time and energy differently.

Ultimately, the open exchange of feelings helped both of them recognize what was causing their marriage to fall apart. The clash in grandparenting styles caused by retirement seemed to be the core problem initially, but it turned out to be just the most visible symptom of a long-running conflict. Finally addressing and resolving it brought their marital intimacy to heights they never thought possible.

Adult Children

As children mature and become adults, their relationships with their parents remain prominent. Often the parent-child dyad is the primary link between the retired parents and the rest of the family. In fact, typically, most of the interaction between older adults and the rest of the family occurs in the presence of their adult children. Notwithstanding its primacy, the adult child–parent relationship requires appropriate changes and transitions in order for it to remain viable, particularly in the arena of decision making.

When parents retire, the relationship dynamic is impacted. For instance, adult children may resent their parents' tendency to involve themselves in their children's decisions without a clear invitation to contribute their two cents' worth. Parents likewise object if their adult children try to usurp their decision making.

Retirement can create tension when one generation fails to understand the needs and expectations of the other. In certain instances, children expect that after retirement, their parents will provide them with more assistance, that they will offer more baby-sitting, run errands for them, and do repairs around the house. If parents don't fulfill these expectations—often because they view retirement as a time to have more fun and less responsibility—feelings are hurt. The parents resent the sense of entitlement that their adult children exhibit, and their children feel disappointed and even betrayed.

Unmet financial expectations also can cause bitterness between adult children and their retired parents, even when the amount of money involved is relatively minor. Some retired people, believing they have to be more cautious about their spending, reduce their spending on gifts for their kids. In one family, the parents used to give each child and grandchild $500 for Christmas. After their retirement, they dropped the amount to $100, and all their adult children, who saw no valid reason for the change, were angry and disappointed.

George, a successful 42-year-old contractor, was embarrassed by his parents' frugality all his life. Even before they retired, they gave modest gifts to their grandchildren, usually ate at cheap restaurants, and were inveterate bargain hunters. Because both parents had good jobs and made above-average salaries, George saw no reason for them to be so miserly. Though he tried to talk with them about this habit while they were working, they were never willing to listen, so he stopped bringing it up.

After they retired, George noticed that his parents became even more frugal. His children, who were teenagers at the time, ridiculed the cheap discount-store presents they would receive from their grandparents, and George was concerned that the kids were losing respect for them. His wife's parents, who weren't any better off financially, were much more generous with the kids. George felt that, as a result, his wife and children were favoring her parents over his.

Not only was he becoming angry at his parents because of their behavior, but also he was getting into arguments with his wife in trying to defend them. He finally talked to her about how much the situation bothered him. He explained that though he didn't agree with their frugality, it was understandable given that they were immigrants who had suffered great financial hardships before coming to this country and still worried that they would need every last dollar to prevent them from becoming a burden on him. In contrast, his wife's parents were fifth-generation Americans who had never experienced much struggle or suffering, so financial scarcity was not part of their heritage. After several such discussions, they managed to reduce the tension somewhat, but his parents' posture remained a tender point for George, his wife, his children, and his parents themselves.

In other cases, the retiring grandparents want to be more involved in the lives of both their adult children and grandchildren, but they are rebuffed. Sometimes adult children are afraid that their parents will become intrusive or that they'll wield too much influence over the upbringing of the grandchildren. They want to ward against any interference with their autonomy and often interpret the grandparents' attempts at involvement as lack of trust or confidence in their parenting abilities. The parents thus resist the grandparents' increased participation, which makes the grandparents feel rejected and hurt.

The situation is more sensitive and problematic when one spouse is adamant about limiting the involvement of the other spouse's parents. The upshot is that the other spouse is torn between loyalty to the parents and loyalty to the husband or wife.

Harold and Grace Foster wanted to spend more time with their grandchildren after they retired. So, as content as they were with city living, they decided to move to the suburb where their son Drew and his family lived, in order to see them more often.

Though Harold and Grace loved Drew and his family, they felt free to criticize certain lifestyle choices they had made and values that were contrary to their own. Grace, who was especially outspoken and opinionated, would often criticize her daughter-in-law, Lea, for being too lenient with her kids. She also reproached Drew for not taking a stronger stand in his marriage and mandating the "Foster" way of doing things: "We insisted that you make your bed before going to school; how could you not require that your children do the same?"

Lea, who was not particularly assertive, could rarely stand up to her mother-in-law and was always fuming after a visit. She would then turn her wrath on Drew for failing to tell his own mother that she was off base in her criticisms.

Eventually, Lea began to respond in a passive-aggressive manner, declining Grace's offers of help and manufacturing excuses why they couldn't come over. Grace caught on that she was being rejected, and her hurt and ire spawned arguments with Harold. She blamed him for their move from the city. Harold became upset with her constant carping about Lea and how their son had "made a mistake" in his choice of a wife. He told Grace she was overreacting, which just made her angrier.

Drew, aware of both the tensions in his parent's marriage and the growing divide between his family and his parents, at my suggestion, arranged an open conversation in which the four of them discussed the problem. Though this discussion didn't fix all the problems or relax all the tension, it did help improve the situation by creating agreement on acceptable boundaries.

Grace realized that she needed to be more tolerant of her son's and daughter-in-law's parenting and less verbally critical when they did things in a way different from hers. Harold agreed to be her sounding board as long as she expressed her criticism to him and not to them. The agreement gave Lea and Drew the space they needed so that they were able to have more interaction with the grandparents with much less conflict and tension. Most important, the grandchildren were able to enjoy family harmony with both their parents and grandparents.

Parents

The "sandwich generation" refers to people who face the double duty of providing care to both younger and older generations, and it's a group to which a growing number of retirees belong. Given that 10 percent of people over age 65 have a child who is also over 65, some retirees may be cast in the roles of child and grandparent simultaneously. And some may also add the challenge of being caregiver to their aging parent.

Gender is an important factor in this regard since women are much more likely than men to be the primary caregiver for older parents. Societal expectations mark caregiving as women's work. Elders' attitudes may help perpetuate such gender biases, as many people in their 80s or older have strong preferences about who should provide their care. Mothers are more likely to turn to daughters than to sons for help, even when both are available.

Often, the woman ends up being the primary caregiver for both her parents and her husband's. Sons often assume caregiving only when a female relative is unavailable, and they tend to perform indirect, intermittent "male" tasks such as finance management and home maintenance. The combination of increased life expectancy and reduced fertility means that some women can expect to spend more years caring for an older parent than they did raising their own children. As of 2011, there are 65.7 million people in the U.S. caring for a family member, according to Caring.com, a resource for caregivers.

The burden of caring for older parents often disrupts plans for the "golden years" and imposes unexpected physical, emotional, and financial costs. Rather than a time of freedom, retirement becomes a time of new demands. Instead of an empty nest, the retirees have a crowded house, including a frail elderly parent and sometimes also "boomerang kids"—young adults who return home because of divorce, unemployment, or the like.

It is no surprise that caregivers resent this dramatic change in their retirement plans and the time impositions. Not only do they undergo stress and a reduction in privacy and leisure activities, but they also may experience conflicts about their caregiving with their spouses, as well as with children, siblings, and even the older parents who are the care recipients.

Retirees whose parents are still alive need to plan for their caregiving responsibilities. Ideally, before an emergency arises and as part of a formal retirement planning process, individuals should discuss living arrangements, finances, and specific responsibilities with their parents and spouses. The caregivers need to be reassured that they are not alone and do not have to do it all on their own. A spouse's participation in the physical aspect of the caregiving, combined with emotional and financial support, is crucial for marital stability.

Other Family Members

Retirement can also change relationships with other family members. The combination of increased leisure time and reduced contact with work friends creates a social vacuum. Some retirees, particularly those who are shy, who have only a few friends, or who are slow to develop new friendships, try to fill this social vacuum by intensifying relationships with family members. They spend more time not only with their adult children and grandchildren but also with siblings, cousins, and nieces and nephews.

Retirees often subscribe to the creed that "blood is thicker than water" and thus gravitate toward people with whom they have a history and a bond. This can be harmful at times to the marital bond, as demonstrated by the following case.

Nicholas started baby-sitting for his niece's children twice a week after his retirement. His grandchildren were older and away at college, and he enjoyed spending time with kids, so it seemed like a good use of his time.

Nicholas's wife, Whitney, had another reaction altogether. She resented the time he was spending with his niece's kids and contended that his niece was "using" him. On several occasions while Nicholas was taking care of her children, the niece stayed longer at work or went out with friends, causing Nicholas to be late to social events that Whitney had planned for them.

Nicholas felt sorry for his niece, who was a single mother scrambling to raise two children on her own without much support. He also sincerely loved the children and saw himself as providing affection, patience, and stability that they weren't getting from other quarters, since one set of grandparents lived out of state and the other were in poor health. Performing this service made him feel useful and needed. Moreover, Nicholas's shy demeanor held him back from becoming friendly with the recent retirees whom Whitney was getting to know through her various activities.

As could be predicted, it didn't take long before Nicholas's preference to be with his niece's children drove a wedge between him and Whitney.

It gradually became clear that they had opposing expectations about with whom they would spend their time.

As they strive to work out an acceptable compromise, the ongoing friction takes its toll on their marital satisfaction and the stability of their relationship.

Inheritance

Retirement raises the profile of inheritance in the lives of retiring couples and various family members. The values, preferences, and potential health concerns that impact inheritance decisions need to be addressed, especially among couples who expect to leave a sum of cash when they die and who have more than one child. The prickly question of wills and how to divide money fairly among children, as well as other people who are close to the couple, can imperil relationships if ignored or given short shrift.

Many couples choose to give each child the same amount, regardless of individual circumstances such as how many children each adult child has, the financial situation of his or her family, and the quality of the relationship with each adult child. For other couples and their families, these considerations bear heavily on how the estate will be divided. The choices can stir bitter arguments that have lasting consequences on a variety of family relationships.

Let's say one child is much more successful financially than the other sibling. The former is a partner in a large law firm, while the latter is an engineer who draws a smaller salary. Both have three young children, and all the families live in the same city and celebrate holidays, birthdays, and other important occasions together.

The lawyer's children routinely receive expensive gifts from their parents for Christmas and birthdays, while the engineer's kids get much more modest ones. The grandparents feel torn: Should they give the engineer's kids more expensive presents to help compensate for the relative lack of wealth, or would this create the appearance that they love these grandchildren more? Similarly, but more far-reaching, the lawyer will have no problem funding his own kids' education, while the engineer will require significant loans. The retired parents naturally are concerned about the educational needs of both sets of grandchildren, and recognizing that their engineer son will need more help than their lawyer son, they decide to leave more money in their will to him.

When the lawyer son and his wife learn about this provision, they're upset. The lawyer complains to his parents, and while the father is adamant about the justification of providing additional help to the engineer's family, the mother believes the lawyer has a legitimate complaint and sides with him. The argument is now no longer as much between parents and child as it is between spouses.

To steer clear of these troubles on the horizon, retired couples should give careful thought to the following elements that can impinge on their decisions and strive to reach accord on their priority:

- *Adult children's spending habits:* The generation gap often creates situations in which parents don't always approve of their adult children's spending habits. While some retirees believe that such lifestyle choices should not influence decisions about inheritance, others feel that they must take them into account. When retired parents perceive their adult child and his or her spouse as wasteful—squandering money on excessive vacations, presents, clothes, and jewelry—it seems fair to them that a sibling who is less wasteful and is in need of money should receive a larger portion of the inheritance. But what if the wasteful lifestyle creates a financial need? Should they leave a greater percentage to the spender on the theory that he needs it more? Or, would they be enabling an irresponsible lifestyle by doing so?

- *The relationship between the retired couple and their adult children:* It's not unusual for retired parents to have a better relationship with one adult child and his or her family than with another. For example, parents are often more involved with a daughter's family than with a son's. Also, external factors such as geographical proximity, work demands, and travel schedules affect the availability of contact between the parties. The question that many couples debate is: Should we leave more to the one we see more and like better than the other?

- *Who does more:* Sometimes retired couples get combative about who does more for them, the premise being that the child who gives them the most help should be rewarded with a bigger share of the inheritance—the daughter who drives Mom to chemotherapy three times a week versus the one who makes sporadic visits. It's a particularly loaded question when the health of one or both retirees declines and they need help. Should they express their gratitude to a more giving child by leaving him or her more money?

As in the previous point, extenuating circumstances can complicate the question. For instance, one child may live closer or work at a job that allows more free time to devote to the parents, or may have a spouse who is willing and able to care for them.

Questions about loyalty, love, betrayal, and fairness are embedded in all of these scenarios, and they can lead to conflict in a retired couple's relationship. The same holds for the decision of whether money should be left to other family members or to close friends. If you leave money to a poor niece to whom you feel close, for example, what about a nephew with whom you also have a strong bond? Inheritance decisions carry numerous emotional and psychological ramifications.

Some people use inheritance to deal with "unfinished emotional business" with certain family members. By leaving less or even no money to John, one has the last word, a final chance to register anger and disapproval. Spouses frequently disagree and have difficulty reaching a decision that feels right to both of them. While some families have open conversations about inheritance in which the parents explain their rationales, particularly when they do not divide the money equally, in other families the subject is off-limits. In the latter case, there is more chance for hurt when children and grandchildren do not understand the reasons for the "unfair" division.

The status of children from a previous marriage can also roil the waters. The relative financial position of a previously married spouse may have bearing on the couple's decisions. Does each leave money to his or her own children and grandchildren, or do they put everything in a new mutual pot and divide it equally?

Gill was a widower who became close with Shelly, who had been a friend of his wife and who was a widow herself. While he still worked, they spent a lot of their free time together, going to the theater, taking vacations, and so on. When Gill received a sudden opportunity to sell his business, the offer was too good to pass up, but after he retired, he felt lonely and vulnerable. He decided to tie the knot with Shelly, hoping that he would feel less lonely that way.

He promised Shelly that he would take care of her financially in return for her company and taking care of him when his health started to decline. At his request, she quit her job so they could spend more time together. In order to please Shelly he also changed his will and left her all of his assets, including the house in which he and his first wife had raised their children. Shelly too had children from her previous marriage, and both sets were happy at first to see their parents remarry.

That state of contentment ended when Gill's children found out about the change in the will. They angrily told him that Shelly obviously cared more about his money than him—a statement that hurt Gill as he too had had doubts about her loyalty. Gill, still feeling vulnerable and dependent in his first year after retirement, didn't want to ask Shelly if he could revise the will so that the house would go to his children after her death. It took him months to gather the courage to bring the subject up.

When he did, Shelly was shocked that he would even think about changing the will, which she saw as a betrayal of his promise to take care of her. For the next few years it remained a bone of contention between them, ruining their intimacy and mutual trust. Gill died without resolving the issue, and his children eventually sued Shelly for the house. If Gill had only addressed this issue at the beginning of the relationship and had been up front about his feelings of wanting to take care of both Shelly and his children, his relationship with Shelly and his children might not have been negatively affected.

Exercises:
Analyzing How Family Matters Affect Your Marriage in Retirement
Exercise One:
The Effect of Grandparenting on Your Marriage

Is there a difference between how you and your spouse conceive the grandparenting role?

Is it the most important thing by far in your life, while your spouse views it as only one of many enjoyable endeavors?

Sometimes the differences are apparent, and retirement throws them into even greater relief for you. Many times, however, couples don't realize that their grandparenting differences are a primary agent of discord in the relationship. In fact, some couples don't even realize that they have grandparenting differences.

Here's a simple exercise that will help you reveal these differences.

1. You and your spouse should respond to this question separately. From the following list, mark every quality that describes how you feel about being a grandparent (mark as many as apply):

☐ useful
☐ loved
☐ a source of family history
☐ used
☐ looked up to
☐ obliged to do too much
☐ young
☐ put-upon
☐ able to provide needed assistance to my adult children
☐ taken for granted
☐ able to show love
☐ underappreciated
☐ able to meet new people
☐ able to have fun
☐ special
☐ able to do new things
☐ more productive

Now compare your responses with those of your spouse. If there are differences, be aware that they can be the cause of tension. You may want to do only fun things with the grandchildren, but your spouse wants to help in any way possible, regardless of how entertaining the activity is. Some differences can coexist without much conflict, while others may scream for negotiation.

The next two questions will help you and your spouse explore what you learned from Question 1. Again, answer both questions individually, and then confer.

2. Being a grandparent is:

    A. The most important role in my life.
    B. On a par with my role as spouse and parent.
    C. One of many roles and activities I enjoy.
    D. Not particularly important.

3. As for the amount of time spent with my grandchildren, I:

    A. Would like to spend more.

    B. Am pleased with the amount.

    C. Would like to spend less.

    D. Would be content seeing them only on special occasions.

Again, look for discrepancies between your answers and those of your spouse. Lack of commonality in all three questions is a signal that your relationship may be, or is being, put under pressure.

Exercise Two:
The Effect of Your Relationship with Your Children on Your Marriage

1. Since you retired, have you noticed any changes in your relationship with your adult children?

If so, what has changed?

What caused it?

How do you feel about this change?

How does your spouse feel about this change?

2. Since you retired, have you had more arguments with your spouse regarding your adult children?

3. Even if you haven't had more arguments, do you suspect that your spouse disapproves or resents how you divide your time, energy, and money among your adult children and their families?

4. Since you retired, has your relationship with your grandchildren in any way caused a problem in your relationship with your adult children?

If so, has that had any negative impact on your relationship with your spouse?

5. Do you have disagreements with your spouse about the division of your inheritance?

Have you discussed your will or how you've divided your inheritance with other family members besides your spouse?

If so, do they agree with your reasoning, or has it created conflict?

If it has created conflict, what have you done to reduce or eliminate tensions?

Exercise Three:
The Effect of Your Relationship with Your Parents on Your Marriage

Have you and your spouse discussed the possibility of providing care to your parents?

Is there agreement between the two of you regarding the scope of the caregiving you are willing to provide:

- Are you willing to take them into your house versus putting them in a nursing home?
- Have you talked about the amount of financial responsibility you'll assume?
- Is there agreement between you and your siblings regarding everyone's caregiving roles?

Sorting through difficult situations such as these ahead of time, and achieving a mutual understanding of what you expect yourself and your spouse to do, will lower their potential to rock your marriage.

Exercise Four:
The Effect of Other Family Relationships on Your Marriage

The final set of questions will help you assess if relationships with other family members have caused problems in your marriage since retirement.

1. Since you retired, have you noticed any changes in the way you interact with different family members?

- If so, what changed?
- Do you like the change?
- What caused the change?
- How does your spouse feel about the change?

2. Since you retired, have you had more arguments with your spouse about how much time you spend with family members?

3. Since you retired, have you had more arguments with your spouse about the specific activities you do or do not do with family members?

4. Since you retired, have you had more arguments with your spouse about the amount of money you spend on family members?

5. Even if you haven't had more arguments since retiring, do you suspect that your spouse disapproves of or resents how you divide your time, energy, or money among family members?

6. Since you retired, has your relationship with a specific family member (e.g., a brother or cousin) caused a problem with other family members?

CHAPTER NINE

Gendered Retirement: The Different Responses of Men and Women

By this point, you have learned that people can have very different reactions to retirement based on numerous factors: how meaningful work was to them, their attitudes toward friendship, relationships with grandchildren, and so on. In this chapter, I'd like to explain why gender could also be a factor to add to the list. It is important to regard retirement as gendered-different for men and women as well as having both individual and couple level experiences.

Understanding the influence of gender in attitudes toward retirement gives couples a leg up in surmounting conflicts when both people are no longer working. In general, men tend to be more satisfied with their retirement than women. Husbands of retired wives are more satisfied than wives of retired husbands. Retirement increases the dependence of retired husbands on their wives and triggers changes in marital roles and marital satisfaction. For instance, some men don't realize that being retired causes them to "cling" to their wives; some women don't attach, at first, enough importance to maintaining their social routines and autonomy. In a short time, these gender-based tendencies are bound to collide. Women resent their clinging husbands who intrude on their friendships with other women; men feel abandoned by their wives and uncomfortable hanging around the house all day.

The recommended cure is for couples to anticipate these gender-related differences and be willing to talk about them honestly and openly. In too many cases, couples fail to see how gender operates at the heart of a conflict and instead become sidetracked by surface symptoms. Rather than replaying the same old arguments, couples need to shed new light on their areas of disagreement. That starts with a recognition of how differently men and women react to life after work.

Gender Gaps: Three Key Differences

This section draws on both research and my own experiences with clients, with the qualification that, as in all discussions of gender differences, the characteristics aren't universally applicable. Some men respond to retirement more like the women described, and vice versa. Still, sufficient data exist to make these generalizations valid. More to the point, these are ones that often bring on post-retirement relationship blues.

- *Retirement is more financially problematic for women:* Retired women in all racial and ethnic groups have fewer economic resources than do retired men. A New York Life survey in 2006 noted that 57 percent of the women surveyed are concerned about funding their retirement past age 85 (vs. 43 percent of men).

    Intermittent careers, jobs in low-paying fields, and lower salaries result in reduced retirement benefits and less money at retirement. In fact, women's retirement income typically is only about one-half that of men's. In addition, women often do not prepare financially for retirement. Traditional female roles in our society emphasize dependence and passivity, encouraging women to rely on their husbands to prepare for retirement. The survey also found 78 percent of pre-retired women feel they should know more about strategies for generating income in retirement (vs. 67 percent of pre-retired men).

    This dependence may render them economically vulnerable but unaware of their financial disadvantage. Moreover, among couples in which the woman is aware of her financial limitation, particularly if it is such that she will not have access to her husband's pension or retirement savings after his death, arguments may flow from her concerns about the couple's budget.

- *Women may find the transition to retirement difficult in ways that men don't:* Researchers comparing how men and women adjust to retirement have sometimes begun with the assumption that women adjust more easily because work often isn't central to a woman's self-image and women are more involved in family activities than are men. What these researchers discovered is that female retirees valued their work as much as their male counterparts valued theirs. Indeed, a 2001 study found that the impact of women's retirement on the marriage is as strong as that of men's retirement. Another study in 2008 found that women tend to have greater problems adjusting to retirement both as retirees and as partners of retirees. Possible explanations are that for women the majority of non-work obligations remained unchanged after retirement, thus the reality of being retired is less appealing than for men who have fewer non work obligations. It is also possible that women find it easier than men to express and admit symptoms and negative feelings.

Researchers further determined that retirement was often easier for men who had developed satisfying leisure activities (golf, fishing, home repair) than for women who were expected to maintain their domestic responsibilities. In effect, since women do not retire from household work and therefore lacked as much leisure time as men, their adjustment was less comfortable. Study after study found that the majority of non-employed older women even up to age 74 did not describe themselves as retired. For them, retirement connoted leisure and freedom from obligations, which their continuing domestic obligations prevented them from experiencing.

Feminist analysts argue that retirement, the demarcation between work and home life, doesn't account for women's experience and that there is a male bias in retirement research as the male experience is assumed to be normative while it doesn't apply to women. Indeed, a study of academic women found that many women do not see themselves as retired. Part-time work, housework, family obligations, volunteering, and continuing education are important to women regardless of whether retirement status applied to them or their husbands. They feel like they never retired from doing something as there are the day-to-day housework and family responsibilities that never end. For example "I'm retired in the sense that I don't have to go to work ....but I'm still involved in things I was involved in previously." Their retirement decisions are often influenced by the decisions of others, or recent economic and work place changes often alleviate women from the responsibility to decide. They often depend on their husband's financial security and his decision to retire influences theirs. Being able to continue to contribute to social life and having social connectedness is important to them in work and retirement. In other words, for women, successful adjustment to retirement can be explained by having compatibility in life goals and personal orientation of having multiple role commitments whether through work or through contributing to social projects in retirement.

Some of these trends and attitudes cause individual problems with retirement for women that in turn produce conflict with the spouse. Others result in more direct marital conflicts. Together, they've created relationship tensions that are far more common today than in years past.

As you can foretell, men who don't realize that women feel this way can spark conflicts with an insensitive remark. One recently retired couple with whom I worked had to confront a weakness in their post-retirement relationship that resulted from the husband's insensitivity to his wife's efforts to maintain their large home without the help of a cleaning service, which they had canceled when she retired. He would assure their adult children that he and his wife were "living the life of Riley," with lots of time to pursue their individual interests. In reality, he had much more time than she did, especially since he rarely lifted a hand to help with the housework. Once, when he came home from a day at the club, he became irate because she hadn't picked up his laundry from the dry cleaner. "You were home all day with nothing to do; how could you have forgotten to pick up the clothes?" That unfeeling remark and the blowup that followed was the final straw that brought them to my door.

- *Men tend to retire for health and work reasons, while women retire for family reasons:* In many cases, men stop working because of work-related reasons: they accept a retirement offer, are downsized out of a job, or face organizational changes that make work less satisfying. In other cases, they leave due to an illness that prevents them from working as hard and as well as they did in the past. Women, on the other hand, often retire to care for a family member who needs assistance. In other instances, their husbands pressure them to join them in retirement, even before they want to stop working.

  This is especially problematic when women are younger than their husbands and are not as advanced in their careers. As a result, women are less likely than men to have achieved their career goals at the time their spouses wish to retire. Also, women often view the later phase of their careers in a different way from men, particularly if they had a discontinuous career history or entered the workforce when they were older. For many women, their final working years represent their last chance to achieve certain professional milestones, rather than the time to start disengaging and phasing down, as many men view the end of their working years.

Women who retire for the "wrong" reason invariably have a tougher time adjusting to retirement, and in these situations, relationship problems often flare up. Loneliness, low self-esteem, oversensitivity to criticism, and even depression are more prevalent among retired women who stopped working against their will than among retired men.

Both spouses should be aware that giving up work takes an emotional toll. I've found that husbands who want their wives to retire sometimes subconsciously choose to be influenced more by sex role stereotypes than by who their wives are. They ignore or discount the emotional investment that their wives have in work. As he pressures her to quit work, he thinks, "It really isn't that important to her." She comes to resent her premature retirement caused by his pressure, and her adjustment period is consequently longer and bumpier, unsettling and disrupting the marital balance.

Why Women Have Trouble with the Transition

The path is smoother when both men and women accept that it's not only men who are subject to the vicissitudes of retirement. I see many clients who have bought in to the policy that retirement is a "male" issue and that women are only marginally affected by this passage. In reality, women are equally affected, though sometimes differently from men.

The first explanation for this relates to the double standard of aging. Physical appearance is generally more important for women's self-image than for men's, especially in our culture, where the feminine ideal is embodied by 18-year-old models with flawless skin and impossibly thin bodies. Aging women are deemed less desirable. Masculinity, on the other hand, is defined by competence, autonomy, and self-control, qualities that aren't inextricably linked to youth and beauty. These social realities present women with a double deficit upon retirement. Having lost physical attractiveness as they age, women who retire also suffer the loss of their work identity. Because women experience two reductions instead of one, retirement may hit them harder than it does men and may mandate a longer recovery period.

Second, for both men and women, having multiple roles fosters good psychological health, and retirement forces people to surrender one of their roles. For working women, particularly those who worked out of choice and not out of financial necessity, giving up multiple roles and the associated psychological benefit may be harder than it is for men. Since women usually aren't under the same social pressure as men to have a career, the loss may be more painful: they're leaving their chosen work, as opposed to men who didn't have the option and "had to work." In other words, some men are relieved to conclude a job that they felt they had to take in order to conform to society's image of who they should be, while for women who elected to work, the positive value they place on it inhibits their letting go and moving on.

Third, more women than ever before admit that they dislike the "housewife" role. Unlike previous generations, baby boomers have been socialized to believe that a woman's place is not necessarily in the home. Many women, particularly those who chose to work, gain much more satisfaction behind a desk or in the boardroom than they do in the laundry room or in front of a stove. They consequently connect retirement to a forced assumption of a role that is less rewarding psychologically. Whether these thoughts are conscious or not doesn't matter. Psychologically speaking, retirement can be synonymous with a backward step.

Given these reasons, couples should heed the following suggestions:

- Men shouldn't expect a wife who has worked for years to enjoy assuming the traditional role of a homemaker just because she's retired.
- Both parties in a relationship should endeavor to keep themselves in top physical shape and maintain an interest in their appearance after retirement in the absence of a work-based impetus to "look good."
- Taking on another meaningful activity—such as through volunteer work or involvement in social clubs—can provide women the satisfaction of performing multiple roles.

Social Activities: Recognizing an Unequal Need to Get Out of the House

As a general rule, social contacts outside the marriage are more important for women than for men after retirement. Married women who are retired show relatively high participation in many social activities, visiting with friends and relatives as well as volunteering. Involvement in community work and participation in clubs and other organizations facilitates many working women's adaptation to retirement, fulfilling needs previously served by their work roles. For women, involvement in volunteer activities is related to retirement satisfaction–not so for men.

Retired married men tend to engage only moderately in social activities after retirement. While men may retain more friends from their working days than women do, they don't see them as frequently as women see their friends. For many retired men, their wives are their main—and sometimes only—social sustenance. They seek fulfillment for their social needs primarily in the marriage. Not only do they expect their wives to be the social director and arrange their social calendars, but they also are often content to have their social lives revolve around the two of them as a couple, rather than including others.

As has been shown, this exclusive reliance on the wife often impairs the relationship, since the woman may see her husband as overly needy and dependent. It's more acute when the husband gives her grief about her wanting to spend time with her female friends and without him. I have found that it is easier for husbands to accept their wives' engagement in volunteer and formal community work than their interaction with friends. The latter makes them feel rejected, while the former does not.

To illustrate the process from problem to resolution, I'd like to share the saga of Lemont and Sylvia.

Having been married for 27 years, at age 72 Lemont retired from his successful heating and cooling business. His son from his first marriage had worked with him for the last seven years, and Lemont felt confident that he could turn the business over to him.

Sylvia, nine years Lemont's junior, owned a flower shop that consumed much of her time and energy. Because of the perishable nature of her product, she felt that she needed to be at the store every day. After Lemont retired, he began complaining about how much she was working and about her not being available to travel with him and take extended vacations. Sylvia was torn between her enjoyment of her business and her desire to make her husband happy.

Sylvia didn't "have to work," since Lemont's heating and cooling business was very profitable, but she loved the creativity involved in flower arranging and enjoyed her relationships with her employees and customers. She also took pride in being a successful businesswoman and "not just a housewife." In the few years before Lemont retired, he had cut back his involvement in his business and gradually stepped up the pressure on Sylvia to do likewise, but she did not comply.

Six months after Lemont retired, their relationship had deteriorated to the point that a wall of unpleasantness separated them. Lemont felt emotionally abandoned by his wife and refused to continue to shoulder his share of the housework, as his way of punishing her. He was essentially saying to Sylvia, "Since you do not care about me, I do not care about you." Sylvia felt used and angry and groused that Lemont was being unfair in his demands. After much deliberation, and in order to save her marriage, Sylvia reluctantly sold her store.

At first, everything was great as they took long trips to Australia, New Zealand, and Thailand. After these excursions ended and they settled into a routine, however, Sylvia grew lonely and irritable. She missed the relationships that her store had afforded her and hadn't found a way to restore her life.

Meanwhile, Lemont was happy as a clam with their new arrangement and spent much of his time tinkering around the house; he was good at fixing things and took immense satisfaction from replastering rooms and fiddling with his car engine. He also was fond of interacting with family members, particularly Sylvia.

But then Sylvia became, in Lemont's words, "no fun." In her words, she became "depressed." He couldn't understand what was wrong with her; to him, she had no legitimate reason to be down. After all, they had money, their health, and strong family relationships.

Sylvia "took the blame" and, assuming that something was wrong with her, entered individual therapy. It became clear to me that the best way to help her was to bring Lemont in too and to educate both of them about the part that gender played in their conflicts.

My first goal was to help them express their unshared pain. Sylvia spoke of her pride in being a successful businesswoman and her disappointment that Lemont didn't appreciate her sacrifice in selling the shop. She felt that he saw it as something that was due him.

She also told him for the first time how hurt she was that he declined to do his share of the housework during the period when she was working and he was not. It communicated to her that he didn't care about her and that he was inconsiderate, selfish, and basically sexist, relegating domestic duties to "women's work" and therefore beneath him.

Lemont explained how much he depended on her for companionship and emotional support and his sense of abandonment when he was home and she was still working. He also admitted that he was not free of "macho stereotypes" and felt it was inappropriate for Sylvia to work when he was no longer working. The therapy helped him realize that instead of coming to terms with his sadness about his retirement and his anxiety about who he is without work, he found it easier to direct his anger at Sylvia. His willingness to face these concerns on his own would in turn free her to manage her own agenda without the drag of his emotional "baggage."

They were able to place their problems in a larger context that includes the trappings of gender. Sylvia found it reassuring to know that many career women—especially those who retire for the wrong reasons—have a more fitful adjustment to retirement than do men and take longer to mourn the loss of a career. As the discussion progressed, her guilt and shame about her "failure" to fully embrace retirement dissipated.

Lemont became much more considerate of his wife's feelings and needs after learning that many retired men become dependent on their wives for the bulk of their social life, to the detriment of the relationship. In addition to taking on his fair share of the housework, he started seeking more social contacts on his own, which surprised and delighted Sylvia. More important, the socializing helped him see that even as a retiree, he still was valued and wanted.

As for Sylvia's loneliness and loss of social interactions, I pointed out that many recently retired career women restore their social networks by contacting old friends, taking up hobbies, and volunteering. Though Sylvia was reluctant to make any of these moves at first—she was concerned that Lemont might feel she was abandoning him again—he and I both encouraged her to pursue this strategy. When she started volunteering and reestablished some old social contacts, she soon began to return to her "old self."

Finally, I suggested they spend a few hours apart every day. Retirement sometimes imposes too much togetherness. Personal differences that had little impact during the working years become destructive when couples are rarely apart. When Sylvia and Lemont started making a conscious effort to spend a part of each day following their individual interests, their relationship noticeably improved. They felt more refreshed when they were together, and sharing new nuggets of information helped them enjoy each other's company more. Spending some time apart reestablished the successful pattern that existed between them pre-retirement, and both felt a greater intimacy than in the past.

Homemakers versus Employed Women

Retired women, who had careers when they were employed and are married to retired men, frequently behave differently from housewives who are married to retired men. According to research as well as my clinical observations, each group experiences different emotions. Some researchers hypothesize that housewives married to retired men might be better adjusted to the homemaker role than retired women of the same age who had worked outside the home. Theoretically, the husband's retirement would restore housewives to their traditional role. In one sense, they somewhat have given up that role when the kids matured and left home, and now that their husbands are retired, these women could return to being care providers and would feel comfortable with increased homemaking responsibilities as well as increased companionship.

It turned out that the opposite was true. While the studies found no difference in psychological well-being between the two groups, other significant differences emerged.

First, homemakers frequently complained about lack of autonomy after their husbands retired. For them, the workload often became heavier. In their traditional roles, they had more meals to prepare and less discretionary time because of the demands of "companionship." In addition, some homemakers "learned that their husbands aren't children;" if they attempted to attend to their husbands' needs as they did those of their children or as they used to do pre-retirement, arguments would result.

Some men started asserting themselves much more than they had pre-retirement as their way of coping with their ambiguity about their self-worth. They resisted their wives' suggestions and misinterpreted them, perceiving that they were being treated like kids and objecting to "being controlled."

One client complained that she fell into a routine that she grew to despise: "I really hate that he expects me to be ready to go with him anywhere at the drop of a hat. At the same time, he resists my suggestions more than he used to before he retired. I feel that I don't have any free time for myself or to do the things that I want; because I have to do the things that he wants. The part that I hate the most is that, since he likes to sit around and do nothing except watch TV, he expects me to do the same and sit next to him. Then he becomes angry when I don't want to just sit there."

Husbands of homemakers also complained about the increased "closeness" of the relationship and their getting in each other's way. As one client put it: "Being together is a nice aspect of retirement, but it can be the reverse too. We argue and fight more now, particularly when it's bad weather and we're stuck at home. I don't think she enjoys my company as much as she used to. I often feel as if the house isn't big enough and that I'm getting under her feet. At other times, she gets mad because I follow her around 'like a lost puppy.'"

Wives who were employed, on the other hand, were more likely to state that retirement improved their marital relationships. In the studies, these women reported more egalitarian and cooperative relationships in retirement, saying that sharing of household tasks created feelings of togetherness. They also seemed to handle the increased time together with greater equanimity. None of the retired women who were previously employed complained about "too much togetherness" or the need to "baby-sit" their husbands.

Part of this reaction has to do with the marital dynamic among traditional couples versus couples in which both spouses work outside the home. In a marriage between a working man and a housewife, the wife tends to conform her personal activities to the husband's schedule and availability. Among couples in which both people were employed, that structuring dynamic does not occur. Or, more accurately, it occurs in the sense that both husband and wife are inclined to accommodate each other's schedules in order to carve out time together. This egalitarian pattern also continues after retirement and may contribute to the higher marital satisfaction reported by these couples.

In another noteworthy finding, retired professional women who saw themselves as having multiple roles—as retired and as homemakers—had lower depression scores and higher self-esteem scores than retired professional women who saw themselves as homemakers only, even though they too were employed pre-retirement. Routine housekeeping activities didn't boost feelings of well-being for either group, but do-it-yourself projects and volunteer activities did contribute to happiness and satisfaction. The combination of concrete social rewards and a sense of accomplishment that they received from these activities reinforced their psychological well-being.

Further, women who were employed often engage in more non-home-based social activities after retirement than lifelong homemakers. Employment limited their social lives during their work years because of lack of time; upon retirement, they can take advantage of the increased time to pursue social relationships. In effect, they replace the lost work relationships with social ones. While lifelong housewives are sometimes content with traditional family relationships as the focus of their social activities women who were employed are more likely to develop new social networks, including informal groups of friends and neighbors and formal relationships involving volunteer activities and community work. These social networks enhanced their satisfaction with life after retiring.

A 2009 study comparing professional and non-professional women's retirement found the following: "Retired professional women spend less time caring for family members as compared to retired nonprofessional women." The researcher suggested that this is probably because they had more money, enabling them to hire caregiving services, and because they are less likely to identify with the homemaker role and place less emphasis on family roles when deciding to retire.

Retired nonprofessional women report that family responsibilities influence their retirement decisions in many instances. They spend more time in family-related activities compared to the professional retired ones who were more likely to spend time in recreational and community service activities. The professional women were also more likely to work part time after their official retirement; their stronger work identities may have increased their interest in returning to work, pursuing social contacts and recapturing feelings of productivity associated with employment. They were also more satisfied with their social support than nonprofessional retired women.

It is possible that the nonprofessional is less satisfied with their social support because they felt burdened by their family responsibilities and the pressure to provide for others. Both professional and nonprofessional retired women, who were employed continuously, were more likely to volunteer in retirement, than those who had discontinuous work histories. Thus they designed retirement to mimic their former work lives and possibly may have acquired valuable skills that are easily applied to volunteer positions.

I've found that if women who were employed much of their lives don't form these social networks after retiring, they're much more likely than housewives to experience feelings of loneliness and even depression.

And, as mentioned earlier, women may have bigger problems with adjustment than men because women who were employed till retirement age and after are motivated and career-focused individuals. For these women the losses associated with retirement, such as loss of identity, social contacts and social status may be more substantial than for men.

In a similar way, a 2004 study found that the decision-making process influences retirement satisfaction not just for retirees but also for their spouses individually as well as the couples' mutual retirement satisfaction. There is spousal influence on the retirement decision, which also affects subsequent retirement satisfaction, but this relationship is moderated by gender. When husbands perceive their wives as having influenced their retirement decisions, both members of the couple report retirement satisfaction. Surprisingly, the opposite is true for women: retired wives and their husbands are more satisfied in retirement when the wives perceive their husbands as lacking influence on their retirement decisions.

Retirement Timing: Who Should Retire First

Although some people have fixed dates of retirement—such as when there is a mandatory retirement age at a company—many others can choose when to stop working. When both people in a marriage work, they often need to negotiate the timing of their respective retirements.

Timing and structuring retirement in a way that would be most beneficial individually and as a couple can be a tricky proposition. It is important to look at partners' influence on each other in the decision about retirement. Retirement is least satisfying under conditions strengthening one partner's power bases or influence. For both husbands and wives, retirement is less satisfying when one's spouse remains employed and has more say in decisions prior to retirement and probably also in the retirement decision. Thus, again, joint retirement is better for marital satisfaction and letting each spouse make their own decision regarding retirement promotes one's sense of mastery and increases the chances for satisfying retirement and marital satisfaction in retirement.

Remember that women who retire for the wrong reasons or are pressured by their husbands to retire endure lengthier and less serene adjustments. On the other hand, studies show that there are substantial benefits to the marriage when the woman retires first or when both people retire at the same time.

The challenges represent "a stage of the marriage relationship that's occurring for the first time in history," said Phyllis Moen, a sociologist at the University of Minnesota. "This is the first generation that's ever had to deal with this, because in the past it was one retirement per family, and that was the husband's," said Ms. Moen, one of the few researchers to study gender and retirement. "Even if women worked, they didn't work too much."

As the 41 million women of the baby boom head toward retirement age, the new era of retirement increasingly includes two careers, diverging ambitions and very different ideas about what to do with the decades to follow.

Some men are threatened by the role reversal; others are impatient to travel or to move someplace warm. Some women resent having their husbands lie about all day, rarely taking on additional housework. A Cornell University study of 534 retirement-aged men and women found that working women whose husbands were retired or disabled were the least happy with their marriages. Working men whose wives stayed home were happiest.

A few reasons why relationships in which men retire first experience difficulties are deviation from traditional male-female roles and unequal division of domestic labor:

- *Wives employment:* after husband's retirement undermines marital satisfaction. It is associated with greater conflict, lower marital solidarity for both spouses and increased divorce potential for wives.
- *Wives retirement:* didn't have such negative impact. The explanation is that wives tend to adjust their work schedule to family needs more

than husbands do so their retirement doesn't have as strong an impact as their husbands' who didn't adjust their schedule as much before. Therefore, there is more 'time-stress' tension regarding time together after the husbands' retirement.

Another possible explanation is that the loss of the provider role affects men in a way that makes them less inclined to consider divorce.

- **Deviation from traditional male-female roles:** In Western societies, men are supposed to be the providers. When he retires and she does not—especially when he chooses to retire and his choice wasn't affected by health problems or downsizing—role reversal occurs. Retired men are often dissatisfied with the continued employment of their wives and the implied shift in the provider role. They find it undesirable to be at home "by themselves" when their wives are at work. It often takes a man with an untraditional, egalitarian perspective to tolerate this role reversal and not feel demeaned by the fact that he isn't working and his wife is.
- **Division of domestic labor:** As stated earlier in the book, retired husbands, as a group, spend less than 8 hours per week on housework, while their wives expend nearly 20 hours on these tasks. Employed wives with retired husbands experience considerable marital distress from this inequality. Men habitually do less than women around the house, but when the external work roles are reversed, women's resentment builds.

While men who retire may do more housework than men who work, they usually direct their energies to traditionally masculine tasks (outdoor jobs such as lawn care or handling financial investments). They seldom take on traditionally feminine tasks (laundry, washing dishes, cleaning the house), which are more numerous than male jobs and often need to be done daily. So, despite the shift in the provider role, women find they're unable to reduce their workloads at home and establish a more equitable division of labor, and they become less satisfied with their marriages.

How all this will impact your marriage in retirement depends on your definitions of gender roles. Among couples in which the man is retired but the woman continues to work, spouses with more egalitarian attitudes are better able to tolerate the shift in the provider role, with no diminution in the quality of their marriage. Among many such couples, the husband increases his participation in housework, including the daily "feminine" chores, helping to equalize the division of labor.

Exercises:
Gender-Based Actions

What can you do to lessen the likelihood that gender biases will throw water on your relationship after retirement? Here are some specific suggestions, in line with the foregoing discussion.

Reasons for retirement

- Be aware of each other's reasons for retirement, and make sure that your spouse retires for the right reasons.
- Avoid pressuring your spouse to retire before he or she is ready or has achieved certain career goals or because you don't want to be home by yourself.

Retirement order

- While joint retirement or woman-first may be the best choice from the couple's perspective, be sure to take each individual point of view into account.
- Have frank discussions about your preferred time to retire and the reasons for that preference. Understanding each other's motives and seeing their validity makes compromise easier.
- If the man wants to retire and the woman intends to keep on working, discuss the possibility of any resulting tension in your relationship, and air your concerns. When both people are open-minded, psychologically prepared, and flexible, this may be all you need to do.
- Assess how egalitarian your values are regarding gender roles. In the case of a man whose traditional values suggest discomfort with a potential retirement role reversal, be sensitive and try to find some creative solutions. I've recommended to some couples that husbands delay complete retirement and find part-time work for a few years, thereby diminishing the impact of role reversal.
- If the man intends to retire before the woman, talk about whether he would be willing to take on more household chores, particularly some of the daily ones that would lessen her load. This is a litmus test; if he balks, this proposed retirement order may create marital problems and lower marital satisfaction unless adjustments and accommodations are made by both partners.

Housework

- Try to create an equitable balance of household labor. Negotiating and trading tasks is a good approach, so that neither of you feels stuck in doing something you hate or find tedious.
- Talk with each other about your housework likes and dislikes. This is the time for a woman to surprise her husband with the news that she takes no great pleasure in washing his dirty socks. It's also the time for a man to admit that he finds washing the dishes meditative and really never enjoyed traditional male tasks such as raking the leaves or manning the barbecue grill.
- Again, if you both can't stand certain household tasks, you can usually hire someone to do them. So, if it's at all financially feasible, bring in an outsider. Spending a little money to save a lot of arguing is worth it.
- If you anticipate problems in the division of housework, consider creative alternatives. For instance, when a working woman protests that her retired husband refuses to increase his household duties, I've recommended that the couple make other concessions, such as going out to dinner more often to lighten the burden of cooking and cleaning up. Hire a cleaning service if he feels emasculated by doing too much housework; in the long run, it would be cheaper than paying for marital therapy or (eventually) divorce lawyers. When you feel that your spouse is making a genuine attempt to be considerate of you and is trying to make your retirement satisfying, you'll find that your relationship will improve.

Finance

- Both spouses must be involved in the financial aspects of their retirement. In the common case of a woman who has always taken a hands-off approach to money matters, going over financial statements together is a good way to start the process and gain financial savvy.
- Share information, and discuss your financial portfolio. When couples have equal knowledge about their assets and liabilities, they're less likely to come to loggerheads about "what we can afford."

Social contacts outside the family

- Women especially should endeavor to create a social network in retirement that goes beyond family members. Women often need more social contact than men at this stage in their lives, and they should pursue everything from hobbies to volunteer activities in order to develop this network.
- Men need to give their wives the freedom and encouragement to develop social contacts. They need to accept that they may have to spend more time alone than they would prefer or to develop activities they can do on their own while women are away from the house doing their thing.
- Women, in turn, should be sensitive to the fact that they are the primary social outlet for their husbands and allocate sufficient time to interact as a couple, reducing the chance that the man will feel lonely or emotionally adrift.

Patience and tolerance

- Recognize that the retirement transition isn't just personal; it affects each of you in different ways. Even in cases in which both people in a marriage worked, one may take longer to adjust or may stumble along the way. Acting impatient and resentful will only delay the transition. Patience is the best stance. In addition, men married to homemakers should be aware that the wife will have to make a transition to retirement as well, since she is unaccustomed to his being home during the week; therefore, his retirement causes change in her world.
- Women who are uneasy with their own retirement need to talk honestly with their spouses about their reservations and recognize that they are not alone in their feelings. I've worked with scores of women who chastise themselves for the long time it takes them to adjust to retirement. It helps when they realize that many other retired career women are in the same predicament. But with good planning and good communication, the transition can be made smoother.

The bottom line is recognizing that there are significant gender-based reactions to retirement and it's important to take measures that moderate rather than aggravate them.

CHAPTER TEN

The Transition: Making It Easier for Yourself and Your Marriage

The Importance of Going Through the Transition as a Couple

I can't stress enough the importance of going through the transition as a couple. Retirement is likely to bring couples "face to face" in a manner that they haven't experienced since the initial years of their marriage.

After the early period during which newly married people get to know each other, warts and all, spouses often lead relatively independent lives. Children usually dilute intimacy as both spouses attend to parenting duties. Careers also become another legitimate way of causing distance in intimate relationships. It is particularly true for people who don't respond well to tension and are conflict avoiders. Working and raising children thus divert partners from acknowledging intimacy problems or dissatisfactions in their relationship.

Bereft of these two diversions at retirement, partners face each other in a way that is foreign to them. Lacking the escape mechanisms that functioned well during their working years, they can no longer retreat from dealing with what's missing in the relationship.

As much as I've emphasized the efficacy of couples' talking openly and honestly about retirement concerns, I would be remiss if I ignored the potential downside of these conversations. Retirement sometimes shakes couples when they suddenly perceive that they have been moving in dramatically different directions for years.

When couples begin to talk about their dreams for retirement, they may be shocked to discover that each person harbors a very different dream; they may learn that their goals are so different as to be in conflict. These frank discussions may suggest that you don't know the person you married as well as you thought, and your spouse can even become an obstacle rather than an ally in achieving your retirement goals. People also frequently find out that their shared goals don't have the same priority to them as individuals. These belated realizations can lead to a state of marital disappointment.

Pre-retirement concerns about marital conflict predict problematic retirement adjustment for both partners. When workers who recently retired experience adjustment problems, their partner's adjustment is hampered too. Partners play an important role in the retirement decision and it is important that each partner feels some control over the decision.

Involuntary retirement, when a person experiences lack of control over the retirement decision, is a risk factor for adjustment problems. Women tend to have greater problems adjusting to retirement, both as retirees and as partners. Possible explanations are: for women the majority of obligations remained unchanged, and the reality of being a retiree is less appealing than to men. Women have an easier time admitting symptoms and negative feelings than men.

Retirement also intensifies patterns of support and communication as the husband-wife interdependence solidifies. The additional time together and the lack of work as a diversion underscore both strengths and flaws in the marital patterns. If two people enjoyed good communication during the working years and provided each other with emotional support, retirement may be blissful and truly the golden years of caring, since this pattern is likely to continue and even grow stronger. On the flip side, marriages in which patterns of support and communication have been weak become much less fulfilling or even unbearable during retirement as the flaws in the marital exchange become more pronounced. Many times, one person needs more emotional support or wants more communication when he or she is no longer working, and if the pattern for this communication hasn't been put in place over the years, it's unlikely to suddenly avail itself in retirement.

Again, the importance of working through the retirement transition as a couple is of critical importance. In theory, men's status as breadwinners may predispose them to plan for retirement independently from their wives planning. Because women usually are relationship-focused, they often make their retirement decision contingent on their husbands or follow the lead of their spouses before making their own retirement decisions. At least, these have been the assumptions of many researchers. However, a 2006 study about retirement planning surprisingly found that wives' planning had a significant influence on their husbands' retirement decisions while these men's planning had no impact on what their wives decided to do. Thus, it's a mistake to believe that retirement planning has an established script based on gender stereotypes.

Work environment affects the planning; for both men and women, a heavy workload leads to more planning, the same planning required by health and financial concerns. At the same time, a high degree of work autonomy and sense of mastery tends to postpone retirement planning as well as the retirement decision for both genders.

Recall our earlier observation: When couples spend more time together, it throws a harsher light on a spouse's annoying habits and idiosyncrasies that were tolerable in previous years. He notices how much time she "wastes" on the phone sharing "nonsense" with her friends; she notices how rude he is in interrupting people. Retirement provides an opportunity for a "second look" at one's spouse, and sometimes people do not like what they see; they start to criticize each other and offer unsolicited suggestions for improvement which, ironically, lowers marital satisfaction.

Another liability is the abridgement of privacy and freedom to "do your own thing." Housewives accustomed to a lot of privacy while their husbands were at work are the most vulnerable. Some retired couples have an "unwritten contract" to spend all leisure time together just as they did during the working years. Therefore, some women purposefully change their behaviors upon their husbands' retirement. They often feel guilty about leaving the husband alone while they pursue their normal social activities, as such behavior is against the "unwritten contract," or they feel compelled to include the spouse.

Most women resent having to change their schedules so their husbands won't be bored, but since women were socialized to be caretakers and they highly value their roles as wives, they often silence their own needs in order to accommodate their spouses' preferences. Some women make a greater effort to entertain their husbands, such as by having more dinner parties, which means more work for them. Other women may drop plans for doing something to which they looked forward because he's not interested in participating.

While they make these choices of their own volition, their caretaking mandate forces them to subjugate their own needs. "Silencing themselves" often gives way to frustration, distress, and even depression when it's internalized or to hostility toward the spouse when it's externalized.

Retirement becomes much easier for couples if they can reduce stress. Unfortunately, the standard advice in this regard— being open and honest with your partner, being tolerant of your spouse's flaws or idiosyncrasies— goes only so far. So, while there's no getting around the fact that retirement can be stressful on a relationship, bear in mind that it can also be a time to grow and develop relationships that weren't possible when one or both of you were working. Increased leisure time together and shared activities provide opportunities for communication, the exchange of new ideas, and developing new and satisfying ways of being together.

Shared leisure in which there is a possibility for fun and stimulating interactions, such as playing mentally challenging games or intellectual discussions of books, is conducive to improved communication, as opposed to watching television, for instance, which tends to be more passive and less mentally stimulating.

Increased time together allows partners to appreciate each other outside the roles they have played during the earlier part of their relationship. I've seen couples create a deeper understanding of each other as they became aware of these outside roles and bond in ways that weren't possible when one or both of them worked. Expressing affection, communicating positive feelings about interdependence, and developing a sense of belonging are all positive possibilities for couples after retirement.

Dealing with Depression

Marital distress and depression are highly correlated at all ages and in all stages. When one or both people in a relationship enter retirement depressed or become depressed due to retirement, the transition to this new lifestyle becomes that much more difficult. As I've noted a number of times, depression can arise at retirement, particularly among individuals who did not prepare psychologically and emotionally. If you forged your identity through work and don't have much to take its place, you are more at risk.

While depression isn't something that can be easily prevented, you can and should be aware that a certain degree of feeling down is normal when you stop working. In order to stop this normal feeling from escalating into depression, you need to be willing to take steps to deal with it. If you don't, you will have more trouble adapting to this new stage in your life than you should.

To prevent depression from spoiling your marriage, you should understand how it emerges in relationships and in retirement. The marital role is the most socially and personally significant role for most people as adults. It provides emotional and physical intimacy, interdependence in sharing resources, opportunities for give-and-take, and a sense of belonging through identification with the couplehood. When people lack this support or can't confide in their spouse, their risk of becoming depressed increases.

Men are much more prone to become depressed as a result of losing autonomy, while women are more likely to become depressed as a result of family problems. For both, depression goes hand in hand with marital difficulties.

Emotional distance in a marriage is most likely to produce depression in women, and women tend to blame themselves for marital distance and distress; they see it as an indication of a personal inadequacy—not being a good enough wife—rather than a relationship inadequacy. Professor Winnie Kung from the School of Social Work at the University of Southern California cites empirical findings indicating that because women are socialized to be the caretaker of the emotional aspect of family life and to value highly their role as wives, they are three times more likely than men to be depressed in unhappy marriages (45 percent versus 15 percent); almost half of all women in unhappy marriages are depressed.

Further, when men experience difficulty adjusting to retirement and become depressed, their wives try to help them alleviate their depression. When they are unsuccessful, they sometimes blame themselves for not being good enough wives. Many of these "internalizing" women then become depressed themselves. Thus, when men have difficulty adjusting and become depressed, their wives may also fall victim, and the marriage takes the brunt.

When women have trouble adjusting to retirement and become depressed, their spouses typically don't blame themselves. Nevertheless, the wife's emotional withdrawal from the marriage can cause the husband to experience lower marital satisfaction as well as depression.

A 2010 study found an important link between marital satisfaction, depression and lack of sexual satisfaction. In this study, the researcher found that lower levels of both marital satisfaction and sexual satisfaction predict psychological distress/depression for both men and women. Older couples with a high level of marital satisfaction exhibited twice more satisfaction with sexual variables (sexual desire, activity, communication, satisfaction and orgasm) and presented much less psychological distress (depressive symptoms, anxiety, irritability, and cognitive problems) than older couples with a low level of marital satisfaction. These finding were true for both genders.

As you can see, depression does not occur in a vacuum but in an interpersonal context, which can create a vicious relationship circle in retirement. Depression is a serious problem for relationships at any time, but more so in retirement, when people frequently are fending off assaults to their self-esteem as they attempt to establish a sense of self-worth without a paycheck. In addition, the increased amount of togetherness after retirement can wear away at relationships when one party is depressed.

Another reason for the link between depression and lower marital satisfaction is criticism. Depressed individuals are more sensitive to criticism and at the same time tend to be more negative, passive, and critical themselves. As a therapist, I've noticed that during interactions between depressed persons and their spouses, both parties see the depressed partner as more negative, hostile, mistrusting, and detached and less agreeable and nurturing than he/she used to be.

Over time, non-depressed spouses who initially offered help lose their patience and start to criticize the depressed partner in "passive" ways, generating more negative feelings. If your spouse is depressed, it's likely that he or she is passively critical and negative because of the depression, shifting the interaction burden onto you and making it harder for you to adjust to retirement, since you're trying to cope with your spouse's off-putting behaviors on top of your own difficulties.

While there is no handy solution to depression, the worst thing to do is ignore it or try to manage it on your own for too long. Recognize that you're not alone. I'm referring not only to the reality that many other retirees become depressed, but also to the fact that your spouse and a therapist can help you find your way out of that depression before it contaminates your marriage and your spouse's well-being.

Sarah was a reluctant retiree. She was 61 when her employer offered her early retirement, which she felt forced to accept. Before the offer was made, she had never given much thought to the subject of retirement.

An executive vice president with a large corporation, Sarah loved both her job and the company. She'd worked there for almost 25 years and assumed she'd stay for at least another 4 years, allowing her to finish a multi-year project of which she was in charge. She was thus taken aback when the CEO told her that declining revenues over the past few years required that they undertake a program to reduce overhead, which included offering "senior" staff early-retirement buyouts.

As much as Sarah didn't want to retire, the company was dangling a generous package which she found hard to refuse. She talked the offer over with her husband, Murray, who encouraged her to accept it, saying that the money would allow them to come pretty close to the financial goal they had set, as well as give them more flexibility to visit their three children and grandchildren, all of whom lived in different cities.

After Sarah accepted the company's offer, she pondered some other job possibilities and even went on a few interviews, but she soured on her prospects when she realized that she would be "starting over." Even with the same level of job at another organization, it would take her years to learn the company's culture and politics and to achieve her current status. Sarah didn't feel she had the patience for such tasks.

Within six months after she retired, Sarah was miserable. Though she loved visiting her children, they had their own lives, and she felt that she was imposing on their hospitality after a few days. She soon sank into a funk, spending most of her time sitting at home in her robe reading trashy novels, not bothering to put on any makeup, and obsessively checking how their investments were doing.

Murray did what he could to cheer her up and nurture her, all to no avail, which frustrated him and made him feel that he was letting her down in some way. Whenever he suggested they do something with another couple or even go out to a play or a movie, activities they used to do quite often, Sarah usually said no. At first, she made excuses—she was tired from her morning swim or was not feeling good—but she quickly gave up the pretense and admitted to Murray that she was depressed.

As a retiree who was looking forward to spending more time with his wife, Murray was disappointed in Sarah's attitude. His disappointment turned to anger when some of their friends stopped calling; he felt that Sarah was isolating them. He prodded her to pursue her painting, for which she never had time when she worked, or even to work part-time as a consultant, but she kept insisting that there was only one job that had any meaning for her and it was gone. He then suggested that she see a therapist to treat her depression, but the suggestion infuriated her because she interpreted it as another put-down.

The couple's relationship withered over the next year. Sarah regularly criticized Murray, he became more defensive, and both became more emotionally withdrawn. As he remarked to family members, Sarah was "not herself." An outgoing, optimistic woman who enjoyed socializing and being fashionable, Sarah had encased herself in a shell that Murray felt powerless to crack. He even had prompted their adult children to talk to her about her foul mood, but they too had minimal success in getting her to do anything about it.

Murray, who had devised a busy and satisfying retirement routine for himself and spent a good part of each day out of the house, began to dread coming home and finding Sarah parked in the same chair in the family room with the same books piled around her. Murray gradually became more and more upset and finally "lost it." Though he had always been even-tempered, he started yelling at his wife. At first, she would yell back, "You don't understand what I'm going through," and they would have worse set-tos than they'd ever had during their long marriage. After a while, Sarah simply stopped arguing and started to ignore Murray.

That's when Murray, at the suggestion of their daughter, decided that they both needed the help of a therapist to save their marriage. Though Sarah had resisted individual therapy, she was much more amenable to treatment as a couple, since she could more readily accept a shared marital problem than an individual failure.

Entering Retirement with the Right Attitude

The account of Sarah and Murray may sound extreme, but it illustrates a problem that plagues many people when they retire. Even when only one spouse has a hardship in adjusting to the change, odds are the marriage will be negatively impacted. When one spouse is blocked, it often prevents the other from fully enjoying life.

Based on research studies, at least one-third of all retirees falter in adapting to this new life stage. Even those who don't experience major problems often exhibit initial vulnerability and emotional instability.

To facilitate retirement transitions and the health of post-retirement marriages, people need to be aware of the following components:

- The reasons for smooth versus rough transitions
- Involuntary retirement
- Characteristics of those who have easy transitions
- Who should not retire
- The importance of psychological retirement planning.

The Reasons for Smooth versus Rough Transitions

Being forced into retirement or feeling that the decision is taken out of your hands fosters a sense of uncertainty and loss of control. It's natural to worry about not working and to become less optimistic about your life, health, and happiness. It follows that when people are forced to relinquish their employment status, regardless of the reasons, they have a harder time enjoying retirement. Many aren't prepared financially and psychologically for life without work.

One way to avoid these negative repercussions is to be as involved as possible in both the decision to retire and the timing. You also should endeavor to finish your work agenda and satisfy yourself that retirement is financially feasible.

To a certain extent, your work circumstances will dictate the degree to which you welcome retirement. People who perceive themselves as having limited autonomy and mobility and whose organizations are rife with annoying bureaucratic red tape are more likely to look forward to retirement. Workers who have fulfilling jobs, experience opportunities to create, and receive other positive benefits have a harder passage.

"Happy" workers must acknowledge the losses that accompany their retirement. When people consciously grieve the loss of their work, they're often able to relinquish the emotional attachment to the objects of work that they left behind and redirect their psychic energy to new objects that give them satisfaction. Less well-adjusted retirees who are unable to break that emotional attachment and redirect their energy stay mired psychologically in what they can no longer have. Sarah is a prime example.

Like Sarah, many retirees demur from talking about missing the substance of their work, the opportunity to make a contribution, their colleagues, and their job challenges. People need to verbalize these feelings and to mourn what they've lost. Obtaining validation and acknowledgment from your spouse for these feelings is part of the cure. To pretend that you don't miss work when you miss it desperately is a serious error that will make your accommodation to retirement more wrenching.

The combination of verbalizing your true feelings and exploring what you need to do in retirement to derive satisfaction and meaning from your life is key. For example, setting new challenges through a hobby, taking a class, honing an area of expertise, or inventing new ways to help people or contribute to a good cause limits the sense of loss that retirement brings.

Going through the ritual of a retirement party can help bring a sense of closure. As achievements are acknowledged and goodbyes are said, this rite of passage reinforces the reality of retirement and helps bridge the move to the next stage.

Retirement due to health problems also makes the transition more of a trial. Poor health can bring on misery and complaint at any life stage, but the fallout can be worse in retirement, when people have more time to focus on their bodies, thus feeding depression and a sense of helplessness, particularly if little improvement is medically possible. While some people can fight through minor illnesses and ignore aches and pains when they're working, health problems in retirement are less easily brushed off.

The link between mental and physical health, which applies at all ages, is pronounced during retirement. Retirees who feel healthy tend to experience psychological well-being. The other side of the coin is that retirees who perceive themselves to be having health problems often have a rough transition from the work world, derive scant satisfaction from their lives, and lose hope for the future.

Financial health, like physical health, is not always something we can control. Nevertheless, people should strive to practice sound financial judgment as they age, with the knowledge that financial woes have the power to compromise one's retirement adaptation and even life expectancy.

Given the volumes of available material on saving for retirement, I don't undertake to cover the same ground. The suggestions here pertain instead to financial implications that can reinforce the psychological transition to retirement. Many people—particularly those who aren't confident that they have sufficient money to retire comfortably—would benefit from creating a "gradual" way to leave work; some employees are able to negotiate phased retirements, retaining part-time or consulting positions for a period of months or years while the nest egg continues to grow.

Gradual retirement not only softens the financial hit—such as to Social Security benefits or pensions—but also imparts a sense of mastery, autonomy, and control. In addition to the good it can do for the retiree, the couple benefits. I've had clients who retired with the recognition that they were cutting it tight, figuring that they would find a way to get by and would live on a stringent budget. What they didn't realize is that by choosing this route, they ran the risk that one or both of them would come to resent their "budget" retirement.

People have different money styles, values, and expectations that might have gone unnoticed while they worked and had a regular stream of income. These silent forces of difference have been known to charge menacingly to the foreground when money gets scarce. One person may blame the other for not earning enough, not saving enough, or spending too freely when they were younger.

Involuntary Retirement

For more and more people, retirement is not a choice.

As more companies trim payroll by phasing out older employees and reducing health insurance costs by cutting the numbers of employees in the higher age/ more costly bracket, we see a trend toward involuntary or forced retirement.

A 2010 study showed that individuals who retired involuntarily experienced poorer adjustment to retirement and lower levels of retirement satisfaction and well-being than those who retired voluntarily. Voluntarily retired individuals experienced higher life satisfaction, physical and mental health, retirement satisfaction, as well as less anxiety, depression and stress. When people experience forced, unexpected retirement, their adjustment to this change is difficult. As mentioned earlier, feeling like you have control over your life has an immense impact on one's self-esteem and emotional positive outlook. Not having much of a say in the timing of retirement challenges the individual's sense of mastery and self-management.

Vocational psychologists state that work functions as the focal point for individuals as they interact with the social, political, economic and social world. Work is essential to psychological health as it promotes connections to the broader world, enhances well-being and provides a means for satisfaction and accomplishment. Individuals who lose their jobs often struggle with mental health problems. The loss of work has consistently linked to problems with self-esteem, relationship conflicts, substance abuse and other serious mental health concerns. Work often allows individuals to fulfill self-determination; the experience of authenticity which is often characterized by feeling that one is in charge of one's life.

Individuals, if forced to retire, don't have this positive feeling of being in charge and in control. An example is Ted, a skilled engineer who had his retirement funds invested in his company's stock where he worked for the last 22 years. When he found out that his firm was going to be purchased by another company, he knew that his pension plan would have a significant drop in value. Ted at age 56, felt he had no choice but to resign before the takeover would happen to save his pension. He felt compelled to protect his retirement investment and very reluctantly left the workforce during an economic crisis which meant it would be a very long time before he could find other employment.

Another example is Stan, a senior scientist for a medium-sized medical laboratory. Stan was 58 and worked in his company for the last 28 years. He was a major contributor to its growth and success. He was greatly respected and admired by other people in his company and therefore felt very secure at his work. Most of his retirement funds were invested in this company, as he also accumulated many stock options over the years.

When he heard news of the company being bought by a much larger company in the same industry, he felt certain he would survive the transition because of his vast experience and being so highly regarded as a professional. Sadly, the new owners brought in a new team of scientists and Stan was out of his job. Because of the specialized nature of his work, he was unable to find a comparable position in the same metropolitan area (he was unable to move as his wife was a tenured professor at the local university and he was responsible for his older ailing parents, as his sister lived too far). He ran through most of his savings while looking for another career opportunity. Too young for Social Security benefits, he was forced to take a job in an auto parts store, at an hourly wage far below his previous salary. He also lost the intellectual challenges he was used to and the high level of respect he commanded. While Stan felt grateful for having some income to avoid depleting his savings, (he was able to secure this job through friends) he was also quite bitter about his circumstances and became very blue and negative.

Similar to Stan is Kathryn who started her career at an advertising company and after 25 years of working there, was offered a retirement package it would have been foolish to refuse from a financial point of view. Although the package was generous and lucrative, she felt hurt by being asked to leave a career to which she devoted herself for so long and where she was in charge of many of the most profitable accounts at the company. She was the one who brought these accounts to her firm and was responsible for the longevity and loyalty these clients exhibited over the years. She also found it very difficult to get hired for another job at 62 years old - three years away from being eligible for Medicare and Social Security benefits. Needing to pay for health insurance by herself without any contribution from an employer resulted in quite a financial bind.

People like Stan, Ted and Kathryn who experience involuntary or forced retirement do not get the benefit of enjoying the "honeymoon stage" of retirement described earlier in Chapter 1. This initial period of feeling freedom from work demands and reduction of stress is missing for them because of the pressure they feel to secure new employment as soon as possible, thus making their adjustment to this new stage more difficult.

Another reason for the more difficult adjustment by individuals going through involuntary retirement is lack of adequate time to plan and prepare. Voluntary work transitions are often made with enough time to consider multiple options and are usually self-initiated with the timing dependent on one's choice based on conditions in the economy, labor market and family situation that are generally favorable.

On the other hand, involuntary transitions are often accompanied by a number of obstacles to opportunity. These include individual barriers, such as not having enough information to make a good decision and not having enough time to prepare for it, nor having the emotional, social and financial support to adjust to the transition. Barriers could also be environmental such as ageism, a slow economy, high unemployment or unpredictable timing of opportunities. The barriers could also be institutional, e.g., unemployment compensation rules or Social Security benefit availability. Individuals faced with involuntary transitions often are forced to make decisions in non-optimal circumstances, without sufficient information alternatives.

Indeed, when companies offer retirement packages or, in other words, put their employees in an involuntary retirement situation, they usually don't give employees much time to consider their options. The offer comes quickly and needs an equally quick response. We often see this in academia – when universities and school districts want to get rid of their more experienced, costly staff. They offer enticing retirement packages which may look good initially, but often lead to a more prolonged and difficult period of adjustment.

The retirement package is not a gift; it is something the employee earned, so at a minimum it requires careful consideration and sound advice from various sources before making a final decision. Not having enough time to consider and evaluate all the options is therefore why the adjustment is harder, as often individuals are full of self-doubt and unsure if they made the correct choice. If you are "forced" to retire at a younger age than what you originally planned and hoped for, because the offer is too good to refuse or because of any other unexpected and involuntary reasons that are beyond your control, you need to accept that your adjustment to this transition is going to be longer and more difficult.

It is important not to despair if you are facing involuntary work termination. Research shows that while voluntary retirement increased positive adjustment in the initial stages, after 6-7 years post-retirement, there were no differences between these and those who retired involuntary. Voluntarily choosing to retire helps people make the retirement a positive experience; however, with time the situational factors surrounding the initial transition to retirement appear to fade as retirees make the necessary changes.

Let's look at what makes it easier and possible to adjust more quickly to this involuntary – forced retirement:

- Having a positive identity as a friend in pre-retirement provides a bridge, an opportunity to increase interaction with friends and become more positive about retirement. This finding was true for both men and women. Thus, having friends and seeing oneself as a good friend contributes to easier retirement adjustment in this unfortunate situation.
- Having social capital also helps those who want to find new employment as they have a larger network of friends who can put them in touch with other opportunities.

- Having higher pension funds was found among involuntary retirees whereas the opposite was true among those who retired voluntarily. While this finding initially might be puzzling, the explanation is that involuntary retirees worked longer hours, contributed more to Social Security and had higher pension funds. They were perhaps pressured by their organizations to retire, while this was not the case the voluntary retirees. They didn't work long hours, didn't have higher pensions and didn't feel pressured from their organizations to retire.

Among involuntary retirees, those who experienced more organization pressure to retire expressed higher satisfaction with retirement despite the involuntary nature of their retirement. This is probably because leaving an unpleasant work environment felt like some sort of relief and gave the retirees a legitimate explanation for their involuntary exit from the labor force.

Similarly to the effect of high organization pressure to retire, having group norms that perceive low ability to continue working were correlated with seeing retirement in a favorable light and predicted retirement satisfaction and easier adjustment.

Optimism and creativity also help those suddenly forced to retire. Seeing forced retirement as a mixed benefit, a chance and opportunity to start a new venture or use one's time to pursue a dream helps in better coping here. So while your view of retirement may be vastly different when retirement is sudden, unplanned and involuntary it may provide an opportunity for bridge employment that would let you follow your heart and work at something you enjoy.

In fact, today some companies are offering start-up funds for entrepreneurs, including Kickstarter.com, a funding source for creative projects. In 2001, Starbucks launched "Create Jobs for USA," a program that makes loans to small businesses.

In the same vein, switching to work with non-profits may be a good fit because such organizations often offer part-time work, appreciate the expertise of older workers and because they often hire short term help for matters such as fundraising, marketing and managing social media strategies. AARP suggests these resources for those pushed out of the workforce who are ready to find new opportunities working for non-profits: Commongood Careers, Idealist.org, Change.org, Bridgestar.org and Civic Ventures' site Encore.org, and The John D. and Catherine T. MacArthur Foundation, which lists non-profit jobs and resources. The AARP site also has a huge roster of nonprofit and philanthropy job boards and employment resources. www.aarp.org/work/working-after-retirment/info-11-2011/non-profit-jobs-for-retirees.html.

In summary, while often people don't have the opportunity to prepare sufficiently for sudden, unexpected, involuntary retirement, they can help themselves. Those who are resilient, flexible, , open to new experiences, and continual learners are also more likely to perceive options and new opportunities and are better able to manage this involuntary transition. Developing a clear and realistic plan for change, maintaining a positive outlook, staying future oriented, having social capital (who you know), identity capital (self awareness of your skills and strengths), flexibility and adaptability all aid in better coping with such involuntary change. Lastly, it is helpful to remember that by using the above-mentioned coping mechanisms, within a few years your level of retirement satisfaction and well-being should be the same as if your retirement was voluntary.

Who Should Not Retire

After reading this book, most of you will find it relatively easy to make the transition and take the steps that are necessary in order to adjust the balance in your life to a successful retirement. But a few of you may say, "Not me! I'm never going to retire!" No matter how hard you try, you can't get your mind around the idea of not working. You're sure that you would be miserable without work and that a gradual adjustment would not do a bit of good.

I would be remiss if I didn't mention the possibility that you may be one of the individuals who are psychologically incapable of living a life without work. While the odds of this are slim, I think it is worth addressing the subject briefly. In the back of your mind, you may wonder if you're really cut out for retirement. You probably are, and the following section will help you realize that avoiding retirement is a healthy option only for a handful of individuals.

Some people have value systems that prevent them from seeing anything positive about retirement; for them it's a bleak time in which one waits to die. Others may harbor extremely negative values about aging, such as the belief that being old means being useless and a burden to others.

Typically, such types have a fleeting retirement honeymoon period or none at all. Rather than feeling great for the first few months and then becoming miserable and disenchanted, they become miserable very quickly. Every day seems the same and they don't feel as if there is anything to look forward to. They can't even look forward to a weekend break or a summer vacation as they did during their work years.

They drift aimlessly when released from the ordered world of work and may become seriously depressed within the first year of retirement. Plagued by fears of the unknown—of financial or physical disaster—they believe their main purpose in life was being a productive member of society and contributing to the support of their family. Without this quest, they are just taking up space on Earth.

This attitude at its worst is caustic to a marriage. Extreme irritability is typical of people who just can't do without work; they snap at their spouses and make people around them uncomfortable. They may also wax eloquent about how great life was when they were working and display complete disinterest in any other topic. Sullen, withdrawn, and lethargic, these souls spend inordinate amounts of time sleeping or lying in bed; some, not even changing out of their pajamas, stare endlessly at the TV.

The spouse of the disgruntled person may want to get away but feel guilty leaving him or her alone. The spouse revolts at having to forgo enjoyable social activities because the partner is too quarrelsome or morose to participate.

David's case is a stark example. Having grown up on a farm in Poland, David worked seven days a week from a very early age, and the concept of play or leisure was foreign to him in childhood. As a teenager, he was sent to a forced labor camp, where hard work was the only reason he didn't die. The lesson he learned during these years was: One must work in order to deserve life.

After the war, he immigrated to the United States, married another Polish immigrant, and had two children. Because he had little formal schooling and spoke English only falteringly, his job outlook was narrow. He found work in factories and often served a double shift to provide for his family. Through his labors, he was able to send both children to college.

His wife retired at 65 and persuaded him to retire when he was 68. She was worried that he might damage his health if he maintained his frenetic pace and convinced him that they had saved enough money so that there was no longer any financial need for him to continue working.

At first, David didn't object to retirement, since part of him felt that he had earned it, but retirement changed David. He had always been kind, quiet, and sweet, but within a month, he sank into a depression. He became mean, loud, and difficult. Nothing pleased him, not even his favorite food prepared by his wife. He couldn't muster any interest in visiting his grandchildren, meeting with friends, going to movies, or any of the other diversions he used to enjoy. He criticized his wife constantly but was furious whenever she left the house without him.

When he came to see me (his wife almost had to drag him into my office), I determined that work was his coping mechanism; it had literally saved his life in Poland. This coping mechanism wielded far more power than any logic. In addition, retirement ran counter to the value system he'd internalized at a young age and required a psychological change that he was not equipped to make.

I suggested that the best remedy for David would be part-time work that would allow him to feel productive. He subsequently found a position at an athletic club where he worked 20 hours per week, arriving at five a.m. and leaving at nine a.m., checking people's membership cards as they entered the club. While this isn't the sort of job that might make everyone feel productive, David responded quickly and almost miraculously by returning to his old good-natured self.

While you might not have been in the same straits as David, in which work was a means to stay alive, you may nevertheless have an overpowering drive to work. This phenomenon is not limited to blue-collar workers. I know of an 84-year-old physician who continues to see patients even though there is absolutely no financial need for him to work. I also know a 92-year-old engineer who has passed on his business to his sons but continues to stop in every day and to drive them crazy with advice.

Without work, these people become depressed. They need to continue on in their field of expertise, as their self-esteem is inextricably linked to the position they held and the respect they received for performing their job.

Does this sound like you? If so, and you find that nothing helps you adjust to retirement and that your marriage is suffering as a result, you may want to consider returning to work. Don't rush into this decision, however. You may just need to get used to the idea of retirement or take up a hobby or volunteer activity that satisfies your desire for a meaningful way to spend some of your time. It's also possible that you and your spouse would benefit from therapy.

Casting a darker shadow over this syndrome, there are cases of people dying unexpectedly soon after they retire, without any apparent medical reason. I'm convinced that in many such cases, the prospect of life without work is a trigger. For them, there was no point to go on living if they couldn't go on working. If you feel this way, by all means pursue a full or part-time job after your initial, unsuccessful retirement.

Characteristics of Those Who Have Smooth Transitions

Joy is associated with a smooth adjustment to retirement. By this I mean that people who are able to enjoy and relish the details of their lives frequently have an even transition. To a certain extent, a joyful demeanor becomes a self-fulfilling prophecy; people who appreciate life in general are apt to find positive aspects to retirement specifically. A willingness to stop and smell the roses helps retirees deal well with the changes.

Similarly, *positive attitudes* about retirement, the future, and aging in general facilitate the adjustment. This trait isn't mindlessness; it's thoughtful optimism. People who have affirmative attitudes look at retirement not as the beginning of the end but as the beginning of the next phase in their lives. They expect their retirement years to be happy, and they look forward to the future. They confront their fears about what may lie ahead, talk about them with others, and set a post-retirement path that feels right and meaningful.

Having an activity that captures one's interest is very helpful here. The psychoanalyst Heinz Kohut proposed that in later middle age, the ability to maintain a sense of self-continuity and direction—to feel that life still has a meaning and there is a task to be performed—is critical, particularly during the retirement transition. This attitude tends to protect against the depression that sometimes accompanies retirement.

As you can deduce, people with negative attitudes about aging tend to go into retirement feeling over-the-hill, useless, or worthless. This antipathy may gnaw at their spouses, and all the more if the spouse has a positive attitude. For someone who is trying to maintain a hopeful, forward-looking attitude, nothing is more irksome than the company of someone who is always looking on the gloomy side of things.

These negativists would be well advised to try to adopt a more positive attitude about aging. I've seen it work. Formerly downbeat people have learned to view retirement as an opportunity to do new things and as a chance to free themselves from boring duties. In many cases, other retired or older people serve as inspirational role models.

Hardiness is a less obvious but no less important trait. Hardy people feel that they can control or influence events in their lives, and they see change as an exciting challenge. As a result, they cope better with stressful events, are less likely to become ill or depressed because of trauma, and are willing and able to make adjustments in their lives that retirement demands. An innate quality, hardiness is not something that people can acquire at retirement age.

Another related subject is *the ability to cope with change*. While some people take naturally to change, others are more rigid. The latter group is more likely to flail upon entering retirement. However, it's the dislike of change rather than retirement per se that sets them adrift. Indeed, a 2010 study found similar evidence that resilience, which is characterized by the capacity of adaptation and development, helps when it comes to retirement. Vulnerable individuals report more adversities than resilient ones in retirement.

I've found that open discussion helps people who have an aversion to the changes that retirement brings. When people are uneasy or on edge about these revised states—from having to live on less money to maintaining self-image without an ego-building job—verbalizing their concerns can help to ease their minds. Often such discussions help people realize that they have a resistance to change in general that predates their retirement. This insight gets them to stop thinking of retirement as the cause of all their worries and enables them to adjust faster and better to this new life stage. When people are willing to talk openly and honestly with their spouses about the changes that trouble them, adapting to retirement is easier, and "silent" anxieties don't degenerate into estrangement in the marriage.

Another trait that eases the retirement transition is *non-work competence.* The knowledge that we are skilled in certain aspects of life adds to our self-esteem. When people retire, they sometimes attribute feelings of incompetence to their separation from work and the recognition that came with it. In reality, most people who feel incompetent post-retirement felt that way in non-work situations even during their work years. Work provided a place to hide this insecurity, allowing them to avoid facing and handling it. Now that this hideout is no longer available, they need to confront their fears that they are "not good enough."

Sometimes this means talking to a therapist, but in many cases, it can be much simpler. Pursuing an interest or activity based on skills and knowledge that were used at work is a great strategy.

Tina, for instance, was racked by the fear that her husband would find her to be incompetent in her new role as a homemaker. Tina had been a highly successful lawyer for most of her life, a crusading public defender who had been lauded by the media as well as various public-interest groups. She felt much less competent, however, when it came to cooking, cleaning, and other domestic chores, which their housekeeper had always handled. She worried that Bob, who retired at the same time, would somehow think less of her, that he would realize that she was "nothing" without her work.

After they retired, Tina took on the domestic chores, assuming that she should be the one to tackle these tasks and that Bob would expect her to do so. During the first few months, she constantly criticized herself for not doing a good job, but she was afraid to share these negative feelings with Bob. Because of this fear and the difficulty she was having with the transition, Tina became unusually quiet and even somewhat depressed.

Her husband couldn't figure out what was wrong and assumed that he must have offended her in some way. It was only when he pressed her about why she was acting so oddly that she owned up to her fears. After he calmed her down by communicating that her homemaking skills had little to do with his love and appreciation for her, he and Tina worked out a better coping strategy, in which they shared homemaking chores.

While Bob joked to her that if what he wanted was a Martha Stewart kind of wife, he would not have married her, he also admitted that he was not immune to traditional sex role stereotypes. He said he was probably guilty of communicating to Tina both that she was responsible for housekeeping chores and his expectations that she should be competent at them.

Bob's willingness to talk to Tina about these issues and to blame himself in part for her reaction helped her stop blaming herself and start focusing on the skills she did possess. In a short time, their relationship righted itself, and the quality of their retirement life shot up.

As you might expect, people who do well in retirement *find life interesting,* while those who don't do so well find life boring. More often than not, behind that boredom lurks a more imposing negativity. Retirees who complain that they're constantly bored often are expressing a form of despair; they are despondent about their life not just now but in the future too.

Anyone who feels this way or whose spouse acts this way needs to form more optimistic goals and expectations regarding retirement. When your expectations about your post-work years are realistic, you have a much easier time of it. This is why I frequently recommend to bored clients that they set new goals in retirement. I've found that when people can strive to achieve a meaningful and fulfilling goal—be it mastery of a new computer program, proficiency at golf, raising money for a favorite charity, or climbing a mountain—they quickly throw off their "I'm bored" attitude, and the underlying negativity is swept away.

In characterizing optimal transitions, we shouldn't overlook a *spouse's attitude* toward retirement. If your spouse is entering retirement kicking and screaming, this is also going to affect your adjustment. At the very least, such a spouse creates stress and anxiety that could detract from your enjoyment of this part of your life.

In addition, if you were looking forward to spending quality time with your spouse, you may be in for a rude awakening by the complaints that he or she is bored, depressed, and so on. Furthermore, this behavior transfers the emotional burden of the relationship onto the non-depressed spouse, who may eventually feel resentful, as Murray did in our earlier example—going from being even-tempered to yelling at Sarah for her inaction. It's not enough, therefore, that you've made a splendid transition from work to retirement. If your spouse is stumped by this transition, it's bound to impact your life satisfaction as well as your ability to achieve your retirement goals.

A trait that many people—younger ones in particular—assume is necessary for a satisfying retirement is sexual gratification and interest. That assumption has not been proved valid. While good sex is a component of a satisfying marriage at all ages, people typically have less sex as they get older. To assume that couples can't enjoy retirement together without frequent sex just doesn't jibe with what I've observed in clients and what the literature indicates. Other expressions of affection such as caressing, touching, cuddling, and holding hands can provide gratification for many couples. In fact, good sex is not strongly associated with overall marital satisfaction in later life, and sexual problems have less effect on marital satisfaction of older couples, particularly when other modes of physical expression exist.

While strong sexual activity isn't typically required for a successful adjustment, *strong social activity* is. People who have many friends and frequently interact with them feel connected to society; the social activity compensates in a way for the loss of social contacts at work. Loneliness is devastating at any age, but it is especially so at retirement, as it tends to increase retirees' worries and even shorten their life span—research indicates that retirees who decrease their social activity level die sooner than retirees who maintain the same level as in pre-retirement.

Retirees who are socially withdrawn are also more likely to be self-centered, reserved, and inhibited and often feel directionless, pessimistic, and depressed. Retirees with lots of friends are able to compare notes, receive feedback and information, and feel as if they belong. They tend to be more energetic as well, compared with those who don't have friends. Social contact can also foster a sense of value by communicating that one is still considered interesting and worth being with. Friendships can thus be an excellent buffer against depression and loneliness and streamline the transition to retirement.

"Stay busy" is common advice for retirees, and it certainly makes sense; you're less likely to be bored or depressed if you're engaged in meaningful activities. But staying busy with meaningless activities—playing monotonous games of shuffleboard or going on frequent cruises as a way to fill time—is not a trait of good adjusters. In fact, it can prevent people from finding meaningful activities and increase feelings of boredom and emptiness. Staying busy, in the best sense of that phrase, means being able to find a life purpose, direction, or goal after retirement. Ideally, people are as passionate about what they're pursuing in retirement as they were when they were working.

Having goals that are mentally stimulating and challenging helps people stay young at heart. As the saying goes, "Age is an issue of mind over matter: if you don't mind it, it doesn't matter." Staying challenged, engaged in learning new things, and involved with people who value and respect you is part of a meaningful life, whether you're working or retired. In retirement, it yields the added benefit of restoring the structure that work used to provide. Plus, retirees who live this type of life often take the opportunity to pursue goals that work made impossible. With the newly gained increase in time and freedom, they set forth on projects that they've always dreamed of doing but couldn't do when they were working. Staying busy in desired and fulfilling activities and daily routines enhances retirees' sense of control and autonomy as well as self-esteem.

The last trait is what I refer to as *time equilibrium.* This concept refers to the time people spend by themselves versus the time they spend with others. Disequilibrium may occur at retirement, not only because you're spending more time with your spouse and less time with others such as coworkers but also because aging is associated with greater introversion. You may feel the need to spend more time taking solitary walks and reflecting. Everyone's time equilibrium is different—one person may need to spend the majority of time alone, and someone else may want to spend a minority of time alone.

The quality of the interaction is far more important than the quantity. Having confidants, intimate friends, and loving relatives offers insulation against stress and contributes to well-being. Superficial relationships held together by gossip and small talk do not. Be aware of what works for you, and adjust your schedule accordingly. In one study, for instance, some married retirees reported spending 40 percent of their daily lives in solitude, and they loved it. My own experience concurs that people who schedule sufficient alone time in retirement tend to be more satisfied than those who attempt to fill every waking hour with activities and superficial contacts as compensation for the loss of their work life.

In summary, we can say that the following traits are associated with a smooth transition to retirement:

- Wanting to retire rather than feeling coerced
- Perceiving oneself as healthy
- Perceiving oneself as having sufficient financial resources for the road ahead
- Seeing retirement in a positive light and having positive attitudes about aging and the future
- Experiencing joy in everyday life
- Finding meaningful and fulfilling activities that offer opportunities for learning and contributing to a worthwhile cause
- Being goal directed
- Avoiding boredom
- Seeing oneself as competent in non-work settings

- Having friends and staying socially engaged while also having sufficient "alone time"
- Embracing change
- Having a spouse who does not have a rough transition

The more of these traits you and your spouse possess, the more likely you'll have a happy and healthy retirement.

Exercises:
Questions to Consider

If you're contemplating retirement, or even if you have already retired but need a plan, answer the following questions before creating your retirement plan:

- When do you want to retire, and why?
- Do you feel that you have enough money for a comfortable retirement?
- What role does work play in your life; in what ways does it provide you with a sense of purpose, belonging, and influence?
- What will you miss most about work?
- How will you substitute for the losses you experience with retirement?
- What makes life not only satisfying but also exciting for you—what is your passion?
- How will you create meaning in your life when you retire?
- How would you like to divide your time among being alone, being with your spouse, and being with other people?
- How will you organize your time so that you have structure, satisfaction, and meaning?
- How can you maintain the best possible level of functioning as you age?
- How will you stay in touch with friends, and will you be willing to pursue new friendships as old ones fade?

Consider the following questions regarding your relationship with your spouse:

- Are you aware of your spouse's retirement goals and if they're compatible with your own?
- Do both of you have realistic expectations and goals, based on your preferences and personalities as well as established patterns?
- What adjustments do you need to make so that your goals will be more compatible?
- What adjustments may be necessary relative to your partner's needs for privacy in terms of time and space?
- How much togetherness do you personally want, and does it match your spouse's feelings?
- What commitments and obligations do each of you have to other family members, and how similar are they?
- Do you see retirement as your own personal concern or as a joint issue?
- Do you expect any changes in your role and behavior as a spouse after retirement?
- Do you expect any changes in your spouse's role as a result of retirement?
- Do you expect changes in your spouse's interests and energy level after retirement?
- Do you expect changes in the division of housework, and does your spouse agree?

Before creating a goal-based retirement plan, you and your spouse should discuss these questions, many of which we touched upon in earlier chapters. By doing so, you'll be able to create a plan that helps each of you fulfill personal goals in retirement but not at the expense of the other's goals.

In fact, you can greatly facilitate the transition to retirement by starting to think about it as a couple rather than individually. Don't, as many people do, become so wrapped up in your anxieties about adjusting to this next stage of life that you're oblivious to the effect on your partner. Adjustment to retirement is done on both levels, as an individual and as a couple.

Relocation

Where people live during their adult life is strongly dictated by their workplace. Retirement removes this constraint or at least allows for new residential choices to be considered. However, the majority of retirees stay in place (96 percent of those surveyed in 2008, according to the US Census Bureau) and if they move it is usually to homes only a short distance away. Indeed Dr. Robert Butler, former head of the National Institute on Aging, has been quoted saying that the best place to retire is the neighborhood where you spent your life.

Between 1985 and 1990, only 4.5 percent of people age 60 and older made an interstate move. However, among 50-year olds, according to a 2005 report conducted by the Gallup Organization, 60 percent of people surveyed said that they daydreamed of finding a small town or rural county to move to when they retire. In another large survey by Del Webb Corporation, 18 percent of today's 50-year olds said that they are planning to move to another state when they retire.

Even if only half of those baby boomers actually move, it would be an enormous change which would have an impact on a large number of people. According to demographer William Frey from the Milken Institute, if the stock market's vicissitudes don't wipe out boomers retirement savings, they are likely to be more affluent and therefore more mobile than any gray generation that preceded them. Thus it is very likely that boomers are not going to listen to Dr. Butler's advice and retire in their old communities. Therefore I would like to address the issue of relocating and its impact on the couple's relationship.

I'm going to focus on long-distance relocation as it is the most difficult one to accomplish successfully (each time relocation will be mentioned it would imply that it's a long distance one). Later in the chapter I'll briefly discuss moving to different housing in the same community.

The retiree's home represents an accumulation of a lifetime, numerous memories, a familiar setting in which friends visit and to which children return for holidays. Home is a critical focal point around which people organize their everyday behaviors and experiences. Retirement means losing work and all the other components attached to it; the professional identity, colleagues, friends who knew you as Professor X or as VP of company Y and not as Mr. X or Mrs. Z. Relocation after retirement also means losing the place where you know the houses, streets, stores, how to get around, and the people, neighbors, doctors, and bank tellers who know and recognize you.

Therefore, relocation after retirement disturbs established family and friendship networks and can increase the feeling of losing control and competence. Losing the familiar environment with all its social attachments and emotional connections, on top of losing one's job is psychologically much more challenging than retiring without relocation or relocation before retirement. The greater challenge is both on an individual level as well as on a couple's level.

Relocation at any life stage often increases the pressure on the couple's bond; relocation after retirement does it even more. Couples who move experience changes in family life differently than those who did not move and retired in place. The interaction between husband and wife can be altered as a result of their retiring to another community rather than retiring in place.

Reasons for relocation

People relocate for many reasons. For some the promise of a residential setting that is consistent with how they want to spend their leisure and recreational time is a significant reason. They have a clear image of a retirement lifestyle that calls for a different environment. For example, golf or fishing. Other couples want to live in a smaller, easier and less expensive place to maintain. This change is often in another state where cost of living is lower. People who move to retirement communities often feel that they are getting a "good deal" for their money and are attracted by the variety of indoor and outdoor events and programs available.

For others the appeal for the move might be meeting other retirees who have similar interests, life concerns or background which provide a good opportunity for new friendships. For many, a favorable year-round sunny climate is the inducement for the move. Better weather is associated with more outdoor activities, ease of getting around, fewer upkeep responsibilities, e.g. snow, ice, and prospects of better personal health, e.g. relief from asthma, arthritis, and minimizing the chances for falling or having an accident due to slippery ice. Indeed a large number of retirees who relocate are "snow birds." They live in warmer states during the fall and winter months, but retain a residence in their original place to which they return during the spring and summer. Another group states that the reason for the relocation after retirement is to be close to children and family. Yet others feel that now their neighborhood no longer holds the same appeal; that they have no reason to stay where they worked or raised their kids, and they can go back to the place they are homesick for; their childhood hometown or a place where they went many times for vacations.

Unsurprisingly, the most popular retirement locations are overwhelmingly in or near places that attract tourists and vacationers. For others, the reason for the relocation is now that one thing is ending, it's time to start something new—a desire for a change in life.

Whatever the reason or reasons for the move, it is very important that couples have elaborate discussions for why they want the move. Do they have similar expectations regarding the goal that would be accomplished by it? How similar are their reasons for wanting to relocate? Many couples find themselves surprised by the significant differences of opinion that exist between them when it comes to deciding where to spend their golden years. Clarifying these reasons before the actual move makes a big difference in easing the adjustment to the move and retirement afterward.

Couples need to be aware that a new location will not necessarily make things better between them. The problems that existed for them in Wisconsin, i.e., she was too involved with their daughter and grandchildren, and they had many fights about that, is likely to surface in other ways too. The lack of agreement they have regarding their roles and obligations to adult children and grandchildren does not disappear after they move.

So realizing, "wherever you go there you are" and having realistic expectations and compatible goals will make a big impact here.

Retirees and people of all ages can be grouped into three distinct and general groups:

- those whose main source of emotional support and satisfaction comes from their spouse
- those who get it from their family and friends
- those who get it from being engaged in different activities

The relocation issue can be very difficult because it brings to the surface mismatched retirement expectations that emphasize these differences. For example, one couple who came to see me was teetering on the brink of divorce, experiencing this mismatched expectation. He was determined to move to Phoenix where he could play golf and grow orchids year round, focusing on activities as the main source for satisfaction, while she insisted on staying in Chicago where their children and grandchildren live, focusing on family relationships as the main source of satisfaction. Thus what they envisioned is not to be found in a particular state, per se, rather the geographic state represents a state of mind.

Characteristics of those who relocate

Many of the long distance relocated retirees have the economic resources needed to make such a move. They are usually affluent and tend to have better than average financial resources. Often, those who relocate are better off economically than those who do not move or those that move only short distances.

In addition to the financial resources, relocated retirees also have psychological resources. Retirees who relocate display values that are at odds with some images of old age. Rather than keeping the status quo in their familiar dwellings, they are ready to "pull up stakes" to change and start something new. They tend to be less risk-averse, possess more adventurous personalities and have a positive orientation toward the future. Often they successfully coped with new roles and situations during their lives. Retirees who experienced a few residential relocations during their working years understand the positive and negative of the transition and usually have less doubt or fear about it.

Another characteristic is that those who tend to be ready to relocate at this life stage did not put down roots or did not get emotionally moored to the community in which they worked. Their main connection was through work and now that work is over they have few ties to the local community, with no reason to remain, which makes it easy to leave.

Health makes a difference in two ways here. On one hand, good health encourages retirees to relocate. They justify the move by saying that they want to do it while they are still in good health and able to enjoy their new life. On the other hand, declining health close to retirement triggers a tendency to move too. However the reasons are different; to be near family members who can help in case there is an additional health problem or physical deterioration.

Indeed, most relocated retirees are met by relatives and friends, eager to provide information and assistance at the new destination. Family and friends provide a source of continuity that eases the transition.

Obstacles to satisfaction in retirement after relocation

The key to successful adjustment is the matching of one's desired retirement lifestyle to a retirement location and accommodations that are found in the new environment. While climate and natural beauty always rank high on the list of reasons retirees give to relocate to their new place, being able to be among people you want to be with, and do what you wish at retirement is more important to long term satisfaction. Golf or fishing may be enjoyable vacation activities. However, the great golf course and the well-run marina may lose their appeal after a year of retirement. At that time, the absence of a good library, theatre or even cable television may cause considerable regret.

In some places, relocated retirees have a hard time developing ties to the new community as they lack workplace or children that usually are the natural way to develop these ties. As a result, retirees are vulnerable to being stigmatized as "outsiders" by the natives. Without making a considerable effort to break through the local xenophobia, retirees are vulnerable to feeling rootless, having only other relocated retirees as their source for potential social ties, which increases their sense of being outsiders.

Retirees who relocated to a retirement community, which means interacting mostly with age-homogeneous people, can have, in addition to the outsider issue, a negative image that they need to deal with. People who move to retirement communities often complain about living in a geriatric ghetto. Thus they view even more unfavorably being stigmatized as outsiders since it implies old, discarded and unwanted. Many do not like to be continually interacting with and surrounded mostly by persons of their own age. They miss the diversity they experienced in their previous setting.

Many retirees have difficulty establishing new friendships and relating to completely new groups of people. They complain about the fact that it seems that everyone already belongs to a clique, and have their own schedules, thus making it harder for them to integrate. People who are shy, less outgoing or with a discerning style of friendship (i.e., choose friends slowly and carefully, are very committed to their friends and see them as not easily replaceable) are particularly vulnerable.

Many retirees suffer from the fact that the transplantation to a new setting diminishes the opportunity to draw on the previous sense of "self." In leaving a community where one has worked, reared a family and achieved a certain social position, one also leaves behind correlated identities tied to that community. A successful businesswoman in a small town in Vermont who had many people come to seek her advice felt surprised by how much she missed that and how angry she felt when her input in the new setting was ignored by others who did not know how "important" she was pre-retirement.

Relocated retirees often miss being known as they used to be. It is as if they are not known or seen for who they are or as they see themselves—the successful entrepreneur, or the brilliant lawyer. The decline in recognition and status that all retirees experience is much more intense when there are no people who knew how important and valuable they used to be. Even when they make new friends, they often feel that the new ones do not know them as they used to be or as they see themselves. The only one that sees them as they see themselves is often their spouse, thus increasing the stress on the marital bond.

Gradual relocation

In order to increase the smooth transition to retirement in the new place, retirees should consider creating a way to do that move in a gradual manner. No one moves to a new place without checking it first or without establishing a pattern of pre-retirement visitation. Increasing the amount of time each year that one spends in the community where one plans to permanently relocate can help to create a smooth transition. It allows people to create social ties in which their work identity is known. It also gives them an opportunity to become familiar with the new place so that they do not feel out of control as everything is unfamiliar. As they live there as seasonal visitors and increase the time, they create a gradual change and shift in their identity too, thus making the transition easier for themselves as well as for their partners.

Gradual relocation also provides them with an opportunity to make sure that the amenities that are important to them and enhance living are readily available. In other words, that the retirement lifestyle they aspire to with all the activities and participations in clubs is possible year round. For some relocated retirees, moving to a place that is close enough to their original home and family is important as it allows them to maintain some consistency in life, e.g. moving to Cape Cop from Boston.

An ideal gradual long distance relocation would look like the following:

- While the couple is still employed, they should start to think and talk about relocation. After an extensive discussion about where the couple would like to live after retirement and for what reasons, the couple starts to go on vacation to the identified location. As time goes by, they increase the frequency and duration of their visits, from one week or long weekends to weeks at a time, encountering how life would be there on a regular basis. Developing social networks, making friends, visiting different clubs or organizations where they can see themselves involved is important to do. This gives people an opportunity to meet friends who know them while their work identity is still intact and increases their ability to integrate into the community rather than being seen as outsiders.

- In the second step, either while still working, if it is possible to work from a different state, or right after retirement, in case the couple can do gradual retirement as well as gradual relocation, the spouses increase the time they spend in the identified location to a few months. A typical example is the "snow birds" spending the winter months in the new location either working or as retirees, and returning to work in their previous community in the spring and summer. Thus at this stage they have both homes, maintaining ties in both places.

- In the third stage, the couple retires and relocates completely to the new location. Some do a reverse pattern in which they spend most of the year in the new location and go back to briefly visit the previous community.

It is important at each stage to have extensive discussion about the relocation. Are the expectations and goals they set for themselves being met, do they encounter surprises or unforeseen issues, do they like the new lifestyle, the friends and activities they are able to be involved in there, what do they miss about the previous community, etc. Couples should give themselves the option of going back if their expectations are not being met, or if they realize that they miss too many aspects of their previous life. Indeed, we sometimes hear about couples who relocated completely for a few years or were snow birds for a while, but later moved back to the community were they spent most of their adult life. A gradual relocation increases the chances that people will find out sooner than later that complete relocation is not right for them as well as ease the transition to the new destination.

Alan Fox, editor of *Where to Retire* magazine (wheretoretire.com), suggests that people not even look for a retirement town any earlier than five years before they are ready to retire. The reason is that some towns are growing so fast that by the time people are ready to relocate it loses its appeal as the cost of living goes up and there are long lines at movie theatres and restaurants. He also recommends that retirees rent for a year before buying a home, as the most common mistake people make in long distance relocation is buying a house in the wrong neighborhood. Lastly, it is important to experience the place before making a permanent commitment during the off-season. It's one thing to vacation at a sea side resort during the high season, and another to shiver through January and February when the wind is blowing in full force.

Pressure on the couple after relocation

As mentioned before, relocation puts extra pressure on the couple's relationship. It's easier not to make a long-distance move – so you can maintain ties with family and friends, keep your concert or theatre subscription and keep visiting your family dentist. Married relocated people may find their partner helpful in assisting their integration into the new setting, and at the same time they might find them also "getting in the way." Away from their friends, family, previous co-workers, and removed from their former community and work setting, the relationship between the spouses is highlighted. They need to renegotiate patterns of interaction on the new turf.

At first, immediately after the move, patterns of interaction arise out of the activity of moving itself. The physical process of moving gives the relocated retirees something to do, thereby easing the transition. It is as if the process of relocation is work in and of itself. As they get involved in packing, unpacking, transforming the summer home into a year-round residence, or other projects like planning a garden, wallpapering, buying or building new book shelves, all these activities fill the void created by leaving the old community and work. The time that spouses spend with each other at this initial stage increases as they need to make decisions together or even do many of those projects together.

As the house gets settled, couples have time to establish social contacts. Often wives are the social directors, in charge of establishing new social contacts, joining clubs, temples, and making new friends. Again, gradual relocation can be helpful, as those who relocate gradually have some existing social contacts rather than needing to completely create new contacts as is the case for those who relocated abruptly; for example, in order to be close to their children.

At this stage, development of independent interests is crucial for successful retirement as is the case for retirees who did not relocate. However, personality differences between the spouses with regard to adjusting to change in general and making new friends becomes even more apparent now and can increase the pressure on the relationship. The spouse who takes longer to adjust to change or to make new friends might resent being "left" and might feel abandoned by the other one who developed new interests faster. In addition, the one who has a hard time making friends might feel dependent on the other spouse; an issue that would not likely have surfaced if they did not move. All the issues discussed in Chapter 4 about togetherness, time and space together vs. alone, need for validation and appreciation, become more demanding and can possibly create more conflicts as retirees relocate.

Often, people also feel that only their spouse really knows them as they want to be known or as they see themselves, and thus may be disappointed by the new friendships. Relocated retirees, more than retirees who stayed in place, are sensitive to not being considered as influential and knowledgeable, and fear they are being perceived as mere retirees. Therefore their need for validation and appreciation from their spouse is higher.

Being in a new place can make the development of new activities and interests, which is so important for a successful retirement, more difficult. Relocated retirees might not know how to go about finding the resources they need or are interested in. Therefore, it's very important to do some checking about those resources pre-retirement or pre-relocation. Here again, gradual relocation is helpful as it gives people the opportunity to find out important information ahead of time.

In summary, relocation after retirement can be the best thing for some people. However, one needs to do it carefully, having realistic and compatible expectations. Doing a gradual relocation as much as possible and being sensitive to personality differences increases the chances for a successful transition.

The following case illustrates a couple whose marital satisfaction suffered by a cultural norm that blocked them from making future plans about relocation.

Mrs. X was referred to therapy by her physician due to her depression. After seeing her once, it was clear to me that not only was Mrs. X depressed, but the entire marital system was in great stress. Therefore I asked Mr. X to come to the sessions to "help me help his wife" as he had refused to come to therapy when his wife asked him to join. In the joint sessions it was very clear how loving and devoted to each other they were. I also learned that the couple emigrated from Greece when they were in their 20's leaving behind large extended families. Mr. X retired two years ago after selling his successful auto-body repair shop. Soon after retirement he became depressed. His depression caused them to fight much more than they used to before retirement, and gradually caused her to become depressed too.

When I asked them what they wanted for themselves for their golden years neither could think of an answer. He said that there is nothing for him to live for and that he is waiting to die. After additional probing about dreams they might have had before, Mr. X mentioned their long-forgotten dream of returning to the village where they were born, on a Greek island, after their retirement and living in a villa by the sea there. They had this dream as a young couple. They were from the same island and immigrated to the US shortly after their marriage looking for a better life. They visited their family in Greece almost on a yearly basis, and retained the attachment to the idea of successfully returning to their village to live out the remainder of their years. Now in their late 60's they were proud of their business and childrearing accomplishments. All children had post-graduate degrees that the parents paid for. They continue to give generous presents to their children and grandchildren, even though their savings were not large.

When I asked them why they do not go back to Greece to fulfill their dream they said that they never talked any more about it and could hardly even remember it without my question. When I insisted and asked again, "So now that you are in touch with the dream, how about going for it? (I asked that because I noticed how much they both lighted up talking about their village), it became clear that the X's feared that they might anger their two adult sons and daughter by moving back to Greece because buying the villa by the sea would reduce their children's inheritance. Their dilemma was that by taking care of themselves they would not be able to continue to help their children. They felt that the cultural norm that children can expect their parents to protect their inheritance was stronger than their own wish and dream for themselves.

Once the dream was recalled, the question that was discussed in the therapy was when do marital responsibilities take precedent over parenting obligations. After the cultural norm was successfully challenged, the X's rediscovered the importance of their original marital dream and the depression eased for both of them. In addition, Mr. X said that he never raised the villa issue as he knew how much his wife was attached to their children and grandchildren and he felt he should sacrifice himself for her. He did not realize that his depression might be related to his sacrifice of which she had no idea. With tears she said that he is more important and if the villa means that he won't be depressed, would start living and stop waiting to die, it is worth it for her. They now were able to address in therapy the issue of how they can be together in a way that is enriching for them, and discuss what they want to leave as a legacy for their children. They were able to see and accept that they would still be loved by their children in spite of leaving a much smaller inheritance and that their legacy would be one of showing how to be a happily married couple later in life. Within a few weeks the X's moved back to Greece to their village. It is almost ten years since the therapy ended and I still get a post card from them every Christmas thanking me for helping them to fulfill their dream and telling me how happy they are. Their children and grandchildren visit them as the X's did when they were younger.

Moving to new housing in the same community or "retiring-in-place"

Many couples use retirement as an opportunity to change housing but to stay in the same area. Examples are moving from the suburbs to a condo downtown, or moving from a house on two to three levels to a ranch house where everything is on the same floor. It seems that these retirees plan ahead for the future for the time when their health might decline and they want to be prepared. At the same time they make a change that is satisfying, gives them great pleasure as it often means a smaller or less expensive home to maintain. The move also gives them an opportunity to do things that they want (moving from the city condo to the suburbs so that they can have a yard and garden to take care of now that they have the time) or to get rid of things that they do not enjoy (moving to a complex where they do not have to shovel snow or mow the lawn). For them the change is not as drastic as for those who choose the long distance relocation, since they stay in the environment they are familiar with. Those who age in place are able to stay in touch with the same friends, the physicians that have known them for the last 20 years and they are knowledgeable about the different resources in their community. Often they have children in the same general area and want to stay close to them. Not having to learn and adapt to a new environment allows them to explore other aspects of their life with greater freedom and courage as their sense of control and competence is not disturbed.

Another change is moving to *a retirement or adult community* in the same general area. The appeal here is the lifestyle that the community offers. All the activities are there; often they can meet new social contacts that share the same interests they do. Another benefit is that usually such complexes offer a good security system and retirees feel safe there, crime has less chance to impact them as well as not having to bother with different maintenance chores like snow shoveling, etc. Most of these adult communities are a little further away from the metropolitan center and retirees like the more suburban, uncongested setting without pollution, high crime rates, bad neighborhoods, crowded streets and disturbing traffic. They often feel like they got a good deal by having all the recreational facilities so close and having a predictable orderly setting and lifestyle.

Residents of adult communities in the same general area where they lived before retirement are less prone to suffer from feeling like outsiders, rejected by the natives, as do long-distance relocated retirees, since they see themselves as natives. Similarly they are less disturbed by 'cliquey groups" as they usually continue to interact with their former friends, often inviting them to join and participate in the activities that are offered and are therefore less dependent on the new social contacts in the adult community.

On the negative side, as mentioned before, people sometimes start to resent the age homogeneity of their complex and some complain that they are continually surrounded mostly by people of their own age. The sight of an ambulance or the sound of a siren becomes an unpleasant reminder of one's age and mortality.

Another complaint is the limit on one's autonomy that living in such adult community entails. There are rules about many subjects that the residents need to obey: for example, what can be planted in the yard, or how long children and grandchildren can stay. Often the residents feel that they have a limited say in running the community so they experience undesirable rules they need to go along with. In order to control their autonomy and decrease the chances that unpleasant decisions will take place, they feel that they have to take a leadership position and become a board member. While for some active retirees this is appealing, to others it is appalling and upsetting that they have to go through all the trouble to make a trivial thing happen according to their liking. Other retirees mention that sometimes there is pressure to participate in the organized activities, thus not having enough time or space for solitude.

In summary we see that there are a lot of options regarding where to live after retirement. It is very important that couples have extensive discussions between themselves, and with other retirees who made the change they are thinking about before they consider where to live. Adjustment to the change often depends on how retirees feel about their new place of residence - whether and how soon they start to consider it home. Having to adjust to a new home on top of losing one's work might be exciting and challenging to some, yet too stressful and disturbing to others. There are no rules about what's best and each couple needs to find out what is the best strategy for them.

This chapter doesn't have questions for you to answer as each situation is so different. Instead of the questions you had at the end of earlier chapters, I suggest you take some time to get clearer on your reasons for wanting to relocate, and be willing to do the necessary research about the location with all necessary details. Having good communication, and sharing in the decision fully, is of crucial importance, combined with being open to the fact that your spouse might feel very differently about this. And remember that although it is a big change, it does not have to be permanent if it doesn't work out, or if you discover that you moved for the wrong reasons and don't like it.

Relocation Resources

The following section offers helpful and practical relocation information.

Publications

Finding the Right Place for Retirement-from 50 Plus Pre-Retirement services,
28 W. 23rd St. New- York, NY, 10010.

America's 100 Best Place to Retire, and the *How to Plan and Execute a Successful Retirement Relocation* booklet from *Where to Retire*, 5851 San Felipe Street, Suite 500, Houston, TX, 77057. www.wheretoretire.com

Organizations

Retirement Living Information Center lists great places to retire, tax rates, and retirement communities. www.retirementliving.com

Senior Housing Net is a comprehensive and easy to use internet directory of senior housing in North America. It has information on over 35,000 senior living communities nationwide. www.seniorhousingnet.com

Top Retirements lists the best and worst places to retire on a variety of criteria. It includes a quiz to help you and your partner choose the best retirement town for you. www.topretirements.com

U.S. Dept. of Health and Human Services, Administration on Aging, www. aoa.gov

CHAPTER TWELVE

The Best Retirement

As you ponder all the relationship changes that couples experience in retirement, I hope you also understand that it doesn't have to be traumatic. Marriages in retirement can be as good as, if not better than, they were in the working years.

Ian and Lina, for example, had a stable marriage while they were working, but both would agree that they weren't particularly close. Ian was a well-known architect with a portfolio of international assignments, and he spent at least a month away from home each year. Lina, who stayed home with the children until they started school, became active in politics. She eventually got a job as an administrative assistant to a state representative and began working long hours.

When Ian and Lina retired, they rediscovered each other. Both admitted that they had taken each other for granted and had lost the spark that ignited their relationship in the early years of the marriage.

The increased time together in retirement turned out to be a blessing for them. It wasn't that they suddenly decided to spend every waking moment together or stopped doing things on their own, but they did luxuriate in having whole evenings to themselves to just relax with each other or take a leisurely walk. Ian remarked, "I forgot how much fun it was just to be around Lina." Lina mused, "I can't remember the last time—before retirement— that we had one of our wonderful conversations; I think I fell in love with Ian in the first place because he was so easy to talk to."

Therefore, take the message of this book as more than simply a way to prevent divorce in retirement. The ideas and exercises can also help you maintain a great marriage or make your relationship even better. Couples often ask me what one thing they can do to increase the odds that they'll have a terrific retired life together. There isn't one thing, but the 10 tips that follow seem to help marriages flourish after retirement.

Ten Steps to Take in Order to Have the Best Retirement Together

Step 1: Say Good-bye to Work. Saying good-bye to work is best done in two phases. The first phase should begin months or even a year or two before retirement. As shown in Chapter Two, you need to think about who you are without work and prepare yourself for life without the structure and routine your job provides. If you're in denial about retirement, you'll be unprepared for the day when you no longer have to get up and go to work. Preparing yourself emotionally can involve visualizing what a typical day or week will be like and accepting that it's going to happen.

Along with this emotional preparation, take some practical steps to detach yourself from work. For instance, if your employer will allow it, reduce your schedule by a few hours per week, or go to a four-day workweek. You may be able to negotiate an arrangement in which you do some work at home rather than on-site. If possible, take longer vacations or schedule more three-day weekends. You may also want to consider turning down projects that will require a significant investment of both emotional energy and time. Ideally, you'll be able to reduce your workload gradually so that when you finally do leave your job, you will have acclimated yourself to retirement and won't be quitting cold turkey.

As it gets closer to your retirement date—three to six months beforehand—move to the second phase of your leave-taking. Begin to assess again what work gives you. How does it help you fulfill your life purpose? What social function does it play in your life? How important is work to your identity? Determine what you're going to miss most when you leave work, and then how you can replace what you're losing in non-work situations. As I've emphasized, volunteering, community service, and hobbies are among the outlets that retirees find useful in forging satisfying identities.

If both you and your spouse are retiring, remember to talk through the "saying good-bye" ritual together. By sharing your feelings about leaving work, you can embark on retirement without the overhang of unarticulated fears or concerns. Men who are macho and expect that retirement will be "a piece of cake" often find that their machismo backfires as they become regretful or depressed without gainful employment. Talking with your spouse about what leaving work means emotionally will help you determine if the aspects you'll miss are similar or different. For many couples, such emotional sharing happens naturally, but if you and your spouse have a pattern of airing emotions only or mostly when there are relationship problems, be proactive: don't wait for a distress signal to get closer to your spouse.

Step 2: Share Expectations. Talk with your spouse about your retirement dreams and how you can achieve them together. Don't be discouraged if your dreams are different; remember that disagreements do not break relationships. In fact, disagreements can strengthen relationships when both points of view are considered, both people feel valued, and resolutions are mutually satisfying.

Frame the discussion in terms of how you can each get what you want out of retirement and where you can yield ground to achieve mutual aims. As discussed in Chapter Three, think specifically about how you would like to occupy your time. Is there a shared activity that will help both of you find a substitute purpose or identity, or will each of you need a different activity or interest?

Talk about whether your expectations are realistic and attainable, individually and collectively. Will you have the requisite financial resources and stamina? For example, a couple wants to travel, but his idea is to buy an RV and travel continuously for a few months, and she is appalled by this plan; she prefers going on one trip for a few weeks and then coming home and staying there before taking the next vacation. In this case, the discussion needs to go beyond their love of travel and all the places they want to see. They need to reach a compromise in which both of them feel that the travel schedule is close to their dreams.

It's also worthwhile to clarify the emotional meaning behind an expectation. If you say you expect to go mountain climbing after you retire, add that you want to do so because it makes you feel adventurous and as if you're leading an exciting life. Understanding each other's feelings helps align spouses to each other's goals.

Couples who are aware of their individual and shared expectations in retirement are primed for bringing them to fruition. When these expectations are hidden, the odds of their coming to pass plummet. Reaching consensus regarding mutual retirement goals and supporting each other in fulfilling individual goals makes couples feel closer and more connected.

Step 3: Address Your Relationship with Money. Some retirees delude themselves that money won't be a thorn because "we have enough" or "we've never had a problem with how we spend our money." It's time for a closer look.

As I've shown in Chapter Five, money is a stickler for many retired couples because the lack of a paycheck changes the status quo.

Couples who have wonderful lives during retirement don't always have lots of money, but each spouse usually has a good understanding of the other's money relationships, and they've taken those relationships into account when planning their new life stage. One person may be a spender and the other an assembler: even though these opposing money styles might not have mattered much during the work years, retirement can upset the apple cart. You both have to recognize the possibility for collision and be willing to veer from your time-honored courses—the spender comes around to spending a bit less; the hoarder eases up and spends a little more. Wills and money given to adult children and grandchildren can also create relationship havoc if you and your spouse are oblivious of each other's money styles or of the values and psychological meaning that each of you associate with money.

Step 4: *Prepare for Mixed Feelings.* While some people enter retirement with dread, most couples look forward to it. Given good health and adequate finances, couples often talk excitedly about what they're going to do after they stop working; now, finally, they'll be able to fulfill lifelong dreams. While it's important to dream, it's just as important to recognize that retirement is not nirvana and that it will require adjustment from both people.

Zack and Nina can testify to that. Zack retired after a 40-year career as a carpenter and cabinet designer. He enjoyed his job and did very well at it, but his passion was fishing. He and his wife, Nina, had a country home in the woods, and during his work years, Zack took every opportunity to go up to the house and fish in the nearby lakes.

Nina enjoyed the country home nearly as much as Zack did, but while both were looking forward to spending more time there, Zack could hardly talk or think about anything else in the year before his retirement. When Zack retired in the spring, he and Nina agreed that they would spend the summer and fall in their country house.

After two months, Zack had stopped fishing, claiming that he was "fished out." While it's true that he spent the first three weeks fishing non-stop, he had been sure that he'd fish every day that he was there for years to come. Now, for some reason, fishing was no longer as pleasurable as it had been when he was working.

At first, he pointed the finger at himself for not being able to enjoy this aspect of retirement. He told Nina that he thought he was one of those people who like something only if they can't have it. He grew sullen and snappish because he could no longer anticipate enjoyment from this activity and there was nothing else that could take its place.

By the end of summer, Nina was ready to pack up and move back to their suburban home. Zack, however, refused, saying that they had a plan and they were going to stick with it; he was sure he would be even more unhappy if they left prematurely.

Zack's problem, which he began to work on in therapy, was that he did not prepare psychologically for retirement and was flummoxed by the mixed emotions that it brings. His honeymoon stage thudded to a halt when fishing lost its appeal. He was stuck in the disenchantment stage of retirement, and it was unlikely that he would wriggle out and move to the reorientation stage at the summerhouse. He had anointed retirement as a perfect state and was bitterly disappointed when it came up short.

Zack realized that he missed the mental stimulation of work and had been unable to acknowledge that at first. He'd been resistant to the idea that retirement could be anything less than paradise. His exclusive focus on fishing was a denial-coping mechanism, a poor substitute for mourning the loss of work.

When he finally accepted that retirement meant having mixed emotions, he was able to stop berating himself for his lack of enjoyment and his slowness in adjusting. Once his self-criticism was quelled, he started thinking proactively about changes that he could make to improve his lot.

In steadying yourself for the ups and downs of retirement, recognize that you and your spouse may not experience the same jolts or be thrown simultaneously. Even if you're retiring from similar professional careers, don't conjecture that you'll have the same reactions to life without work. Maybe you'll go through a honeymoon period in which you absolutely love your retired life for ten months and then become restless, while your spouse becomes restless much sooner.

As delineated earlier in the book, retirement is a process with different stages, and once you graduate from the honeymoon to the disenchantment stage, you want to proceed as quickly as possible to the reorientation stage. Here again, one member of the pair may need more time than the other for the process to take hold—he's ready to move on and establish a new routine, but she's still getting reoriented. In these instances, one person can become impatient with the other.

Try not to. Harboring resentment while your spouse goes through the process will only complicate and delay their reorientation. Remember that everyone reacts to retirement differently. If you can accept that the transition period can be a bit of an emotional roller coaster, you'll probably be able to keep the relationship from being bruised or scarred. People who have the best relationships in retirement aren't filled with unbridled optimism about the future but rather are realistic about the mixture of emotions infiltrating the progressive phases of the journey. They also are tolerant and patient with themselves and their partners and allow each other to take the time they need to readjust.

Step 5: Address Issues as They Surface. Retired couples who have wonderful relationships still disagree from time to time or have gone through a stage of frequent arguments. As mentioned earlier, self-validated intimacy does not assume "sameness" and allows for individual differences to exist. When you're both finally retired and spending more time together, it's a mistake to overlook relationship problems, hoping that they'll go away by themselves. If you attempt to bury your resentment now, it will eventually emerge as emotional distance between you and your spouse, which is a relationship killer. You're not going to make your relationship perfect by ignoring whatever irritates you.

Expect disagreements in your relationship to come to the fore after retirement. Being out of sync is a normal aspect of every relationship, and conflicts are inevitable and tend to burst forth more often or with more intensity during a period of change. Dissimilar reactions to the change are unavoidable, and couples handle these reactions with the greatest aplomb when they acknowledge the disagreements, address the conflicts promptly, and have differentiated selves that enable them to listen respectfully to each other's point of view.

Don't be discouraged when old issues resurface; it's the sign not of a weak relationship but of one in transition. An argument that a couple had about money early on in the marriage may be replayed now that income isn't coming in regularly. Trust that if you resolved it before, you'll resolve it again.

Rely on negotiation techniques to settle differences. Here are four that I've found to be effective:

- *Get in touch with your feelings and share with your partner the symbolic meaning behind them:* As I've discussed before, in most cases, when couples experience a conflict, the real disagreement is not about the specific item. What they are fighting about is the symbolic meaning that is attached to that specific item. It's not that you really mind vacuuming the living room before the guests are coming, what you resent is feeling like you don't have autonomy. Being able to talk about the symbolic meaning allows each spouse to explain him- or herself, be understood, and usually come up with solutions.

- **_Talk with your spouse about how you've changed:_** Communicate how your attitudes or behaviors have evolved since you stopped working. Perhaps you need to explain that you feel lonely and incompetent since you lost your work identity, and that's why you're spending so much more time with the grandchildren. Or, you don't feel that you have anything to say to your younger friends because they're still working and you're not, and that's why you refuse to go out with the Smiths anymore.

  Be aware of what's different about you, and try to articulate it. It's easy for your spouse to misinterpret the reason you're acting differently and assume that it's something he or she has done. Talking openly about the subject and the feelings behind it is a way to clear the air and to get a better idea of how to resolve it.

- **_Search for a middle ground:_** Sometimes the solution is as simple as finding a compromise between your position and that of your spouse in retirement. Digging in and holding one position may be only bothersome during the working years but devastating during retirement. When partners continuously practice middle-ground thinking and make an effort to give a little, the relationship invariably benefits.

  A common misconception is that we become more stubborn and uncompromising as we age, but I've seen plenty of retirees become more flexible and amenable to compromise. For example, some people like to plan their activities, while others like spontaneity: being willing to give and take makes each approach doable and enhances satisfaction.

- **_Trade:_** If no middle ground can be surveyed, be willing to participate in an activity you generally dislike—say, cooking dinner for a week—in exchange for doing something you really want to do but your spouse does not, such as taking your grandchild on a three-day fishing trip. This kind of trading allows each spouse a turn to do something that really lights his or her fire and allows both to feel that they're being flexible and considerate of each other, without giving up too much.

  Mature and well-differentiated individuals are able to put their partner's priorities on par with their own and to find a way to participate in their agenda even when it contradicts their own. When your partner's happiness is as much of a concern as your own, there is usually a satisfying resolution even if it means that you "agree to disagree."

Step 6: Custom-Design Your Days, Weeks, and Months. Happy retired couples don't just drift from day to day, week to week, month to month. They plan their activities based on their needs as individuals and as a couple. Some people are adrift without a regular schedule and need to replace the framework that employment provided; scheduled activities can be a good substitute for the regimen of a job. More important, a custom-designed calendar formalizes the process of getting needs met. Activities may skew toward one of the two people if there isn't a clear process to ensure that both spouses are happy with how they're spending their time.

To that end, create a calendar that meets not only both people's activity needs but also each spouse's personality and interests. It should also distribute time alone and together with friends and family. Everyone has different visions for optimizing leisure time, so expect some disagreements as you draw up this schedule. Be flexible, and use the calendar as a tool to arrange at least some of your time independently as well as together. You don't need to account for every hour of every day, but you should do enough scheduling so that you both feel that you're getting your needs met. Schedule time to do things by yourself and give your spouse the same courtesy.

Look for things you enjoy doing as a couple; you may come upon activities that you did together years ago but stopped because of more pressing demands. This is a good time to reprise them. Aim for a range of physical, social, and intellectual outlets. Retired couples should be active and enjoy a stimulating life. Relationships suffer when two people are sitting around feeling as if life has passed them by.

Don't rely on your spouse to be the exclusive social planner, even if that was his or her bailiwick when you were working. Planning should be a joint activity in which you take turns initiating social dates, visits to children, playing tennis or golf, and other outings.

These efforts should also include maintaining old friendships and establishing new ones, which takes effort. As mentioned in Chapter Seven, it's common for retirees to lose touch with old friends, especially if work kept you in contact with them. Similarly, think about ways to meet new people, and schedule events at which it's likely you'll be introduced to people who share your interests. Doing individual activities and meeting separate people will stimulate your relationship.

Step 7: Stay Mentally Active. This tip is especially important to those who had jobs that were intellectually stimulating. Some retirees feel as if they're deteriorating mentally and that the condition is age related. While Alzheimer's and other diseases of age are real problems, most retirees lose a mental edge when they allow themselves to while away their time staring at the television and engaging in other non-thinking activities.

Relationship tension can result if one spouse descends into this passive mode while the other is intellectually afire. The latter may light in to the former for sitting glued to a chair all day or for not taking an active part in the world. Just as detrimental, they may find that they have less and less in common, in terms of both their activities and subjects of conversation.

Staying mentally active doesn't mean reading Shakespeare and attending art exhibits, though those certainly can be components. It's a simple matter of acquiring new skills and knowledge, and that can incorporate everything from tackling a new hobby to joining a book club to taking art classes. Through learning new skills and acquiring new knowledge, retirees maintain a sense of personal effectiveness, competence, and involvement. Two people who are mentally active and are continuously learning also have a lot more to talk about with each other; they are overflowing with ideas and information to share.

Step 8: Give Each Other Physical and Emotional Space. In a very real sense, couples must learn to live together differently in retirement to avoid tripping over each other. Just about every couple will be at home together for a much higher percentage of the time than when one or both of the spouses worked, and the amplitude of togetherness can be grating. Retirees commonly lament that they no longer have any privacy or that the spouse is "suffocating" or "crowding" them. Therefore, it's important to respect each other's need for autonomy and try not to be the cause of more work. Both men and women can make their own lunch as well as serve the other snacks some of the time. Don't nag. Don't expect your partner to be at your beck and call. Being a good spouse does not mean dropping whatever you were doing when your spouse calls you.

Couples who do well in retirement recognize the imperative of giving each other space. They "allow" each other to pursue an individual agenda without criticism or ridicule. If necessary, they assign a certain period each day as "free time." This way, each person has a sense of power in the relationship to do what he or she wants, even if their spouse dislikes a particular activity. They remember that retirement means freedom from obligations and that they are now people of leisure—they can spend hours at their favorite store without being dunned or ridiculed. Giving each other space can also be as straightforward as just staying out of the other person's way at certain times, rearranging the home environment, or re-dividing the living space so that each person has a private room. One popular method is to convert the basement or attic into a study or an office. Happily married retired couples also share their routines with each other; they know when each is going to be home, when one's friends are coming over for the weekly card game, when one's going to be out of the house for an extended period. This way, each person can plan for alone time at home.

If needed, get a second phone line so that both of you can talk without being disturbed. You don't want your spouse staring holes in you while impatiently waiting for you to finish your conversation. Along the same lines, make sure you don't eavesdrop on each other's telephone conversations; don't listen on the other extension unless you are issued an invitation to do so. Likewise, if sharing one computer is making you frazzled, get a second one to avoid off-line bickering about whose turn it is to go on-line.

Also be extra-sensitive to each other's preferred routine and desire for some peace and quiet. If your spouse is trying to start each day by meditating, change your routine of running the dishwasher first thing in the morning or vacuuming; wait until your partner is done. If you're trying to go to an aerobics class every morning and need the car to get there, your spouse should not insist on running errands at the same time. Sharing your preferred routine, the "map" of your daily or weekly schedule, helps avoid run-ins and integrates your spouse into your preferred pattern.

Recognize that providing each other with emotional space is not a sign that the relationship is coming apart. It's easy to misperceive the need for space as a desire to get away from the other person. You really do not need to know the precise details of what your spouse is doing at any given moment. Don't tap your foot impatiently while the other watches a football game or talks on the phone. Not having enough personal space causes serious resentment. In actuality, giving each other the gift of solitude may revitalize the relationship and give you each more to offer the other when you're together.

Step 9: Celebrate Your Sexuality. Do not mistake your biological or genital prime with your sexual prime. In retirement, you probably will need a little more time to have an erection and orgasm or you'll need to use a lubricant for vaginal dryness. However, all these normal physiological changes should not prevent you from expressing yourself sexually and enjoying erotic intimacy with as much vigor and intensity as when you were younger.

Sexual intimacy requires letting someone know you as you know yourself, and that is only possible when you have some degree of identity and maturity. Passion and desire for your partner are the most important factors when it comes to sexual pleasure. Your age, the shape of your body, and how fast your genitals respond are secondary and almost irrelevant.

In retirement, having more time means that you have the freedom to engage in sex whenever you're in the mood. Now that you don't have to rush somewhere in the morning, starting the day by making love might be a new way to enjoy your sexuality and relationship. Sex is one of the best ways to maintain intimacy. Retired couples can also broaden the repertoire of their sexual intimacy, find new ways to engage their partner, lengthen the duration of their sexual encounters, and increase their pleasure.

When you retire, you have much more freedom and time to articulate your passion for your partner in sexual expressions. Without the children at home, a rat race to run, or the stress of work turning sex into one more task to be finished, you'll have many more opportunities for great sexual heights and even a second honeymoon, so be open to this opportunity.

For those of you who have health problems that interfere with your enjoyment of unrestricted intercourse, remember that even if your sexuality is diminished, your sensuality is not. Therefore you are always able to express your sexual intimacy through an erotic touch, cuddling, or caressing. Whatever changed in your body, it should never prevent you from expressing yourself sexually and sensually through touching, hugging, kissing, and fondling.

Step 10: Celebrate Your Body. Getting plenty of exercise and eating right is essential at all life stages, and it should not be neglected at retirement. Many retirees say that staying in great shape helps them adjust to retirement, giving them a strong sense of vitality and physical well-being.

Unfortunately, retirement can lead some people to the conclusion that exercise is pointless, that there's no longer any reason to look sharp, since they're not being judged by bosses, customers, and other constituents anymore. They may also stop worrying about gaining weight now that they don't have to put on a show at job-related functions or compete with people who are younger and slimmer than they are. Another hindrance is that many people lose their sports partners when they retire—they played tennis with a colleague every other day at the local club. Without the usual partner at hand and the proximity of an athletic club, they don't exercise as frequently.

Don't feed on these fallacies. Recognize that such thinking is indicative of negative values about retirement. In addition, physical activity increases brain activity, improving your mood. Self-image is as important in retirement as it was before, and it can wilt when our bodies get out of shape. When we are in good shape and feel attractive, it's easier to accept the physical changes of aging.

Being in poor physical condition can impair relationships. For instance, because of weight gain or lost muscle tone, one partner is too self-conscious or unwilling to walk along the beach or engage in other physical activities that formerly were integral parts of the couple's life. When couples make a commitment to maintain their physical health, putting the accent on exercise and proper nutrition, they can do more enjoyable activities together such as touring, taking "adventurous" vacations, or even learning to cook healthy meals. By doing all that, they will have a better chance of living both longer and better together.

Do not expect you or your partner to be able to take in and implement all ten tips immediately. Some may be easier for you to apply than others, as they are less foreign and relate more to your established dynamics. Remember that being aware of the different steps you can take in order to achieve your vision of a desirable retirement will help you more fully enjoy your life and relationship. Hopefully, these ten steps have helped you clarify and begin to design your own version of the best retirement. With this insight you may find yourself feeling and then telling your loved one, "for better or for worse. . . *and also* for lunch."

Retirement Past, Present, and Future

Retirement has many meanings. It refers to the ending of and formal withdrawal from a job, a demographic category, an economic condition, a social status, a developmental stage in the human life span, the start of a transition to old age, and a lifestyle dominated by leisure pursuits.

Due to better health care and nutrition, people are living longer and today we see more and more centenarians - individuals who reach their 100th birthday. Because of increasing longevity, and the trend toward retirement at age 65, people are spending more of their life as retirees. In 1900 a man could expect to spend only 1.2 years— about 3 percent of his life—in retirement. By 1980 the expectation had risen to 14 years—about 20 percent of his life—and by 2000 to 18 years—nearly 25 percent of his expected life span.

In many ways, our current culture has defined and continues to redefine retirement. Years ago, retirement was what happened to workers at the age of 65 when they were eligible to receive Social Security or other pension plan benefits. Retirement was looked forward to with great anticipation, in part because work often involved a hefty amount of regimentation, limitation, and boredom. Retirement was also regarded with a sense of entitlement. People said to themselves, "This is what I am entitled to have and deserve to get after years of work. I am reaping the fruits of my labor." Retirement had a very positive connotation and was referred to as the "golden years."

Retirement is a much more complex issue today, as people are retiring at all ages and for various reasons. In fact, as stated in the January 2012 issue of the *American Psychologist*, the designation of the retirement status has become somewhat meaningless and ambiguous because there are overlapping criteria. It includes numerous forms of transition from work to other activities, it potentially occurs at different stages of working life and is compatible with other activities that contribute to the well-being of oneself and society at large. We see people in their fifties accepting early retirement packages from one organization and then becoming employed with another company, or starting their own business, or returning to work when they become bored with their retirement. Indeed as stated in the same issue of *American Psychologist*, researchers are unable to agree on a single definition of retirement and therefore have challenges studying it.

Additionally we are seeing a trend toward "episodic" careers in which people switch from one field to another; they may start out as a teacher and then decide to become a chef. All this moving about requires more time, and so full retirement may not be a reality until they reach their seventies or eighties.

Other considerations include gender: Women who began their careers later in life because they took time out to raise children balk at retiring until they've achieved their career goals instead of at the traditional retirement age. As more and more people begin to work out of their homes, the entire concept of work will be transformed. There will soon be an entire generation in which a considerable percentage of its people will never know what it's like to work in an office. For them, retirement will have far less of a social impact than for previous generations.

As the rules regulating the age eligibility for Social Security benefits change because of demographic and economic reasons, so do our cultural attitudes, values, and views of retirement.

In 2011, the first Baby boomers reached age 65. It is projected by the U.S. Census Bureau that by 2030 the percentage of the population aged 65 and over will rise to 22 percent (from its current state of 13 percent), while the number of Americans under 55 will be almost unchanged. In addition, the depletion of Social Security funds that these shifts could cause, or the tax increase that may be borne by younger workers to avoid this depletion, could have a considerable impact on retirement. It's fair to assume, however, that younger workers will resent paying higher taxes to fund the retirement of older workers, and such sentiment might create more changes in retirement policies.

Another very important factor is the state of the economy, particularly unemployment rates. When unemployment rates are low it affects the demand for older workers and we could see companies offering incentives to older workers to stay employed and postpone retirement. On the other hand, when unemployment rates are high we could see general resentment toward older workers who postpone retirement, and prevent younger workers from having employment and being able to provide for their families.

Because of this, *the future of retirement should be discussed within the context of several demographic, economic, and cultural trends that are currently underway.* As people live longer and better; as society diminishes ageism with the negative connotations to old age and acknowledges that seniors can continue to be productive; as work, productivity, and youth continue to be the preferred cultural values; as more people continue to derive a sense of identity, self-esteem, and satisfaction from their work; and as the economy alters financial stability, our view of retirement will change and could possibly take on different connotations.

Indeed since this book was first published, we've seen many articles and studies that emphasize the value of work for emotional well-being. They talk about how work past traditional retirement age can boost health, keeping people sharp and fresh in mind and body. In this edition "bridge employment" is discussed in Chapter 3 - a new concept that didn't appear in the literature when the first edition was published.

We think that creativity, entrepreneurship and innovation are the exclusive province of young people. But it turns out that there's a growing group of people in their 50s, 60s, and beyond who are applying their experience to solve major problems in society. One example is a man in San Francisco who wanted to join the Peace Corps when he was young but couldn't afford to do it. He spent 35 years in the food distribution business. His wife passed away in his late 50s, he re-evaluated his priorities and went to work in the Vista Program, the food bank in San Francisco, where he discovered that food banks were just giving out canned food. He knew that growers throughout the state were wasting an enormous amount of "blemished" but edible produce. He created the Farm to Family Program, which in 2010 distributed 100 million pounds of fresh food to these food banks throughout the state of California.

As stated in the January 2012 of the *American Psychologist*, retirement has been defined by an underlining negative notion – what people are NOT doing; not working or not seeking work. Instead, I suggest that we define retirement by a positive notion, providing people an opportunity to imbue their lives with enhanced virtue and meaning regardless of their employment status. Retirement can be a time when one experiences self-actualization that enhances well-being and provides novelty, challenges and excitement

A lot of retirees possess the skills and desire to contribute to society as well as pursue old or new careers. For many, retirement is a catalyst to try something new rather than an opportunity to relax, travel or have endless leisure.

So check in with yourself and your spouse. Consider the complexities, opportunities and changes in today's world and in your own personal situation.

Regardless of what is the cultural trend and connotation of retirement when you retire, this stage of life deserves the same thoughtful consideration as earlier stages. You want to ensure your retirement years will be your reward for the years you invested in your working life. It can include new challenges that energize and excite you and your marriage. And your marriage deserves the same care as it enters the retirement phase. May it be for you a time of self-fulfillment and growth in your relationship.

Acknowledgements

I owe a tremendous debt of gratitude to several people who have helped me throughout this project. My agent, Bruce Wexler, who believed in this book from the time it, was only an idea in my head. He read every word I wrote, and in turn made this book a reality. Thanks also go to Leslie Bjorncrantz at Northwestern University Library who made my initial literature search much more manageable. My friend and colleague, Judy Bakshy, offered helpful observations. To Margo Gordon I owe an especially heartfelt gratitude, not only for years of support and friendship, but also for her expertise and speedy assistance in a time of need. Last, I wish to convey deep thanks to those friends who kept asking me about the book progress and were supportive and encouraging of the idea of releasing both the first and second edition of the book. You know who you are and your sincere interest and genuine caring means a lot to me.

Most important, I'm deeply appreciative of my family. I'm profoundly grateful to my parents, *the late* Israel and Cila Frankel, who each in their own unique way made me aware of the heavens and hells of retirement. Special recognition, appreciation, and credit also go to my entire immediate family, who stood by me through all the steps of this project and were always available whenever I needed them. My husband, Ram, whose tireless love, unwavering encouragement, and faith in my work, combined with his dry wit that still keeps me bent over laughing, nourished me and kept me going at times of sickness and health. His caring took on many forms: a source off which to bounce ideas, an ear to vent my frustrations, and a hand that offered a soothing cup of tea. My three children, Tomer, Shelly, and Eldad, were always there to help me find the right words to express an idea, to remind me that it was time to play or go to bed, who were tolerant of the millions of interruptions my word-processing questions caused them, and who, on numerous occasions, calmed me down by explaining that I did not cause irreversible damage to the computer or the book by pushing the wrong key.

When it comes to this updated second edition, I must mention again my husband Ram who valued this book from its initial creation and whose insistent and determined pushes over the last few years made me take upon myself this revision. Without his persistent "naggings" this second edition would not have come to life. I would not have been able to accomplish this updated version of the book without the immense help of my editor, Helen Gallagher. She provided extremely valuable advice and guidance. She helped me navigate through the maze of publishing books. I'm convinced this updated book would be much less without her. Special thanks to my publisher Christopher Robbins at Familius who worked zealously with me to bring this second edition to fruition, involved me in the decision about many details of this edition in a manner that made this publication a real joint venture. I would like to thank my daughter-in-law Monika Black for her help with the computerized literature search. I also would like to thank my daughter Shelly for her last minute amazing editing touches which improved sections of the book that I had problems with. I don't have enough words to thank my son Tomer for all his computer help. His skills putting the first edition of the book into a document on the computer that could be edited made this process so much faster and more manageable and efficient. In addition, his technical help with different aspects and tasks of this revision were extremely valuable. Last and definitely not least, his patient answering the millions endless and repeated questions I had about word processing and working with two documents deserves a special award.

Without all of their steadfast love, support, and encouragement, both my work and my life would be measurably impoverished.

Selected Bibliography

Citations

Adelmann, P. K. Psychological Well-Being and Homemaker vs. Retiree Identity Among Older Women. Sex Roles 29, no./1993, 195–212.

Askham, J. Marriage Relationships of Older People. Reviews in Clinical Gerontology 4, no. 3, 1994: 261–6.

Atchley, R. The process of retirement: Comparing women and men, *American Psychologist*, Vol. 63(4), 2008, 25-26.

Blieszner, R., and V. H. Bedford, eds. *Handbook of Aging and the Family*. Westport, Conn.: Greenwood Press, 1995.

Blustein, David L., The Role of Work in Psychological Health and Well-Being: A Conceptual, Historical, and Public Policy Perspective, *American Psychologist*, May-June, 2008, 228-240.

Bonsdorff, M., Shultz, K., Leskinen, E., Tansky, J., The Choice Between Retirement and Bridge Employment: A Continuity Theory and Life Course Perspective, *Intl. Journal Aging and Human Development*, Vol. 69(2), 2009, 79-100.

Brougham, R. & Walsh, D.A., Early and Late Retirement Exits, *Intl. Journal Aging and Human Development*, Vol. 69(4), 2009, 267-286.

Cliff, D. R. 'Under the Wife's Feet:' Renegotiating Gender Divisions in Early Retirement. The Sociological Review 1993: 30–53.

Coyle, 3. M., ed. *Handbook on Women and Aging*. Westport, Conn.: Greenwood Press, 1997.

Davey, A. & Szinovacz, M., Dimensions of Marital Quality and Retirement, *Journal of Family Issues*, Vol. 25(4), 2004, 431-464.

Dorfman, L. T. Health, Financial Status, and Social Participation of Retired Rural Men and Women. Educational Gerontology 21 1995, 653–69.

Gall, T. L., D. R. Evans, and J. Howard. The Retirement Adjustment Process. Journal of Gerontology 52B, no. 3, 1997, 110–17.

Halford, W. K., and H. 3. Markman, eds. *Clinical Handbook of Marriage and Couples Interventions*. New York: Wiley, 1997.

Hallowell, E. M., and W. 3. Grace. Money Styles. In *Money and Mind*, eds. S. Klebanow and E. L. Lowenkopf. New York: Plenum Press, 1991.

Hersen, M., and V. B. Van Hasselt, eds. *Handbook of Clinical Geropsychology,* New York: Plenum Press, 1998.

Hershey, D. & Mowen, J., Psychological Determinants of Financial Preparedness for Retirement, *The Gerontologist*, Vol. 40(6), 2000, 687-697.

Higginbottom, S. F., J. Barling, and E. K. Kelloway. Linking Retirement Experiences and Marital Satisfaction. Psychology and Aging 8, no. 4, 1993, 508–16.

Hildon, Z., Montgomery, S.M., Blane, D., Wiggins, R.D., Netuveli, G. , Examining Resilience of Quality of Life in the Face of Health-Related and Psychosocial Adversity at Older Ages: What is Right About the Way We Age? *The Gerontologist*, Vol. 50(1) 2010, 36-37.

Johnston, T. Retirement: What Happens to the Marriage. Issues in Mental Health Nursing 11, 1990, 347–59.

Klebanow, S., and E. L. Lowenkopf, eds. *Money and Mind*. New York: Plenum Press, 1991.

Kulik, L., The Impact of Men's and Women's Retirement on Marital Relations: A Comparative Analysis, *Journal of Woman & Aging*, Vol. 13(2), 2001, 21-37.

Kung, W. W. The Intertwined Relationship Between Depression and Marital Distress. Journal of Marriage and Family Therapy 26, no. 1, 2000, 51–60.

Kupperbusch, C. Levenson, R., Ebling, R., Predicting Husbands' and Wives' Retirement Satisfaction from the Emotional Qualities of Marital Interaction, *Journal of Social and Personal Relationships*, Vol. 20(3), 2003, 335-354.

L'Abate, L., ed. *Handbook of Developmental Family Psychology and Psychopathology*. New York: Wiley, 1994.

Lee, G. R., and C. L. Shehan. Retirement and Marital Satisfaction. Journal of Gerontology 44, no. 6, 1989, S226–30.

Melton, M. A., M. Hersen, T. D. Van Sickle, and V. B. Van Hasselt. Parameters of Marriage in Older Adults. Clinical Psychology Review 15, no. 8, 1995, 891–904.

Moen, P. A Life Course Perspective on Retirement, Gender, and Well-Being. Journal of Occupational Health Psychology 1, no. 2, 1996,131–44.

Moen, P., Huang,Q., Plassman,V., Dentinger,E. , Deciding the Future: Do Dual-Earner Couples Plan Together for Retirement? *American Behavioral Scientist*, Vol. 49(9), May, 2006, 1-22.

Moen, P., Kim, J., Hofmeister, H., Couples' Work/Retirement Transitions, Gender, and Marital Quality, *Social Psychology Quarterly*, Vol. 64(1), 2001, 55-71.

Monk, A., ed. *The Columbia Retirement Book,* New York: Columbia University Press, 1994.

Myers, S. M., and A. Booth. Men's Retirement and Marital Quality. Journal of Family Issues 17, no. 3, 1996, 336–57.

Nussbaum, J. F., and J. Coupland. *Handbook of Communication and Aging Research*. Mahwah, N.J.: L. Erlbaum Associates, 1995.

Nussbaum, P. D., ed. Handbook of Neuropsychology and Aging. New York: Plenum Press, 1997.

Nuttman-Shwartz, O., Is There Life Without Work, *Intl. Journal Aging and Human Development*, Vol. 64(2), 2007, 129,147.

Nuttman-Shwartz, O., Like a High Wave: Adjustment to Retirement, *The Gerontologist*, Vol. 44(2), 2005, 299-236.

Okun M, August. K., Rook, K., Newsom, J., Does Volunteering Moderate the Relation Between Functional Limitations and Mortality? Social *Science and Medicine*, Vol. 71(9), 2010, 1662-1668.

Osborne, J.W., Commentary on Retirement, Identity, and Erikson's Developmental Stage Model, *Canadian Journal on Aging*, Vol. 28(4), 2009. 295-301.

Pina, D. L., and V. L. Bengtson. Division of Household Labor and Well-Being of Retirement-Aged Wives. The Gerontologist 35, no. 3, 1995, 308–17.

Pinquart, M, & Schindler, I., Changes of Life Satisfaction in the Transition to Retirement: A Latent-Class Approach, *Psychology and Aging*, Vol. 22(3), 2007, 442-455.

Potocnik, K. Tordera, N., Peiro, J.M., The Influence of the Early Retirement Process on Satisfaction with Early Retirement and Psychological Well-Being, *Intl. Journal Aging and Human Development*, Vol. 70(3), 2010, 251-273.

Price, C.A. & Balaswamy, S., Beyond Health and Wealth: Predictors of Women's Retirement Satisfaction, *Intl. Journal Aging and Human Development*, Vol. 68(3), 2009, 195-214.

Price, C.A. & Dean, K.J., Exploring the Relationship Between Employment History and Retired Women's Social Relationships, *Journal of Women & Aging*, Vol. 21, 2009, 85-98.

Reitzes, D. & Mutran, E., The Transition to Retirement: Stages and Factors That Influence Retirement Adjustment, *Intl. Journal Aging and Human Development*, Vol. 59(1), 2005, 63-84.

Sandberg, J. G., and J. M. Harper. Depression in Mature Marriages. Journal of Marriage and Family Therapy 25, no. 3, 1999, 393–406.

Seligman, M. E. P., and M. Csikszentmihalyi, eds. Special Issue on Happiness, Excellence, and Optimal Human Functioning. American Psychologist 55, no. 1, 2000.

Simmons, B. & Betschild, M, Women's Retirement, Work and Life Paths: Changes, Disruptions and Discontinuities, *Journal of Women & Aging*, Vol. 13(4), 2001, 53-70.

Schnarch, D. Passionate Marriage. New York: Holt, 1997.

Smith, D. & Moen, P., Retirement Satisfaction for Retirees and Their Spouses: Do Gender and the Retirement Decision-Making Process Matter? *Journal of Family Issues*, March, 2004, 262-281.

Szinovacz, M. Couples' Employment/Retirement Patterns and Perceptions of Marital Quality. Research on Aging 18, no. 2, 1996, 243–68.

Szinovacz, M. ed, Women's Retirement: Policy Implications of Recent Research, Beverly Hills, CA: *Sage Publications*, 1982

Szinovacz, M. & Davey, A., Retirement and Marital Decision Making: Effects on Retirement Satisfaction, *Journal of Marriage and Family*, Vol. 66, May, 2005, 387-398.

Szinovacz, M., D. J. Ekerdt, and B. H. Vinick, eds. Families and Retirement. Newbury Park, Calif.: Sage Publications, 1992.

Szinovacz, M., and P. Harpster. Couples' Employment/Retirement Status and the Division of Household Tasks. Journal of Gerontology 49, no. 3, 1994, S125–36.

Theriault, J. Retirement as a Psychological Transition: Process of Adaptation to Change. International Journal of Aging and Human Development 38, no. 2, 1994, 153–170.

Trudel, G., Turgeon, L., Piché, L., Marital and sexual aspects of old age, *Sexual and Relationship Therapy*, Vol. 25(3), August, 2010, 316-341.

Trudel, G., Villeneuve, L., Préville, M., Boyer, R., Fréchette, V. Dyadic Adjustment, Sexuality and Psychological Distress in Older Couples, *Sexual and Relationship Therapy*, Vol. 25(3), August, 2010, 306-315.

Van Solinge, H. and Henkens, K., Couples' Adjustment to Retirement: A Multi-Actor Panel Study, *Journal of Gerontology*, Vol. 60B(1), 2005, 811-820.

Van Solinge, H. & Henkens, K., Adjustment to and Satisfaction with Retirement: Two of a Kind? *Psychology and Aging*, Vol. 23(2), 2008, 422-434.

Vanzetti, N., and S. Duck, eds. A Lifetime of Relationships. Pacific Grove, Calif.: Brooks/Cole Publishing, 1996.

Vinick, B. H., and D. J. Ekerdt. Retirement: What Happens to Husband-Wife Relationships? Journal of Geriatric Psychiatry 24, no. 1, 1991, 23–40.

Wells Y., DeVaus, D., Kendig, H., Quine, S., Health and Wellbeing Through Work and Retirement Transitions in Mature Age: Understanding Pre, Post and Retrospective Measures of Change, *Intl. Journal Aging and Human Development*, Vol. 69(4), 2009, 287-310.

Yogev, S., and J. Brett. Perceptions of the Division of Housework and Childcare and Marital Satisfaction. *Journal of Marriage and the Family* 47, 1985, 609–18.

Index

Abandonment, fear of, 99
Accomplishment, work-related, 37-39
Acquisitive (friendship style), 138-139
Active-isolate activities, 58
Active-social activities, 58
Adult Children, 163-166, *See also* Inheritance
Ageism, 23, 99
Aging, 79
Altruism, 62
Assemblers, (money style), 109, 111
Assistance, friendship and, 136
Authoritative (grandparenting style), 161
Baby boomers, 243
"being in the flow" 53
Belonging, friendship and, 136
Boredom, 212
Bridge employment, 64-65
Career women, 185, 192
Caregiving, 166
Change, 200, 207, 210
Close relationships, 74, 140
Co-dependency, 23,
Communication, 124, 194
Community, 58
Conflict, 27
Conversation, 17-18, 37, 55-56, 75-76
Creative stimulation, 56-57
Criticism, 128
Csikszentmihalyi, Mihaly, 53
Death, 98, 17
Dependency, 75
    fear of, 99, 152-153
Depression, 28, 208
    dealing with, 196-198
Detached (grandparenting style), 161
Differentiation, 73, 236-237
Discerning (friendship style), 138-139
Disclosure, friendship and, 136
Disenchantment, 20
Distant (grandparenting style), 161
Dorfman, Lorraine, 12
Dual-career couples, 27
Empty nest, 29, 86, 166

Enjoyment vs. pleasure, 51-52
Entrepreneur, 65
Exercise, 54
Expectations, 26, 38
Expectations of retirement, 233
External motivation, 53
Family, 156-171
    adult children, 163-166
    as reason for retirement, 156-157
    grandchildren, 156-159
    other family members, 167-168
    parents, 166-167
Family of origin, 76
Flow, 53, 58, 63
Formal (grandparenting style), 160
Foster Grandparent Program, 63
Friendship, 135-153
    gender differences, 137-138
    increased importance in retirement, 142-144
    marital tensions, 140-142
    obstacles to maintaining, 148-153
    styles, 138-139
Fun seeker (grandparenting style), 160
Gender, 120-130 179-189
    depression, 196-198
    friendship and,137-139
    housework and, 121-122
    impact on marriage, 120-130, 176-189
    money issues and, 102, 104-105
    parental relationships and, 166
    reasons for retirement and, 177-179
Grace William, 109
Grandchildren, 156-159
Grandparenting styles, 159-163
Hallowell, Edward, 109
Happiness, 12-13, 28, 52, 59, 73, 121, 141, 186, 200, 237,
Hardiness, 210
Health, 179
    financial, 202
    mental-physical link, 201
    through friendships, 142
Helping others, friendship and, 136
Homemakers, 123, 184-186
    lack of autonomy, 185
    husbands of, 188-189
Housework 120-129
    marital dynamics and, 120-122
    responsibility after retirement, 123-129
    setting the terms, 129

Immortality grandparenting and, 160
Independent (friendship style), 138-139
Influential (grandparenting style), 161
Inheritance, 168-170
Innate tendencies, 74
Inner-directed relationships, 59
Intellectual stimulation, 55-56
Intimacy pattern stages, 83-88
  before children, 83-85
  child raising, 85-86
  empty nest, 86-87
  retirement, 87-88
Intrinsic motivation, 52
Involuntary, forced retirement, 202-207
Joy, 209
Kohut, Heinz, 210
Kung, Winnie, 197
Leisure time, 50
Life expectancy, 166
Life of leisure, 57-58
Life purpose, 40-42, 50
Loneliness, 136, 180
Meaningful Work, 24
Mental activity, 196
Middle ground, 237
Migration, 151-152
Mixed feelings, preparing for, 234
Money, 97-112
  addiction to, 108
  adult children, 164
  balance, 100-102
  earning and handling, 102
  psychological meaning of, 97-98
  retirement and psychological impact of, 98-100
  retirement, marriage and, 106
  styles, 109-110
  upsetting the balance, 100
  values about, 102
Non-work competence, 211
Obstacles,
  to keeping friends 148-153
Outer-directed relationships, 59
Paradox of togetherness versus separation, 73
Parents, 166-167
Passion, 53
Passionate Marriage (Schnarch), 73
Passive (grandparenting style), 161
Personal identity, work related, 35, 37-38
Personal well-being, 59

Physical space, 83-84, 86
Physical stimulation, 53-54
Plato, 57
Pleasure vs. enjoyment, 51-52
Positive attitude, 210
Pre-retirement, 20, 42
Pre-retirement stage, 20
Purpose, 24-26
  creative stimulation and, 56-57
  finding the right activity,
  intellectual stimulation, 54-56
  leisure to discover, 57
  physical stimulation, 53-54
  volunteerism and, 58-60
  work as source of, 24
Reflected sense of self, 73
Reliving the past, grandparenting and, 160
Relocation, 217
  after retirement, 218
  gradual, 222-224
Reorientation stage of retirement, 20
Resource (grandparenting style), 160
Retired Senior Volunteer Program (RSVP), 63
Retirement
  satisfaction vs. adjustment, 42
Retirement event, 20
Retirement phase in intimacy pattern, 87-89
Retirement planning, psychological, 22-23
Retirement psychological process, 19
Retirement satisfaction, 42-43
Retirement stages, 20
Right attitude, 200
Role models, lack of, 26
Routine stage of retirement, 20
Schedule, regular, 27, 238
Schnarch, David, 73
Safe haven, (grandparenting style), 161
Sedentary-isolate activities, 58
Sedentary-social activities, 58
Self-validated intimacy, 73
Senior Companion Program, 63
Service Corps of Retired Executives (SCORE), 63
Sexual Intimacy, 78-80
Sexual relations, 78-80
Skeptics (money style), 110
Smooth vs. rough transition, 200-201
Social activities,
  gender and, 181-184

Social contact, 80, 146
    grandparenting and, 160
Social interaction, 35, 36-37
Social integration, friendship and, 136
Social Security, 202, 204-205
Socialization, 75-78, 143
Spenders (money style), 109, 111
Status, 35
Structure, grandparenting and, 160
Structured time, 35-36
    grandparenting and, 160
    work as, 35
Subjective well-being, 25, 59-60
Suicide, 145
Support and reassurance, friendship and, 137
Supportive (grandparenting style), 161
Surrogate parent (grandparenting style), 160
Technology, 74
Time equilibrium, 214
Togetherness-separation,
    balance, 30, 72-90
    intimacy pattern stages and, 83-88
    paradox, 73-74
Trade, trade-off, 237
Transition, 21, 193-215
    characteristics of couples with smooth, 200-202
    depression and, 208
    for homemakers vs. employed women, 208
    gender impact on, 177-188
    spouse's attitude toward, 212
Under-involved (money style), 109-110
Unknown, fear of, 99, 208
Valued elder, grandparenting as, 160
Values, 63
    about money, 97, 102-103, 110-112
    discovery of, 25, 63
Volunteerism, 58-63
Well-being, 25, 43
Who should not retire, 208
Women's movement, 26
Work
    as structured time, 35-36
    identity, accomplishment, and status, 35, 37-40
    increasingly meaningful, 24
    saying good-bye, 232
    social interaction, 35, 36, 37
    work identity, 180
Work involvement, 38
Workaholics, 35

About the Publisher

Familius was founded in 2012 with the intent to align the founders' love of publishing and family with the digital publishing renaissance which occurred simultaneous with the Great Recession. The founders believe that the traditional family is the basic unit of society, and that a society is only as strong as the families that create it.

Familius' mission is to help families be happy. We invite you to participate with us in strengthening your family by being part of the Familius family. Go to www.familius.com to subscribe and receive information about our books, articles, and videos.

Website: www.familius.com
Facebook: www.facebook.com/paterfamilius
Twitter: @familiustalk
Pinterest: www.pinterest.com/familius

Helping Families Be Happy